HECTOR BERLIOZ

A SELECTION FROM HIS
LETTERS

Berlioz in 1845; from a lithograph by Prinzhofer, Vienna. Berlioz thought it a good likeness, though he denied that he ever wore rings or carried a cane; this is stated on a presentation copy of the picture, signed "H. Berlioz non Dandy".

HECTOR BERLIOZ
A SELECTION FROM HIS LETTERS

selected, edited and translated

by

HUMPHREY SEARLE

LONDON
VICTOR GOLLANCZ LTD
1966

MADE AND PRINTED IN GREAT BRITAIN BY
THE GARDEN CITY PRESS LIMITED
LETCHWORTH, HERTFORDSHIRE

CONTENTS

EDITOR'S PREFACE

NEARLY A HUNDRED years after his death Berlioz is at last
being recognised as the great composer he was, and whereas
even thirty years ago performances of his works were compara-
tively rare, and there was still a good deal of prejudice against
him in certain quarters, in the years since the second world
war his reputation has steadily increased and one can now
hear his major works with reasonable frequency—though even
so the operas remain more neglected than they should be. The
story of his life has always been well known from his *Memoirs*,
and many of his letters have been published in various selections :
but, apart from Barzun's *New Letters* (Columbia University
Press, 1954) which contains 100 letters or extracts from letters,
many previously unpublished, with parallel French and English
texts, there appears to be no modern edition of his letters in
English. His letters are in some ways even more vivid than the
Memoirs for they describe his reactions to events at the actual
time they happened, and they often fill gaps and correct in-
accuracies in the *Memoirs*, which in any case do not cover the
last five years of Berlioz' life.

Berlioz was a voluminous letter writer : at all times of his life
he felt the need to pour out his feelings to his friends and family.
A volume of this size naturally cannot include all the letters that
he wrote : what I have tried to do is to make a selection from
the most interesting ones so as to illustrate Berlioz in his many
and varied moods and in his relations to his art, his loves, his
family and his friends, and I have added short linking notes so
that the book may be read as a continuous story of his life, told
as far as possible in Berlioz' own words. I have limited myself
to private letters, with the exception of a few letters written to
editors of newspapers, and I have not included the "open letters"
which Berlioz intended for publication as newspaper articles :
these have mostly been reprinted in the *Memoirs* or Berlioz' other
writings. I have also only included two letters written to Berlioz
by other correspondents, and I have avoided reproducing the
private letters which Berlioz himself included in the *Memoirs*.
Even so the task of selection has not been easy, and all I can

hope is that from this book there may emerge a rounded picture of Berlioz as a man and artist of the most remarkable kind. To this end, I have extracted short passages from some letters, and elided (or even condensed) others.

I am indebted to Jacques Barzun for kind permission to quote from his own translations.

A chronology records the main events of Berlioz' life, and a bibliography gives a list of Berlioz' main prose writings and the chief collections of his letters in French, as well as a list of books on Berlioz.

H. S.

CHRONOLOGY

1803 Berlioz born, 11 December at Côte-Saint-André, Dauphiné.

1806 His sister Nanci born.

1814 His sister Adèle born.

1815 Studies flute and guitar.

1816 Love for Estelle. Literary discoveries: Virgil, La Fontaine, Florian. Earliest compositions.

1820 His brother Prosper born.

1821 Berlioz in Paris as medical student. Discovers Gluck and French opera.

1822 His first cantata, *The Arab Horse*.

1823 Begins studying with Lesueur. Publishes first essay on music.

1824 Second essay on music.

1825 Mass completed and performed on 10 July. Hears *Der Freischütz*.

1826 Completes cantata *The Greek Revolution*. Admitted to Conservatoire. Working on *Les Francs-Juges*.

1827 Writes *Mort d'Orphée*. Sees *Hamlet* and *Romeo and Juliet*, first sight of Harriet Smithson.

1828 *Waverley* and *Francs-Juges* overtures written. First concert of his works, 26 May. Second in Prix de Rome contest. Discovery of Beethoven and Goethe. Composes *Roi de Thulé*.

1829 Writes *Cléopâtre* and *Eight Scenes from Faust*.

1830 Writes *Irish Melodies*, *Tempest Fantasia*, *Symphonie Fantastique* and wins Prix de Rome. Love affair with Camille Moke. Meets Liszt.

1831-2 In Rome. Engagement with Camille broken. Revises *Symphonie Fantastique* and prepares *Lélio*. Both performed in Paris.

1833 *Rob Roy* overture played. Various concerts. Music critic of the *Rénovateur*. Married to Harriet Smithson, 3 October.

1834 Writes *Harold in Italy*. Sketches libretto of *Benvenuto*. His son Louis born, 14 August.

1835-6 Adopts career as conductor. Helps Louise Bertin put on her opera *Esmeralda*. Music critic of the *Journal des Débats* and the *Gazette Musicale*.

1837 *Requiem*. Reconciliation with family.

1838 *Benvenuto Cellini* finished and performed: its failure. Death of his mother. Paganini's gift after hearing *Harold*.

1839 Writes *Romeo and Juliet*. Death of Prosper. Receives Legion of Honour. Wagner in Paris.

1840 *Symphonie Funèbre et Triomphale*.

1841-3 Supervises production of *Der Freischütz*. Publication of *Nuits d'Eté*. Affair with Marie Recio. First German tour.

1844–5 *Roman Carnival* overture. *Treatise on Modern Instrumentation and Orchestration* and *Voyage Musical* published. Separation from Harriet. Visit from and concerts with Glinka.

1846 Trip to Austria, Hungary and Bohemia. *Requiem* given again in Paris. *Damnation of Faust* completed and performed; severe financial loss.

1847–8 First trip to Russia. First trip to England. Begins Memoirs. Death of his father. *Hamlet* Funeral March written.

1848 *Te Deum* written. Founds Philharmonic Society in Paris.

1850–1 Begins *Childhood of Christ*. Death of his sister Nanci. Final version of *Corsair* overture. In London for Great Exhibition.

1852 *Benvenuto* successfully produced by Liszt in Weimar. *Requiem* in Paris. Conducts Beethoven's Choral Symphony in London. Publishes *Evenings in the Orchestra*.

1853 Fourth trip to London; *Benvenuto* fails again. Trip to Germany. *Flight into Egypt* a success in Paris.

1854 Finishes *Childhood of Christ*. Death of Harriet. Marriage with Marie Recio. First version of Memoirs completed.

1855 Liszt organises second Berlioz Festival in Weimar. *Te Deum* performed in Paris. Trip to London and meeting with Wagner.

1856 Trip to Germany; success of *Benvenuto* and *Faust*. *Nuits d'Eté* orchestrated. Elected to Institute. *The Trojans* begun. First Baden concert.

1857 His illness becomes worse. Poem of *The Trojans* and most of the music finished.

1858 *The Trojans* finished. *Romeo* at Baden. Illness increasing.

1859 *Grotesques de la Musique*. Two scenes from *The Trojans* performed at Baden concert. Directs production of *Orpheus*.

1860 Death of his sister Adèle. *Beatrice and Benedict* begun.

1861 Directs revival of *Alceste*.

1862 *Beatrice and Benedict* finished. Death of Marie. *A Travers Chants* published.

1863 Trip to Weimar and Löwenberg. *Childhood of Christ* given in Strasbourg. Cut version of *The Trojans* performed in Paris.

1864 Resigns from *Journal des Débats*. Visit to Estelle.

1865 Memoirs sent to printer. Trip to Geneva to see Estelle and to Dauphiné to see nieces.

1866 Rehearses *Armide* and directs revival of *Alceste*. Conducts *Faust* in Vienna.

1867 Death of his son Louis, 5 June. Second trip to Russia.

1868 Trip to Monaco and Nice, falls on the rocks. Illness. Last visit to Institute to vote for Charles Blanc, 25 November.

1869 Berlioz dies, 8 March in Paris.

LETTERS

To the publisher Pleyel

La Côte-Saint-André, 6 April 1819

Sir,

I have several pieces of music of my composition which I wish to have engraved. I am therefore writing to you in the hope that you will be able to realise my ambition. I would like you to take on the publication, with full rights, of a medley for six solo instruments on selected airs, the instruments being flute, horn, two violins, viola and cello. Please be good enough to see whether you can do it, and how many copies you can let me have. I would be grateful if you would be so kind as to reply as soon as possible telling me how long it will take you to engrave it, and whether it is necessary to register the parcel. I have the honour to be your obedient servant

Hector Berlioz

Pleyel replied with a refusal on 10 April: Berlioz had already written in similar terms on 25 March to the publishers Janet and Cotelle, with the same result.

To his sister Nanci

Paris, 13 December 1821

... Short of fainting, I could not have had a greater experience when I saw Gluck's masterpiece *Iphigeneia*. Imagine first of all an orchestra of eighty musicians who perform with such perfect ensemble that one would think it was a single instrument. The opera begins. You see a vast plain (I tell you, the illusion is complete) and further still the sea. The orchestra presages a storm: black clouds slowly descend and cover the plain—the theatre is only lighted by flashes, in the most telling and truthful fashion. There is a moment of silence: no actor on the stage: the orchestra murmurs dully: you seem to hear the soughing of the wind (you know how in winter you can hear it speak!). Gradually the excitement grows, the storm bursts, and you discover Orestes and Pylades in chains, led by the barbarians of Tauris who sing a frightening chorus: "We must have blood to atone for our crimes". It's about the limit of what one can stand: I defy the hardest-hearted being to stay unmoved at the sight of these two wretches longing for death as their greatest hope—and when it turns out that it is Orestes' sister Iphigeneia, the priestess of Diana, who must sacrifice her brother, well, it is ghastly.

I can't describe to you even approximately the sense of horror one feels when Orestes, overwhelmed, falls down and says: "Calm is restored to my breast". While he sleeps, you see the shade of his mother whom he has killed, she is hovering about with other spirits brandishing infernal torches above his head. And the orchestra! It's all in the orchestra. If you could only hear how every situation is depicted in it, especially when Orestes seems calm: there is a long held note in the violins suggesting tranquillity, very *piano*: but below, the basses murmur like the remorse which, despite his apparent calm, throbs in the heart of the parricide.

But I forget myself. Farewell, dear sister: forgive me these digressions and be assured that your brother loves you with all his heart. Give my love to everybody at home.

To his sister Nanci

Paris, 20 February 1822

... You may think that these affairs [dances] are very different from ours—not at all. The only difference is that instead of having sixteen people there are sixty, and the floor is so crowded that one must always be careful where to put down one's feet. Dress is uniformly white for the ladies and black for the men. The orchestra! You probably imagine it is superb. Well, it does not begin to compare with ours. Just think: two violins and flageolet. Isn't it pitiable? two violins and a flageolet, and those three wretches could only play contredanses taken from the ballets I've heard at the Opéra: you can imagine the contrast....

The next day we went to the Feydeau to hear Martin: that evening they were giving *Azémia* and the *Voitures versées*. Ah! what a compensation for the violins and the flageolet! I absorbed the music. I thought of you, sister! How pleased you would have been to hear it! Perhaps you would like the Opéra less; it's too highbrow for you, while this touching, enchanting music of Dalayrac, the gaiety of Boieldieu's, the incredible *tours*

de force of the women, the perfection of Martin and Pon-
chard.... Yes, I would have thrown my arms round Dalayrac's
neck had I been near his statue when I heard this air to which I
cannot give an epithet: "Thy love, O sweetest daughter", I felt
nearly the same when I heard at the Opéra in *Stratonice* "Pour
your grief into your father's breast". But I cannot undertake to
describe such music to you.

Azémia ou les Sauvages by Nicolas Dalayrac (1753–1809) had a
plot vaguely similar to that of Shakespeare's *Tempest*. *Les
Voitures versées* was by Boieldieu (1775–1834) and *Stratonice*
by Méhul (1763–1817). Martin was a well-known baritone at
the Opéra-Comique.

To Rodolphe Kreutzer

[Paris, ? Spring 1823]

O genius!
I succumb! I die! Tears choke me! *The Death of Abel!*
Heavens! What an infamous public! It feels nothing! How can
one move it?
O genius! and what shall I do myself if one day my music
should depict passion? How shall I be understood if the public
does not crown, carry in triumph or prostrate itself before the
author of everything that is beautiful?
Sublime, heart-rending, pathetic!
Ah! I cannot stand any more: I must write! Whom shall
I write to? To the Genius! No, I dare not.
I write to the man, to Kreutzer ... he will laugh at me ...
I don't care—I would die if I kept silence.
Ah! if I could only see him, talk to him, he would listen to
me, he would see what is happening in my ravaged soul; per-
haps he would restore to me the courage which I have lost, seeing
the insensitivity of these lepers, who are hardly worthy of listen-
ing to the buffooneries of that jack-in-a-box Rossini.
If the pen did not fall from my hands I should never finish.
AH! GENIUS!!!

Hector Berlioz.
Pupil of M. Lesueur.

Kreutzer was Director-General of Music at the Opéra: Berlioz'
sincere but comic letter was written after a hearing of Kreutzer's

opera *The Death of Abel*. Berlioz hoped that Kreutzer would perform a work of his at one of the "concerts spirituels" which took place regularly at the end of Lent: he also hoped that an interview with Kreutzer would persuade Berlioz' father that music could be a worth-while career for Hector, but his efforts proved fruitless.

To Lesueur

[Côte-Saint-André, June 1824]

. . . I was received by my family as I expected, with much affection. I did not have to bear my mother's unfortunate and useless remonstrations, which only distressed us both; however Papa recommended me as a precaution never to speak of music in front of her. On the other hand I often speak of it to him. I told him of your curious discoveries in ancient music, which you kindly showed me. I could not really persuade him that the ancients knew harmony: he was full of the ideas of Rousseau and other writers who supported the contrary opinion. When I quoted to him the Latin passage from Pliny the Elder, which gives details of the method of accompanying voices and shows how easily the orchestra can depict passions by the use of rhythms different from those of the vocal parts, he was astounded and confessed to me that there was no reply to such an explanation. . . .

Jean-François Lesueur, 1761–1837, was Berlioz' teacher at the Paris Conservatoire: Berlioz was greatly attached to him.

To his father

Paris, 31 August 1824

. . . I am driven voluntarily towards a magnificent career (no other epithet can be applied to the career of an artist) and I am not in the least heading for perdition. For I believe I shall succeed. Yes, I really believe it. There is no longer any point in being modest about this, since I have to prove to you that I am not drifting haphazardly. I think, indeed I am convinced that I shall attain distinction in music: all the external evidence points that way; and within me the voice of nature is stronger than anything reason can urge against it. I have every conceivable chance in my favour if you will back me. I begin young, and I shall not have to give lessons, like so many others, to support myself. I have a good knowledge of certain branches and the rudiments of others—enough to be able to master them in time. And certainly I have experienced passions sufficiently strong not to be found wanting whenever it will be necessary for me to depict or give them voice.

...Make it only a mere twelve hundred francs: that's enough for me even if music should never bring me anything. In short I want to make a name for myself, I want to leave on this earth some trace of my existence, which is by no means an ignoble feeling—and so strongly do I feel it that I would rather be Gluck or Méhul dead than what I am in the flower of my manhood....

...As M. Lesueur was telling me again yesterday, he became a great musician before he became a learned musician. He acquired his general information at college like everybody else, and it was only later that he deepened his knowledge of certain sciences when he saw how they bore on music. If I haven't yet gone in for Greek, Hebrew and mathematics, I assure you it won't affect my chances as a musician.

This is the way I think, the way I am, and nothing in the world will change me. You could cut off my allowance or force me to leave Paris, but I do not believe you would want to make me lose the best years of my life. Farewell, dear Papa: read my letter over and do not ascribe it to some excited impulse. I have perhaps never been so calm. I kiss you tenderly, as well as Mama and my sisters.

Your respectful and loving son,
H. Berlioz.

To Humbert Ferrand

[Paris] 29 November [1827]

...My Mass was performed on St. Cecilia's day, with twice as much success as the first time. The small corrections which I made to it have improved it a great deal. The *Et iterum venturus* especially, which failed the first time, was performed magnificently this time by six trumpets, four horns, three trombones and two ophicleides. The chorus which follows, which I had performed by all the voices in octaves, with a burst of brass in the middle of the phrase, produced a terrific impression on everybody. I kept my sang-froid till then, and it was important not to get agitated, I was conducting the orchestra; but when I saw this picture of the Last Judgment, this proclamation sung by six basses in unison, this terrible *clangor tubarum*, the cries of fright from the multitude represented by the chorus, everything in fact rendered exactly as I had conceived it, I was seized by a convulsive trembling. I managed to master it until the end of the piece, but I was then forced to sit down and allow my orchestra to rest for some minutes: I could no longer stand upright and I was afraid that the baton would slip from my fingers. Ah! if only you had been there. . . .

I speak to you of all this with fire, my dear friend: but you do not know how little importance I attach to it [here he is referring to the Prix de Rome competition]. For three months I have been prey to an unhappiness from which nothing can distract me, my disgust with life has reached an extreme point; even the success I have just achieved has only lifted for a moment the grievous weight which oppresses me, and it now lies on me more heavily than before. I cannot give you the key to the enigma here: it would take too long, and I do not think I could form the letters if I tried to tell you about it. When I see you again you shall know everything. I will finish with this sentence which the ghost of the King of Denmark addresses to his son Hamlet:

Farewell, farewell, remember me.

Humbert Ferrand was a life-long friend of Berlioz: he wrote the libretto of Berlioz' opera *Les Francs-Juges*. The performance referred to is that of Berlioz' early Mass, written in 1824–5, and first performed on 10 July 1825. This performance took place on 22 November 1827 at Saint-Eustache: Berlioz conducted, for the first time in his life. He then destroyed most of the Mass, but kept the *Et Resurrexit* and used part of it both in *Benvenuto Cellini* and in the *Tuba mirum* of the Requiem. The second paragraph refers to his passion for Harriet Smithson, the Irish actress who at that time was appearing as Ophelia and Juliet with an English company in Paris. She later became Berlioz' first wife.

To the Press

Paris, 16 May 1828

Dear Sir,

Allow me to have recourse to your kindness and to ask for

the assistance of your journal so that I may exonerate myself in the eyes of the public from the grave accusations that have been made against me.

A rumour is going round the musical world that I intend to give a concert consisting entirely of my music, and already blame is being attached to me. I am accused of temerity, and the most ridiculous presumptions are being ascribed to me.

To all this I shall reply that I simply wish to make myself known, in order to inspire, if I can, some confidence in the writers and directors of our opera houses. Is this desire blameworthy in a young man? I do not think so.

But if there is nothing reprehensible about such an object, why should there be in the means I am using to accomplish it?

Because concerts have been given which consist entirely of the works of Mozart and Beethoven, does it follow that in doing the same thing I have the absurd pretensions that are imputed to me? I repeat that in acting thus I am only using the simplest method of making my dramatic efforts known.

The temerity which leads me to expose myself before the public in a concert hall is quite natural. My excuse is that for the last four years I have knocked at every door, to no avail. I cannot obtain a libretto to set, nor get a production of the one I have on hand.

I have tried in vain all the usual means of getting a hearing except one, to which I am now resorting, and I think I cannot do better than to take as my motto this line of Virgil :

Ulla salus victis nullam sperare salutem.
"To the vanquished the only salvation is to hope for none."

My concert, I know, will have all the disadvantages of programmes that are made up of only one man's work, but at least good judges will be enabled to decide whether that work shows any promise.

Your humble servant,
Hector Berlioz.
Pupil of M. Lesueur.

This is one of four identical letters sent by Berlioz to the press, in connection with the concert of his works which he gave on 26 May 1828: the letters were published in the *Gazette musicale*, *Corsaire* and *Figaro*. The concert consisted of the overtures *Les Francs-Juges* and *Waverley*, the *Greek Revolution*, the *Resurrexit* from the Mass, and an aria and a trio with chorus from *Les Francs-Juges*.

To Humbert Ferrand

Paris, Friday 6 June 1828

You must be burning with impatience to know the result of my concert. I have only waited in order to send you the papers too. Triumphant success! After the applause at the general rehearsals of Friday and Saturday I had no misgivings....

Our beloved Pastorale was ruined by the chorus, who instead of counting their bars waited for a signal which the conductor did not make, and only found out they had not come in just as the whole thing finished. But oh, the *Resurrexit*! and oh, the applause! As soon as one round finished another began. No longer able to bear it in my corner of the orchestra, I lay on the kettledrums and wept....

As for the overture to the *Francs-Juges*, I must tell you what happened at the first rehearsal. As soon as the orchestra heard that tremendous solo for trombone and ophicleide to which you have put the words of Olmerick in the third act, one of the violins stopped and shouted: "Ah! ah! the rainbow is the bow of your violin, the winds play the organ, the seasons beat time!" Whereupon the whole orchestra started off applauding it, although they hadn't heard the whole passage: they had interrupted the playing to applaud. On the day of the concert this introduction produced an effect of stupefying power which is difficult to describe. I found myself next to the drummer, who, holding my arm, which he seized with all his strength, could not stop himself crying out convulsively at intervals: "It's superb!... It's sublime! It's terrifying! It makes one lose one's head!" With my other arm I held a tuft of my hair which I pulled furiously. I wanted to cry out, forgetting that the work was by me: "It's monstrous! Gigantic! Terrifying!"...

All the Opéra people were present, and there was no end to the congratulations. The most pleased were Habeneck, Dérivis, Adolphe Nourrit, Dabadie, Prévost, Mlle Mori, Alexis Dupont, Schneitzoeffer, Hérold, Rigel, etc. Nothing was lacking to my success—not even the criticisms of Panseron and Brugnières, who say my style is new and bad, and that such writing ought not to be encouraged.

My dear, dear fellow! in pity send me an opera. *Robin Hood*! How can I write without a book? For heaven's sake finish something! ...

To Humbert Ferrand

28 June, eight hours later

I come, not from M. Laurent, but from Villeneuve-Saint-Georges, ten miles from Paris—I ran there all the way from my home.

I didn't die of it—the proof is that I am writing to you. How alone I am!—all my muscles tremble like those of a dying man! O my friend, send me a work, throw me a bone to gnaw. How beautiful the country is! What abundant light! All the people I saw on the way back looked happy. The trees rustled softly, and I was all alone in this immense plain. Space, distance, forgetfulness, grief, rage surrounded me. In spite of all my efforts life escapes me, I catch only fragments of it.

At my age, with my character, only to have harrowing sensations! On top of this, the persecutions of my family begin again, my father doesn't send me anything more, my sister wrote to me today that he was persisting in this. Money—always money! Yes, money does bring happiness. If I had a lot of it I could be happy, and death is not happiness, it lacks a great deal.

Neither during ... nor after ...
Nor before life?
When then?
Never.
Inflexible necessity.
Yet my blood circulates: my heart beats as if bounding with joy.
I am really in excellent form: joy is what I want, for God's sake, joy!

To Humbert Ferrand

Sunday morning

Dear Friend,

Do not worry about my aberrations—the crisis is past. I cannot explain in a letter, which might go astray: but I beg you not to breathe a word of my state of mind to anyone, it might get round to my father and distress him. All that I can do is suffer in silence until time changes my fate. . . .

Yesterday's wild excursion did for me entirely. I can hardly move. . . .

Adieu.

Laurent was the director of the English and Italian theatres: Berlioz was due to discuss with him the question of an Italian opera on Virginius, in collaboration with Ferrand, but his passion for Harriet Smithson brought on the temporary derangement described in these letters.

To Humbert Ferrand

Grenoble, 16 September 1828

. . . Come as soon as you can, I beg you: your music awaits you.

We will read *Hamlet* and *Faust* together. Shakespeare and Goethe, the mute confidants of my life, oh! come. No one here understands this passion of genius. The sun blinds them: they merely find it bizarre. The day before yesterday, in a carriage, I set the Ballad of the King of Thule in Gothic style, I will give it to you to put into your *Faust*, if you have one. . . .

To Humbert Ferrand

Paris, 11 November 1828

Forgive me for not writing sooner: I was so ill, so stupid, it was better to wait.

La Fontaine has rightly said: "Absence is the greatest of ills". She is gone: she has been at Bordeaux for a fortnight, I live no more, or rather I live only too much: my sufferings are impossible: I have hardly the courage to fulfil my new functions. You know that I have been appointed Superintendent of the Gymnase-Lyrique. I am in charge of the choice and replacement of players, the hiring of instruments, and looking after scores and orchestral parts. I am involved in all this at the moment.

Subscribers are coming in: so are malicious anonymous letters. Cherubini sits on the fence wondering whether to help or hinder us, and we go calmly on. . . .

I have not been Chateaubriand: he is in the country, but I will speak of your piece directly I do. . . .

To M. Sosthène de Larochefoucault, Superintendent of Fine Arts
                        Paris, Friday 12 November 1828
Two months ago the jury of the Royal Academy of Music
received a ballet on Faust. M. Bohain, who is the author of it,
wishing to give me the opportunity of being produced on the
stage of the Opéra, has entrusted to me the composition of the
music of his work, provided that the management agrees. I
have set to music the greater part of the poems of Goethe's
drama: my head is full of *Faust*, and if nature has gifted me
with any imagination, there is no subject on which it could
work with greater advantage....

These letters refer to the work which eventually became the
Eight Scenes from Faust: Gérard de Nerval's French translation of Part 1 of Goethe's *Faust* had appeared shortly before.

To Humbert Ferrand
                                    Paris, 2 February 1829
...Three days ago I was in a delirium of joy for eleven
hours: Ophelia is not so far from me as I thought: there is
some reason, which everyone refuses to tell me until later, why
it is impossible for her to speak openly at the moment. "But,"
she said, "if he really loves me, if his love is not of the kind
which it is my duty to disregard, then a few months' waiting will
not exhaust his constancy." She is to leave soon for Amsterdam
with her mother: Turner, their secretary, could not help emerg-
ing from his British phlegm when he said: "I will succeed, I tell
you, I am sure of it: if I go with her to Holland, I am sure of
sending you some excellent news shortly". I am assured that I
shall have some lines from her hand in reply to my letter, which
will be given to her at Amsterdam. Oh God! What will she say
to me?

To Humbert Ferrand
                                    Paris, 9 April 1829
Ah! poor dear friend! I did not write to you, because I was
incapable of it. All my hopes were dreadful illusions. She has
gone, and in going, without pity for my anguish, of which she
has been the witness two days running, she has left me only this
reply which someone has brought me: "Nothing could be more
impossible"....

Here is *Faust*, dear friend. Could you, without stinting your-self, lend me another hundred francs to pay the printer? I would rather borrow from you than from anyone else: yet had you not offered I should not have dared to ask. Your opera *Francs-Juges* is magnificent. You are indeed a poet! That finale of the Bohemians at the end of the first act is a master-stroke. I do not believe anything so original has ever been done in a libretto before. Yes, I repeat, it is magnificent. . . .

As the *Faust* ballet never materialised, Berlioz completed his *Eight Scenes from Faust* and had them published at his own expense.

To Goethe

rue de Richelieu No. 96, Paris
10 April 1829

Monseigneur,

Faust having been my regular reading for some years, I have pondered on this astonishing work so deeply and lovingly (although only able to see it through the mists of a translation) that it has come to exercise a kind of spell over me. Musical ideas have associated themselves in my mind with your poetic ideas, and despite a firm resolve never to unite my feeble strains to your sublime accents, little by little the temptation became so strong, the spell so potent, that the music of several scenes came to be written almost without my knowledge.

I have just published my score; and however unworthy an offering it may be, I take the liberty today of rendering homage by sending it to you. I do not doubt that you will have already received a large number of compositions of all kinds, inspired by your prodigious pen, so I have every reason to fear that, coming after so many others, I am merely bothering you. But, living as you do surrounded by fame and glory, even if the peti-tions of the humble cannot touch you, at least I hope you will forgive a young composer who, his heart uplifted and his imagination set on fire by your genius, cannot restrain a cry of admiration.

I have the honour to be, Monseigneur, with the most pro-found respect, your very humble and very obedient servant.

Hector Berlioz.

Goethe was charmed by Berlioz' letter, but as usual in musical matters showed the score to his old friend Zelter, the teacher of Mendelssohn, who replied damning the work as a series of "coughs, snores, croakings and expectorations". Goethe never replied to Berlioz.

To Humbert Ferrand

Paris, 3 June 1829

No word from you for three months. Why is it? Does your father suppress our letters? Or can it be that you at last believe the slanders you hear of me? ...

I got a pupil, so managed to pay the printer.

I am very happy, life is charming—no pain, no despair, plenty of day dreams: to crown all, the *Francs-Juges* has been refused by the Opera Committee! They find it long and obscure, only the Bohemian scene pleases them: but Duval thinks it remarkable and says there is a future for it.

I am going to have it translated into German and make an opera like *Freischütz* of it, and if I win the prize perhaps Spohr, who is not jealous but most helpful to young musicians, will let me try it at Cassel. ...

I have had no word from you since I told you of the futility of my hope. Nothing more has happened. This passion will kill me. People have said so often that hope alone can support love! I am certainly the proof of the contrary. Ordinary fire needs air, but electric fire burns in the void. All the English papers ring with cries of admiration for her genius. I remain unknown. When I have written an immense instrumental composition, which I am thinking about, I want to go to London to have it performed. If I could I obtain a brilliant success under her eyes! ...

To Humbert Ferrand

[Paris] 15 June 1829

... I am writing a life of Beethoven for the *Correspondant*, and cannot find a minute for composition—the rest of the time I copy out parts. What a life!

The "immense composition" mentioned here eventually became the *Symphonie Fantastique*. The prize referred to was the **Prix**

de Rome, for which the subject was the *Death of Cleopatra*.
Berlioz had come second the previous year, but no prize was
awarded in 1829.

To Humbert Ferrand

[Paris] 15 July 1829

. . . I am sorry I did not send your music before, but I may as
well own that I am short of money. My father has taken another whim and won't give me an allowance any more, so that
I could not afford the thirty or forty francs for the copying. I
could not do it myself, as I was shut up in the Institute. That
abominable competition is of the utmost importance to me—my
only chance of getting the filthy lucre, without which life is
impossible. Auri sacra fames quid non mortalia pectora cogis?
[Sacred hunger for gold, what do you not force human beings
to do?] My father would not even pay my expenses for the
Institute. M. Lesueur did so for me. . . .

To Humbert Ferrand

[Paris] 21 August 1829

. . . Forgive the delay. My excuses are the Academy Competition and the "new pangs of my despised love". My heart is the
scene of a horrible blaze, a virgin forest kindled by the thunder-
bolt : sometimes the fire seems assuaged, then a gust of wind, a
new lightning stroke, the cry of the trees perishing in the flame,
reveal the terrible power of this devastating scourge. I will spare
you a description of the latest blows.

That grotesque competition has seriously damaged me with
my parents.

Boieldieu says I go further than Beethoven, and he cannot
even understand Beethoven : and that to write like that I must
have the most hearty contempt for the Academicians! Auber
took me aside at the Opéra and told me much the same thing,
and then added : "You hate the commonplace, but you should
never be afraid of writing platitudes. The best advice I can give
you is to write as insipidly as possible, and when you have got
something which sounds to you horribly flat, you will have just
what they want!"

That is all very well, but when I write for butchers and
bakers and candlestick-makers I certainly shall not go to the
passion-haunted, crime-stained Queen of Egypt for a text. . . .

To Humbert Ferrand
                    [Paris] Friday evening, 30 October 1829
...Oh Ferrand! Ferrand! why were you not here for my concert? Yesterday I was so ill that I could not crawl: today the fire of hell that inspired my *Francs-Juges* overture courses through my veins....

All my heart, my passion, my love are in that overture.

To Humbert Ferrand
                              Paris, 6 November 1829
...Mlle Marinoni had just come on the stage to sing an Italian aria: profiting by this moment of calm, I wanted to slide between the desks to take a pile of music from a bench: the public saw me, then the shouts and bravos began again, the artists joined in, a hail of bows fell on the violins, the basses, the desks—I was almost ill. And never-ending embraces: but you were not there!

...Going out, after the crowd had left, the artists waited for me in the courtyard of the Conservatoire, and as soon as I appeared the applause began again in the open air. In the evening at the Opéra the same thing, a regular ferment in the orchestra and the foyer. O my friend, why aren't you here! Since Sunday I have had a mortal sadness, this shattering emotion has knocked me out: my eyes are full of tears all the time, I would like to die.

The receipts totally covered the expenses and I even gained 150 francs, of which I must give two-thirds to Gounet, who so kindly lent it to me—I think he is more in need than you. But my debt to you troubles me, and as soon as I can get enough together to be worth sending you shall have it....

The concert took place at the Conservatoire on 1 November 1829, and included Berlioz' *Waverley* and *Francs-Juges* overtures, the Concert of Sylphs from *Faust* and the *Resurrexit* from the Mass, as well as Beethoven's E flat piano concerto and some smaller items.

To Humbert Ferrand
                              Paris, 2 January 1830
...I do not know where to turn for money. I have only two pupils, they bring me in forty-four francs a month: I still owe

you money besides the hundred francs to Gounet—this eternal penury, these constant debts, even to such old and tried friends as you, weigh on me terribly. Then again your father cherishes the absurd idea that I am a gambler—I, who never touch a card and have never set foot in a gaming house—and the thought that he disapproves of our friendship nearly drives me mad. For pity's sake, write soon!

To Humbert Ferrand

Paris, 6 February 1830

... Again, without warning and without reason my ill-starred passion wakes. She is still in London, yet I feel her presence around me. All my memories reawaken and combine to torture me. I listen to the beating of my heart, it is like a sledge-hammer, every nerve in my body quivers with pain.

Woe upon her! Could she but dream of the poetry, the infinite extent of such love as mine, she would fly to my arms, even though she should die in my embrace.

I was just going to begin my great symphony (*Episode in the Life of an Artist*) to depict the course of this infernal love of mine. I have it all in my head, but I can write nothing. ...

To Ferdinand Hiller

[Paris, ? March 1830]

My dear Ferdinand!

I must write to you again this evening—this letter will be perhaps no happier than the others. But no matter—

Can you tell me what is this overwhelming power of emotion, this faculty for suffering which is killing me?

Ask your seraph, the angel who has opened to you the gates of heaven.

Oh, let me not cry out!

Wait a moment—my fire is going out.

O my friend, do you know! To relight it I have burnt the manuscript of my prose elegy! Always tears, sympathetic tears, I see Ophelia shedding them, I hear her tragic voice, the rays from her sublime eyes consume me.

O my friend, I am so unhappy! inexpressibly unhappy!

I have spent some time drying the floods that have fallen from my eyes—while I saw Beethoven looking at me with severity, Spontini, far above ills like mine, regarding me with pity and indulgence—and Weber, speaking in my ear like a familiar spirit, awaiting me in a happy country to console me.

All this is crazy—completely crazy, from the point of view of a domino player in the Café de la Régence or a member of the Institute.

No, I still mean to live.

Music is a heavenly art, nothing surpasses it but true love— the one will always make me as unhappy as the other, but at least I shall have lived.

> suffering, it is true—
> with madness, cries and tears
> but I should have—
> NOTHING!

My dear Ferdinand! I have found in you all the signs of true friendship, my own friendship for you is also true, but I fear it will never bring you the calm happiness which one finds far from volcanoes—

> absolutely beside myself,
> incapable of saying anything
> RATIONAL

today it is a year since I saw HER for the last time—oh! unhappy woman! how I loved you—trembling I write, HOW I LOVE YOU!

If there is another world shall we find each other again?
Shall I ever see Shakespeare?

Will she know me? Will she understand the poetry of my love? Oh! Juliet, Ophelia, Belvidera, Jane Shore, names that hell repeats unceasingly.

truly:

I am a most unhappy man, a being almost alone in the world —an animal burdened with an exhausting imagination, eaten up with a boundless passion which is rewarded only with indifference and scorn: yes! but I have known some musical genuises, I have laughed in the gleam of their lightnings and I grind my teeth only at the unhappy memories.

Oh! sublime ones! sublime ones! annihilate me! summon me to your golden clouds! deliver me!...

Reason says to me

"peace, fool, in a few years there will be no more question of your agonies than of what you call the genius of Beethoven, the passionate sensibility of Spontini, the dreamy imagination of Weber, the colossal power of Shakespeare!

Go, go, Henriette Smithson
and   Hector Berlioz

will be reunited in the oblivion of the tomb, which will not prevent other unfortunates from SUFFERING AND DYING."

Ferdinand Hiller (1811–85) was a German musician who lived in Paris from 1828–35 and became friendly with Berlioz. Although he lived only a few streets away, Berlioz was impelled to pour out his sorrows to him through the post. The letter above took up four enormous pages of folio size. It marks a change in Berlioz' attachment to his inaccessible Ophelia, as may be seen from the following.

To Humbert Ferrand

Paris, 16 April 1830

...Since my last letter I have passed through some terrible squalls, my vessel cracked at every seam but finally righted itself, at present it rides passably. Some horrible truths, discoveries which cannot be doubted, have put me on the way to a cure, and I think it will be as complete as my natural tenacity will allow. I have just sanctioned my resolution by a work which satisfies me completely, and of which this is the subject: it will be set forth in a programme and distributed in the hall on the day of the concert:

EPISODE IN THE LIFE OF AN ARTIST
grand fantastic symphony in five movements

First Movement: in two parts, composed of a short adagio, followed immediately by a fully developed allegro (surge of passions, aimless reveries, delirious passion with all its facets of tenderness, jealousy, rage, fear, etc., etc.).
Second Movement: Scene in the country (adagio, thoughts of love and hope troubled by dark presentiments).
Third Movement: A ball (brilliant, headlong music).

Fourth Movement : March to the Scaffold (fierce, resplendent music).

Fifth Movement : Dream of a Witches' Sabbath.

And now, dear friend, here is how I have fashioned my novel, or rather my story, whose hero you will recognise....

[Here followed the original programme of the *Symphonie Fantastique*.] I have just written the last note. If I can be ready by Pentecost, the 30th of May, I shall give a concert at the Nouveautés, with an orchestra of 120; but I am afraid I shall not be able to have the parts copied in time. For the moment I feel stupid : the frightful intellectual effort of producing the work has tired my imagination and I would like to be able to sleep and rest continuously. But though my brain is drugged my heart is awake and I feel most strongly that I miss you. When, dear friend, shall I see you ?

To Humbert Ferrand

Paris, 13 May 1830

...Your letter comforts me, dear friend : how good it is to be blessed with a friend such as you ! It is so rare, my dear Humbert, to find a complete man, with a soul, a heart and an imagination : so rare for characters as ardent and restless as ours to meet and to be matched together, that I hardly know how to tell you what happiness it gives me to know you.

...You need not fear for me with Henriette Smithson : I am no longer in danger from that quarter. The symphony is not a deed of revenge. It is certainly not in that spirit that I wrote the Witches' Sabbath. I pity and despise her. She is an ordinary woman, gifted with an instinctive genius for reproducing the torments of the human soul without ever having felt them herself, and incapable of understanding a feeling as great and lofty as that with which I honoured her.

...The rehearsals of my symphony begin in three days : all the parts are copied—there are two thousand three hundred pages—nearly 400 francs worth of copying. I hope to goodness we shall have good receipts to pay for it all. It being Pentecost, all the theatres will be closed. And you alone will not be there ! Even my father wishes to come. Ah, but my symphony !

I hope that wretched woman will be present. Many people at the Feydeau are plotting to get her there. But I rather doubt it. She certainly won't go if she reads my programme. She

could not but recognise herself. What will people say? My story
is so well known.

To his father

Paris, 28 May [1830]

My dear papa,

I am just back from the country, where I have been since
the beginning of this week, staying with a rich Spaniard whom I
know, to whose daughter I gave some composition lessons last
year.

The father and mother are extremely friendly towards me,
and they have invited me to go and see them in the country so
many times that as my concert is not taking place I took the
opportunity to go. When I got back I found Mama's letter: the
idiotic bookseller whom I had told to put your volume in the
post was waiting for me to fetch it.

This is why my concert has been postponed. The German
Theatre was giving one that evening at the same time: and the
Conservatoire was giving another to let the King of Naples hear
the symphonies of Beethoven. The Duchesse de Berry asked the
Conservatoire to do this, and it will be extremely brilliant. We
would not have had many people at the Nouveautés even if I
had been able to put on my concert: we should have been
without singers, since Haitzinger and Mme Schroeder, who had
promised to sing for me, are obliged to sing at their own
theatre, and without orchestra, since the one I had counted on
bringing to the Nouveautés was engaged for the Conservatoire
and the German Theatre. I cannot have my symphony performed by an orchestra as meagre as that of the Nouveautés. I
send you Friday's *Figaro* which had already announced the concert and inserted the programme of my symphony as it will be
distributed in the hall at the performance. It is causing an
incredible stir, everybody is buying or stealing the *Figaro* in the
cafés. We had already had two rehearsals, very bad ones, but
it would have gone passably after five or six other sessions.

I was not mistaken when I wrote it. Everything is as I had
thought. Only, the March to the Scaffold is thirty times more
frightening than I expected. I cannot put on another concert
before All Saints' Day in November. After that Habeneck has
offered me his services, we will put on the symphony as one does

a grand opera, and the performance will be what it should be, tremendous.

Farewell my dear papa, I embrace you affectionately.

Your affectionate son,

H. Berlioz.

To Humbert Ferrand

Paris, 24 July 1830

... All that love offers that is most tender and delicate, I have from her. My enchanting sylph, my Ariel, my life, seems to love me more than ever: as for me, her mother keeps on saying that if she had read in a novel the description of a love like mine she would not believe it true.

... I am shut up in the Institute for the last time: I must have that prize, on which our happiness depends so much. Like Don Carlos in *Hernani*, I say: "I will have it". She is anxious about it too, and to reassure me in my prison Mme Moke sends me her maid every other day to give me news of them and take back news of me. God! how I shall reel when I see her again in ten or twelve days! We'll still have many obstacles to overcome, perhaps, but we will. What do you think of all this? Is it conceivable? An angel like her, the finest talent in Europe, is mine! I hear that M. de Noailles, in whom her mother has great confidence, has pleaded my cause, despite my lack of money. Oh, my dear friend, if you could hear her think aloud the sublime conceptions of Weber and Beethoven, you would lose your wits....

"Ariel" was a young pianist named Camille Moke, with whom Ferdinand Hiller had previously been in love. *Hernani*, Victor Hugo's much discussed play, was first performed in Paris on 25 February 1830. The prize was the Prix de Rome, for which Berlioz was entering for the fourth time.

To Humbert Ferrand

Paris, 23 August 1830

... I have won the Prix de Rome. It was awarded unanimously—a thing that has never been known before. What a joy it is to be successful when it gives pleasure to those one adores!

My sweet Ariel was dying with anxiety when I took her the news, her delicate wings were all ruffled till I smoothed them with a word. Even her mother, who does not look too favourably on our love, was touched to tears....

On the 1st November there is to be a concert at the Théâtre Italien. The new conductor, Girard, whom I know well, has asked me to write him an overture for it. I am going to take Shakespeare's *Tempest*: it will be a piece of an entirely new kind, for piano, chorus and orchestra.

My great concert with the *Symphonie Fantastique* is to be on the 14th November.

I do not want to go to Italy. I shall go and ask the King to let me off this ridiculous journey and allow me my scholarship in Paris.

As soon as I have collected the money you so kindly lent me you shall have it. Good-bye, good-bye. I have just come from Mme Moke's, a moment ago I held the hand of my adored Camille: that is why mine trembles so much and I write so badly. However she did not play me Weber and Beethoven today. Good-bye.

P.S. That wretched Smithson girl is still here. I have not seen her since her return.

To Humbert Ferrand

[Paris] October 1830

I'm writing to you in a corner of a café on the Champs-Elysées, while the setting sun slants through the dying leaves of the young trees surrounding my retreat. I've been talking about you all day to someone who understands or rather divines your nature....

You will be glad to hear that I am to be heard at the Opéra. All thanks to Camille! In her slender form, bewitching grace and musical genius I found Ariel personified. I have planned a tremendous overture which I have submitted to the musical director....

Farewell—my arm is getting cold from the marble on which I'm writing. My thoughts turn to the unfortunate Ophelia: stiff, chill, the dank earth, Polonius dead, Hamlet living. Oh! she is indeed unfortunate. Through the failure at the Opéra-Comique she has lost more than 6,000 francs. She is still here: I met her recently. She recognised me with the greatest sang-froid. I suffered all the evening, and then I went to the gracious Ariel to tell her about it: she said to me smiling: "Well, you aren't in a bad state! YOU didn't have a failure?" No, no, no, my angel, my genius, my art, my thought, my heart, my poetic life: I suffered without complaining: I thought of you: I adored your power: I blessed my recovery; from my delicious island I braved the bitter waves which broke there: I saw my ship wrecked, and looking at my leafy hut I blessed the bed of roses on which I was to rest. Ariel, Ariel, Camille, I adore you, I bless you, I love you, in one word, more than the poor French language can tell you: give me an orchestra of a hundred musicians and a chorus of a hundred and fifty voices and I will tell you....

To Humbert Ferrand
[Paris] 19 November 1830

Just a few lines in haste to tell you that I am giving a gigantic concert at the Conservatoire—The *Francs-Juges* Overture, the Sacred Song and the Warriors' Song from the *Mélodies*, and *Sardanapalus* with one hundred performers for the CON-FLAGRATION, and last of all the *Symphonie Fantastique*.

Come. O do come. It will be terrific. Habeneck conducts. *The Tempest* is to be played a second time at the Opéra. It is new, fresh, strange, grand, sweet, tender, surprising. Fétis wrote two splendid articles on it for the *Revue Musicale*. Someone said to him that I was possessed of a devil. "The devil may possess his body, but by Jove! a god possesses his head,' he replied.

The *Tempest* Overture referred to in the previous two letters eventually became the final number in *Lélio*, the *Fantasia on The Tempest*.

To Humbert Ferrand
[Paris] 7 December 1830

You really must come: I had a wild success. The *Symphonie Fantastique* was received with shouts and acclamations: they had to repeat the March to the Scaffold, and the Witches' Sabbath was quite overwhelming in its Satanic effect. I have been asked to repeat the concert on the 25th [*sic*] of this month, the day after Christmas....

To Humbert Ferrand

[Paris] 12 December 1830

... I leave Paris at the beginning of January. My marriage is fixed for Easter 1832, on condition that I do not lose my pension, and that I go to Italy for a year. My blessed symphony has done the deed and won this concession from Camille's mother....

Oh, I am in a state of intoxication! Since she heard my Witches' Sabbath, Camille calls me her "Lucifer", her "dear Satan"....

The proposed concert did not come off, and Berlioz had to leave for Italy before the end of the year.

To Rouget de Lisle

Paris, 29 December 1830

Sir, I have just received your letter, and I am leaving in a few hours. I am forced to travel to Italy in order not to lose the pension which goes with the Institute prize: so I shall be deprived of the honour of seeing you till my return. I am very annoyed about these tiresome circumstances: one of my most cherished dreams has always been to know personally the author of the *Marseillaise*, and were it not for this damnable journey I would jump at the opportunity he so kindly offers me. I can only curse the more bitterly the tyranny of routine which exiles me from France at the moment when my presence in Paris could be advantageous, and thank you, Sir, for the flattering letter with which you have kindly honoured me.

I have the honour to be, Sir, your devoted servant and sincere admirer.

Hector Berlioz.

The letter referred to was one from Rouget de l'Isle complimenting Berlioz on his orchestration of the *Marseillaise* and suggesting a meeting.

To Stephen de la Madelaine*

Paris, 30 December 1830, at two
in the morning

I am leaving: but happily without fear: my Ariel, my angel,
* 1801–68. A singer, later critic, theatre manager and musical bureaucrat.

can no longer be taken from me : we are so bound together that only our own wills can separate us. During my exile I will try to write some large work and on my return we will shake the musical world in an uncommon way. Meanwhile try to make a breach in what remains of the academic edifice. I leave in six hours.

To Ferdinand Hiller
La Côte-Saint-André, 9 January 1831
I am at home once more, deluged with compliments, caresses and tender solicitude by my family, yet I am miserable : my heart barely beats, the oppression of my soul suffocates me. My parents understand and forgive....

To Ferdinand Hiller
La Côte-Saint-André, 23 January 1831
I have just made a tedious trip to Grenoble, spending half my time ill in bed, the other half in paying visits of which each was more boring than the last : I got back yesterday after passing an exhausting day saying nothing. My father, who had heard of my state from my mother, embraced me smiling and told me that there was a letter from Paris for me : I understood from his manner that it was from madame ... : in fact it was a *double* letter : I became calm again : I was as delighted as I could be in such an execrable exile. Now comes yours today to disturb my calm. The devil take you ! Why do you need to tell me that I am luxuriating in despair, that *no one* is worried about me, "Least of all the people I am in despair about" ?

First of all I am not in despair about *people* : next let me tell you that if you have your reasons for judging severely the person I am in despair about, I also have my reasons for assuring you that now I know her character better than anyone. I know that S H E is not in despair : the proof of that is that I am here and that if she had persisted in begging me not to leave, as she did several times, I would have stayed.

Don't give me your Epicurean advice, it is not of the least use to me. It only leads to minor happiness and I don't want that. Happiness on a grand scale or death, poetical life or annihilation. So don't talk to me about superb women with splendid figures, and the roles which beings dear to me *may or may not* be playing in my distress, for you don't know anything about it—who told you?

How can you tell what she thinks? What she feels? Because you saw her gay and apparently happy at a concert why should you draw conclusions adverse to me? If it comes to that you might have said the same of me if you had seen me at a family dinner at Grenoble with a pretty young cousin on each side of me....

My letter is brusque, my friend, but you have upset me terribly. I shall be here for another nine days at least. If you could write me another letter, by return, it would give me great pleasure. Tell me what the world says of my marriage, if you have heard any talk about it.

To Ferdinand Hiller

La Côte-Saint-André, 31 January 1831

Although my overpowering anxiety still endures, I can write more calmly today. I am still too ill to get up, and the cold is frightful here....

Yes, my dear friend, I cannot reveal to you the cause of a terrible distress which I suffer and shall perhaps continue to suffer for a long time yet, but which must remain a secret: it concerns circumstances of my life which are unknown to anyone, Camille excepted: at least I have had the consolation of telling her about it, without—but enough.

Although I am compelled to be mysterious with you on this matter, I don't think you are right to be mysterious with me on other matters. So I beg you to tell me what you mean by this last sentence in your last letter: "You wish to make a sacrifice: I have long been afraid of one which unfortunately I have many reasons to believe you will make one day". What sacrifice are you talking about? I urge you in your letters never to speak in ambiguous terms, especially in connection with *her*. It tortures me. Don't forget to tell me frankly what it means....

Hiller, Berlioz' predecessor in Camille's favours, had been hinting that Camille, to whom Berlioz was now officially engaged, was not appearing to miss her fiancé very much. In spite of his anxiety Berlioz embarked for Rome, finally arriving there in the middle of March. However, still not having heard from Camille, he started back towards France on 1 April.

To Horace Vernet
                          Diano Marina, 18 April 1831
...*An odious crime*, an abuse of confidence of which I have
been the victim, has put me in a delirium of rage from Florence
to here. I was flying back to France to exact the most just ven-
geance: at Genoa a moment of giddiness, the most inconceiv-
able weakness broke my resolution, I abandoned myself to
childish despair: but I got away with swallowing a lot of salt
water, being harpooned like a salmon, lying a quarter of an
hour stretched out dead in the sun and vomiting violently for
an hour: I don't know who fished me out. People thought I
had fallen by accident from the town ramparts. But at last I am
alive: I must live for my two sisters whose death would have
been caused by mine, and for my art. Although I am still shaking like a ship firing to port and starboard, I promise you on
my honour not to leave Italy: it's the only way of preventing
myself carrying out my plan....

To M. M. Gounet, Girard, Hiller, Desmarets, Richard, Sichel
                                       Nizza, 6 May 1831
...I have made the acquaintance of Mendelssohn. He is a
wonderful fellow. His skill as a player is as great as his genius,
which is saying a great deal. Everything I have heard of his
has always delighted me. I am convinced he is one of the greatest
musical talents of the age. He has been my cicerone. Every
morning I went to his house. He would play me a Beethoven
sonata: we would sing from Gluck's *Armide*: then he would
take me to see all the famous ruins which, I confess, did not
move me very much. He has one of those clear, pure souls that
one does not often come across: he believes firmly in his
Lutheran creed, and I'm afraid I shocked him terribly by
making fun of the Bible.
    I have to thank him for the only pleasant moments I had
during my time in Rome.
    I was devoured by anxiety, I received no letter from my
faithful fiancée, and but for M. Horace I would have left at
the end of three days—I was so desperate at not having heard
from her when I arrived. At the end of the month, still not
hearing, I left on Good Friday, abandoning my pension in order
to go to Paris and find out what was happening. Mendelssohn
wouldn't believe that I was really going, he bet me a dinner

for three that I wouldn't go, and we ate it with Montfort on Ash Wednesday when he saw that M. Horace had paid for my journey and that I had engaged my carriage.

At Florence I had a bad throat: I stopped there and had to wait until I was well enough to go on: while there, I wrote to Pixis asking him to tell me as quickly as possible what was going in the Faubourg Montmartre: he didn't reply to me: I told him I would wait for his letter in Florence, and in fact I waited until the day I received the admirable letter of Mme Moke. It is impossible for me to describe what fury, rage, hatred and love combined I felt in my isolation. . . .

This letter is an incredible model of insolence! You must see it to believe it. Hiller knows better than anybody how the whole affair began: and I know that I left Paris with her engagement ring on my finger, given in exchange for mine: I was called "my son-in-law", etc. . . . and in this astonishing letter Mme X tells me that she had never agreed to the request which I had made to her for the hand of her daughter: she earnestly begs me not to kill myself, dear kind soul!

Now I am quite recovered and can eat as usual: for a long time I couldn't swallow anything except oranges. At last I am saved, they are saved: I come back to life with delight, I throw myself into the arms of music and feel more keenly than ever the pleasure of having true friends. I beg you all, Richard, Gounet, Girard, Demarest, Hiller to write me each a separate letter. I shall not cross the frontier: Vernet reminded me yesterday that there was still time and that my pension was not lost. I wrote to him that I would promise on my *honour* not to leave Italy: I took advantage of a moment of sanity to bind myself in this way. . . .

P.S. I have almost finished the overture on *King Lear*: I have only the orchestration to complete. I am going to work very hard.

Mme Moke's letter announced that Camille was marrying M. Pleyel, the piano manufacturer. Berlioz at once decided to return to Paris and kill Camille, her fiancé, her mother and finally himself. In Genoa an impulse momentarily led to his clumsy attempt at suicide related in the letter to Vernet, and on the way to the Riviera he gave up the whole scheme and wrote to Vernet, who was the director of the French Academy in Rome, to find out if he could still be reinstated there: if he left Italy he was bound to give up his stipend in Rome. Meanwhile he remained in Nice, which was still part of Sardinia at that time, until he received Vernet's reply saying that he could return to Rome without further apologies.

To Humbert Ferrand

Nice, 10 or 11 May 1831

Well, Ferrand, I am getting on. No more rage, no more revenge, no more trembling, gnashing of teeth, no more hell in fact!

...If your silence means laziness on your part, it is too bad of you. When one comes back to life, as I have done, one feels the need of a friendly arm, an outstretched hand.

Yes, Camille has married Pleyel. I am glad of it now. I see now the perils that I have escaped.

What meanness! what shabbiness! what apathy! what infinite—almost sublime—villainy, if sublime can go with ignobility (I have stolen that new phrase from you).

I am going back to Rome in five or six days—my pension is not lost....

P.S. My repertoire has just been increased by a new overture. Yesterday I finished one on Shakespeare's *King Lear*.

To Thomas Gounet

Rome, 14 June 1831

...I wrote the words on the way from San Lorenzo to Rome, during my recent journey: I had left the carriage behind me, and on the road I wrote on my briefcase. The music is finished too: I only have to copy it. There are six monologues and six pieces of music, solo songs, chorus, orchestra alone or chorus and orchestra. I am sorry I can't show you my attempts at literature and profit by your advice, but this is only postponed. For the verse, I did not amuse myself by running after rhymes: I wrote metrical prose only occasionally in rhyme—that is all that is necessary for music. It was Moore who gave me the idea for the work. Anyway the presence of music is justified by my [text] and I have presented the subject in a dramatic framework. The plot begins after the dream of the Witches' Sabbath, at the moment where the artist comes back to life.

This trip has enriched me with three new works: the overture *King Lear*, the one on *Rob Roy* and the Mélologue: I don't know what this is worth, but I know that my journey to Nice cost me one thousand and fifty francs : I am so happy that my purpose was not attained that I don't regret this money today.

This refers to *Lélio, or The Return to Life*, a sequel to the *Symphonie Fantastique*, in which Berlioz incorporated various previously written pieces, such as the Chorus of Shades, the Chorus of Brigands and the Fantasia on *The Tempest*, as well as the motto theme of the *Symphonie Fantastique* itself.

To his parents

Rome, 24 June 1831

...I went to Tivoli last Saturday, at two in the afternoon, in the middle of the dusty heat. There were two of us. We got three-quarters of the way there but then felt exhausted and hailed a passing carriage. It's fifteen miles from Rome to Tivoli. We arrived at half past eight, and next morning got up at four and went straight off exploring. I've never seen anything so exquisite : the waterfalls, clouds of powdery spray, the smoking clefts, the fresh cool river, the caves, the innumerable rainbows, the olive groves, the hills, the country houses, the village—the whole thing is enchanting and unique. The people there are very handsome, but they beg even more than they do in Rome; only, their begging hasn't the unpleasantly debased quality of the Romans'. They do it quite brazenly—they name the sum they want, and laugh as they do so, as if it were a joke between you. Some young men and women, aged between twenty and thirty, who were harvesting and saw us go past, shouted out : "Hey, sir, come on, give us half a *paolo* (five sous), give us a *baiocco* (one sou), what's it to you ?"...

The evening before last, I felt some emotion for the first time in our convent. There were four or five of us sitting in the moonlight round the fountain on the little staircase which leads to the garden. We drew lots for who should fetch my guitar, and as the audience consisted of the few fellow-students whose company I can bear, I did not need any pressing. As I was beginning an aria from *Iphigeneia in Tauris*, M. Carle Vernet appeared. After a couple of minutes he began to weep and sob out loud, then he fled into his son's drawing room, crying out in a choked voice : "Horace, come here !" "What is it, what is it?" "We're all in tears". "Why, why, what's happened?" "M. Berlioz is singing us some Gluck. Oh, how right you are (turning to me), it's overwhelming. You know, you're a melancholy man, I understand you, I do, there are people who—". He couldn't finish. But no one laughed. The fact is we were all moved. I was in the mood, it was night, I felt quite free from anxiety beneath that resonant porch, and I let myself go as if I had been alone....

To his sister Adèle

Tivoli, 8 July 1831

I'm here, next to the big waterfall—I'm writing this in a little temple of Vesta, three-quarters preserved, by the edge next to where the water goes over into the ravine. There's a little table in the middle, no doubt where they used to keep the sacred fire. I've brought some tea here and my guitar. I feel terribly upset. On my way to Hadrian's villa this morning I asked some boys I met for news of Antonio, a child of fourteen who had acted as my guide the first time I came here; I had liked him at once, and felt extraordinarily drawn to him, without quite knowing why. They told me he had been ill for ten days. When I returned from wandering among the ruins, I was shown his house, and went up and found his mother and his young sisters round his bed, in a wretched, dilapidated room. He was asleep, and looked dreadfully pale and drawn, but still beautiful, with that Raphael-like beauty that I have not seen anywhere else but in Italy...I went and fetched some money; when I got back he was awake, and recognised me but could not speak. I gave his mother what I could. She tried to get Antonio to make an effort to thank *lo signore francese*, but he couldn't say anything intelligible, I could only understand the great lack-lustre eyes turned towards me. Then the mother began to weep and to say that she didn't know what to do, they had tried applying leeches to his head but he cried all the time, what an unhappy woman she was, yet she could not believe the *madona* wouldn't preserve her son for her. I said he would be in bed for some time yet but for sure the *madona* would save him. I couldn't do any more: I felt as if I were stifling, and I fled. I climbed the hill behind Tivoli. At the top there is a battered old wooden cross; I sat down at the foot of it, and looked at the stupid city of Rome in the distance, and the immense plain around it and the winding

Anio, and the lakes a long way off shining in the sun; I stayed there a long time... That wretched woman with her *madona* keeps coming into my mind. I keep seing poor Antonio, who was so blithe and gay a few days ago and now is dying....

To his family

Subiaco, 17 July 1831

How Nanci would be delighted with this country, and how Adèle could shine, climbing the mountains (I remember our expedition to the Saint-Eynard, with Adèle thirty yards ahead of us all the way)... The mountains! I came back from there an hour ago... Oh, how I breathed, and gazed, and lived! Not a cloud to be seen. I clambered up for half an hour and then lay on the top, lulled by a soft, delicious breeze....

To Charles Duveyrier*

Rome, 28 July 1831

... Your words were not lost on me: the warmth and passion with which you preached the doctrine to me at first astonished me rather than moved me: but in this case, as in all other things, one must let time act. Since I left you new storms have broken over me: vileness and turpitude had plotted my undoing: as you have perhaps heard, Camille has married Pleyel, in spite of the strongest and most sacred bonds, to the detriment of her honour and reputation. Don't let's say any more about it.

Since my return to Rome I have met one of us, Cendrier the architect: † we have often spoken of you and Saint-Simon. His cool and calm conviction made me think a lot. I read with avidity a number of issues of the *Globe* which someone lent me recently and my last doubts have been completely removed. In all that concerns the political reorganisation of society I am convinced today that the plan of Saint-Simon is the only true and complete one, but I must tell you that my ideas have not varied in the least in all that concerns the supernatural, God, the soul, an afterlife, etc. I do not think this need be an obstacle to my joining my hopes and efforts to yours for the betterment

* Duveyrier (1803–66) was the editor of the Saint-Simonian periodicals *L'Organisateur* and *Le Globe*: he later became a playwright and political pamphleteer.

† François-Alexandre Cendrier (1803–92) became chief architect for the Paris–Lyon railway, and built the termini in Paris and Lyon.

of the most numerous and poorer class, for the natural ordering
of talents and for the destruction of any kind of privilege, which,
hidden like vermin in the folds of the social body, have up to
now paralysed all efforts which attempt to remedy it. Write to
me about this : I will reply to you at once to let you know my
ideas about the way in which I can be used musically in the
great work when I return to Paris.

To Ferdinand Hiller
                                    Rome, 17 September 1831
...Nothing pleases me more than this vagabond life in the
woods and among the rocks, with these friendly peasants, sleeping by day on the banks of the torrent, and in the evening dancing the saltarello with the men and women who regularly come
to our inn. I make them happy with my guitar : before I came
they only danced to the tambour de basque, and they are
delighted with this melodious instrument. I go there to escape
from the boredom which kills me here. For some days I have
managed to get over it by going hunting : I left Rome at midnight so as to get there at dawn : I wore myself out, I died of
thirst and hunger, but I didn't get bored. The last time I shot
sixteen quail, seven marsh birds, a large snake and a porcu-
pine....

Has Mendelssohn arrived yet? His talent is enormous, extraordinary, superb, prodigious. You can't suspect me of partiality
in saying this, for he frankly told me that he understood
nothing of my music....

To Thomas Gounet
                                    Rome, 28 November 1831
...My hatred for everything which they have the impudence
to honour with the name of music in Italy is stronger than ever.
Yes, their music is a whore : from a distance its appearance
suggests a licentious character : at close quarters its dull conversation reveals a stupid beast.

I have only got rid of one of my prejudices : this is against
the Italians, whom I find as good people as any others, especially
those in the mountains, of whom I have seen the most. So I
often go to visit them : my wretched illness makes new progress
every day in Rome : I don't know any other remedy except
flight when the attacks get too bad. As soon as I feel more tormented by *spleen* than usual I put on my hunting jacket, I take

my gun and go off to Subiaco whatever the weather is. A week ago I made the journey from Tivoli to Subiaco in a furious rain which lasted all day. Last month I came back from Naples on foot across the mountains, through the woods, rocks and high pastures, and I only took a guide once. You wouldn't believe how delightful such a trip can be: its fatigues, its privations, its moments of danger, all this enchanted me: I spent nine days which I shall remember for a long time.

I won't speak to you of my various impressions, of Vesuvius, Naples, Pompeii, etc.: I would have too much to say, only I always find that nothing equals the sea. But we'll talk, we'll talk about all that....

To Humbert Ferrand

Rome 8 January 1832

Why did you not tell me of your marriage? Of course I believe, since you say so, that you did not get my letters, but even so how could you keep silence?...

Your *Noce des Fées* is exquisite: so fresh, so full of grace, but I can't make music for it yet. Orchestration is not advanced enough: I must first dematerialise it, then perhaps I may think of treading in Weber's footsteps.

I send you an idea for a three-act opera. Here is the skeleton, which you will clothe with flesh and sinew:

The Last Day of the World

The world ruled by an all-powerful tyrant, the height of civilisation, the extremes of corruption; a pagan court; a handful of religious people, suffered to live in freedom by the contempt of the tyrant; war, victory, a triumph, with pitched battles fought between slaves in the arena; atrocities. The leader of the faithful, a kind of Daniel rebuking Belshazzar, denounces the despot's crimes, and reveals that the prophecies are about to be fulfilled, and that the end of the world is at hand. The tyrant in amused scorn forces the prophet to be present at an appalling orgy in his palace, in the course of which a parody of the Last Day is enacted by him and his wives and eunuchs; but while it is being performed the earth quakes, angels sound gigantic trumpets, the True Christ appears, the Judgment has come.

That of course is as far as the work goes.

Tell me if the subject appeals to you. Avoid detailed effects:

they are lost at the Opéra. And if possible don't be tied by the
absurd bond of rhyme, leave it out altogether whenever there is
no point in it, as is often the case. . . .

To Thomas Gounet

Rome, 17 February 1832

. . . I shall leave here at the beginning of May : I shall go to
Grenoble, playing a trick on M. Horace who will think I am in
Milan. From there I will make a trip to Paris, and you can
imagine what joy it will be to return to you, and music, and
our teas at the Café de la Bourse, and our excellent dinners at
Lemardelay's, and the stories and the chatter : for we can allow
ourselves these, we who aren't married. Aren't you bitten by this
matrimonial madness which seizes them all? My sister too has
just married a judge of the tribunal of Grenoble. Albert Duboys,
whose "Cantata for the Duchesse de Berry" you remember, together with the rather odd letter which was attached to it, is
getting married too, to a rich beauty from the department of
Drôme. Auguste, Ferrand, Edouard Rocher, de Carné, all, all
got married this year : look out for yourself : "Birds, preserve,
preserve your freedom!"

To Gasparo Spontini

Rome, 29 March 1832

. . . You know too well how to distinguish truth from false-
hood to doubt the feelings I entertain for the great man
whose name alone is enough to bring a glow of enthusiasm to
my cheeks. The continuous agitation in which I have lived, the
heartbreaks, the storms of every kind which I have experienced
during the past year will have to be my excuse. I was hardly in
Rome for two months at a time : I was continually on the
move, to Florence, Genoa, Nice, Naples, into the mountains, on
foot, with the sole purpose of tiring myself, of dulling my senses
and resisting more easily the spleen which tormented me. It
would be tedious for you to know the causes of this spiritual
malady from which I am far from being cured. My life till now
has been a strange tissue of adventures and painful experiences,
of which the last episode is only the least. You will remember
perhaps having tried to dissuade me from a marriage which I
was on the point of contracting when you were in Paris. Your
advice, which I now see was sound, was powerless against

passion : a month after my departure this passion was dead, destroyed by the broken faith of her who had inspired it. I realise the extent of the danger I have escaped and I congratulate myself on being able to enjoy my freedom.

My musical observations in those parts of Italy which I have visited are far from redounding to the credit of the *bel paese* : I have found only childishness, pettiness, servile imitation, platitude and an utter lack of great ideas and genius. I have seen poor incompetent performers, wretchedly ignorant maestri, and both categories so convinced of their superiority to the rest of Europe that I could only smile at them in pity. They often reminded me of La Fontaine's baby mouse who, never having left its hole, on its first outing mistook a molehill for the Alps.

Oh ! how far it is from this little world, half artistic and half commercial, to that which you created around you ! that majestic, brilliant, harmonious, poetic world which surrounds you like a glorious halo ! Where are the scores of *La Vestale, Cortez, e tante altre divine sorelle*, with their noble expressiveness, their passionate élan, their royal manner ? Where are the noble choruses and fiery orchestra whose vibrations have so often shaken my whole being ? In Berlin, in Berlin I shall find again my adored idols, even more richly adorned than in Paris : in Berlin I shall at last be able to quench fully my thirst for the true sublime which devours me and which has only been aggravated by the Italian sun.

Berlioz had met the composer whom he so much admired towards the end of 1830 and had been well received by him. Spontini gave him an introduction to his brother, who was a monk in Italy.

To Ferdinand Hiller

Florence, 13 May 1832

I arrived yesterday and found your letter. Why do you not say whether the sale of my medal realised enough to pay the two hundred francs I owe you ? ...

I left Rome without regrets. Life at the Academy had grown intolerable. I spent all my evenings with the Director's family, who have been most kind, and whom I like a great deal. They said goodbye to me with such marks of friendship and affection that I was quite moved, particularly as I had not expected any such demonstrations. Mlle Vernet is prettier and her father younger than ever.

It moved me to see Florence again. It's a town I adore. Everything about it pleases me, its name, its sky, its river, its setting and surroundings—I love it all. I've renewed acquaintance with an old pupil of Choron's, Duprez, who is the fashionable singer here: he has a salary of fifteen thousand francs at the Pergola Theatre, and has into the bargain a genuine and considerable talent and a delightful and accurate voice, and knows music. He is not an actor, like Nourrit, but he sings better, with a fresher and more individual timbre. He'll be the rage in Paris in a few years, I'm certain. He sang at my first concert, before you came to Paris. Last night, during an interval, we enjoyed ourselves reminiscing about that period of our lives. We've both advanced a few steps since then—me five or six, he twenty or thirty....

My sensations are so curiously confused that I cannot explain them even to myself. I know no one, I have not had any adventures here, I am utterly alone. Perhaps that is what affects me so oddly. I seem to be not myself but some stranger, some Russian or Englishman, sauntering along the Lung'Arno. Berlioz is merely a distant acquaintance. I act the dandy, spend money, lounge about like a fop. I don't understand it....

To Josef Dessauer

Milan, 23 May 1832
...Here is my itinerary: until November in Dauphiné, then to Paris till February, thence to Munich and finally to Berlin.

Dessauer (1798–1876) was a composer of operettas and lieder who mostly lived in Vienna: Berlioz had met him in Paris.

To Thomas Gounet

La Côte-Saint-André, 11 June 1832
My very dear Gounet,

Give me your news quickly, I beg you. You can imagine how I am worried about you in the middle of all these dreadful nonsenses. I arrived from Rome a few days ago: I stopped in Florence, Milan and Turin. I am supposed to be in Italy, and in consequence cannot show myself in Paris till November, where I shall give a concert, if Heaven permits, and from there go to Berlin.

Why did you leave me during that awful time without giving me a sign of life? There is no need to write me long letters if you haven't time: a few lines will be enough.

As soon as I get your answer, which I hope will be soon, I will send you a little letter for Cazalès whose contents I'll explain to you: it should, I think, enable you to get the money which I have owed you for such a long time. I treat you very badly, it is true, and I am afraid that you may say of me like Lucullus: "I could not treat your friends like that..." But no, frankly, I am not afraid of that: you know very well that you have given me the right to regard you as one of my best and most stalwart friends.

As the regulations of the Academy confine me to Italy for the rest of this year, don't talk too much about my arrival in France: it might compromise M. Horace and myself. However I would be very glad to have news of Lesueur: try also to inform me what's happening to my other acquaintances, Desmarest, Prévost, Casimir, Turbry, Girard, if you can.

Hiller is in Frankfurt, I got a letter from him in Florence. Didn't he saddle you with a parcel for me?

I am going to see Ferrand at Bellay next week: nevertheless address your reply to the Côte.

Farewell, my dear friend.

Ever.

The "nonsenses" referred to were the outbreak of cholera in Paris on 26 March, and various political upheavals which took place between March and June.

To Madame Horace Vernet
La Côte-Saint-André, 25 July 1832

You have set me, Madame, a new and most agreeable task. An intelligent woman not only permits me to send her my random thoughts, but undertakes to read them without noticing their ridiculous side to much. It is hardly generous of me to take advantage of your kindness but aren't we all selfish? For my part I admit that whenever such a temptation comes I shall fall into it with the utmost alacrity. I should have done so sooner had I not on my descent from the Alps been caught like a ball on the bound and tossed from villa to villa round Grenoble.

My fears that on returning to France I might have to parody Voltaire and say: "The more I see of other lands, the *less* I love my own country" were without foundation: all the glories of the glorious kingdom of Naples are powerless beside the ineffable charms of my beautiful valley of the Isère....

Of society however I cannot say the same. The advantage is entirely with the absent, who are not "always wrong", in spite of the proverb. Despite my Herculean efforts to turn the conversation, the good people here *will* insist on talking art, music and poetry to me, and you know how provincials talk! They have the most extraordinary notions, theories which make an artist's blood curdle in his veins, and on top of it all the calmest assumption of infallibility. To hear them talk of Byron, Goethe or Beethoven one would think these were respectable bootmakers or tailors with rather more talent than their colleagues. Nothing is good enough, there is no reverence, no respect, no enthusiasm. Thus, though living in a crowd, I am utterly, cruelly alone, and am parched for want of music. No longer can I look forward to my evening pleasures with Mlle Louise and her piano, to the sublime adagios which she was kind enough to play to me and to play again, when I obstinately made her do so, with the same unruffled patience and beauty of expression. You smile, Madame? No doubt you murmur that I know neither what I want nor where I want to be—that in fact I am half mad. To which I reply, I know perfectly well what I want, and as to my madness, since there is a general disposition to humour me, and there are many circumstances in which it pays to be thought mad, I make the best of it.

My father thought up recently a remarkable method of making me a good boy. He decided to marry me off. Presuming, rightly, or wrongly, on information given him, that my approaches would be well received by a very rich person, he urged me very strongly to offer myself to her, for the unanswerable reason that a young man who will never have a heritage of more than a hundred thousand francs should not neglect to marry a person who had three hundred thousand at present and the expectation of as much to come. I treated this as a joke for some time: but as my father became more insistent I had to declare categorically that I felt myself incapable of ever loving the person in question and I was not for sale at any price. The discussion ended there, but it upset me terribly, for I thought my father knew me better. . . .

I would have liked to send Mlle Louise some small composition of the kind that she likes: but what I had written did not seem to me good enough to earn the smile of approval of the gracious Ariel, so I followed the advice of my self-esteem and burnt it.*

As I promised M. Horace, I will not go to Paris before the end of the year, and as soon as I have unleashed my vocal and instrumental broadside, will leave for Berlin under full sail. But I see that I am taking unmerciful advantage of your kindness and will conclude by asking your pardon for my garrulity.

To Ferdinand Hiller

La Côte-Saint-André, 7 August 1832

What a queer, elusive, piquant, teasing witty creature is this Hiller! Were we both women I should detest her: were only she a woman I should simply hate her, for I loathe coquettes. As it is, "Providence having ordered all for the best", as the pious say, we are luckily both men. No, my dear fellow, you being you naturally "could not do otherwise" than make me wait two months for your letter: naturally also I "could not do otherwise" than be angry with you as a result. However, as I was not wounded to the quick by your neglect I wrote you a second letter and then burnt it, remembering Napoleon's wise remark: "There are certain things that should never be said. Still less should they be written." Oh Napoleon, Napoleon! Now you've gone and let my enthusiasm escape. However, to save you from such a calamity I won't talk of him and his relics in Lombardy and of how I trod in his mighty footsteps on my way back to France. Instead I'll tell you about three grave mistakes in your letter. Since you are learning Latin I shall turn schoolmaster.

No. 1. There should be no accent on *negre*.

No. 2 *DE grands amusements*, not *des*.

No. 3. *Il est possible que Mendelssohn L'AIT*, not *l'aura*. Take thou good heed unto my lesson. Ouf ! . . .

I spend my time copying my Mélologue :† I have been two months at it hard and still have sixty-two days' work. Do I not

---

* "Ariel" in this case refers, of course, to Mme Vernet's daughter Louise.

† *Lélio.*

persevere? I am ill for lack of music, positively paralysed: then I still suffer from that bilious trouble which sometimes keeps me in bed. However I am up to-day, getting ready for the next attack.

I am going to see Ferrand: we have not met for five years. You see extremes meet. He is more religious than ever and has married a woman who adores him and whom he adores.

To Thomas Gounet

Paris, 6 November 1832

I have just arrived. I am staying at rue Neuve-Saint-Marc, No. 1, in the former rooms of H. Sm...It's curious! I'm longing to embrace you: this evening at eight at the café Feydeau.

To F. B. Seghers

Paris, 16 December 1832

My dear friend,

I am very tired, overwrought, extinguished, dead, and yet I must stick to my arduous path. I am going to give my concert again, perhaps to-morrow week, can I count on your help again? I think I will come out of it all right in spite of the increased expenses, all the fixed costs having been paid.

Farewell, I am so sad not to be seeing H. Smithson to-night that my mind is a blank. Last evening was full of tears for *both of us*. She has a deep and true sensitivity with which I did not credit her: I love her as on the first day, I think I am sure of being loved by her, but she trembles, she hesitates and doesn't know what to decide: how will it all end?

Farewell, I will tell you when the rehearsal is. Habeneck is all for my staying longer in Paris, so that he can put on my symphony at the Conservatoire Concerts.

The devil knows what he really thinks: but let us only judge actions. Farewell again.

Your sincere friend,
H. Berlioz.

The concert on 9 December consisted of the *Symphonie Fantastique* and the premiere of *Lélio*. Harriet Smithson, though not invited by Berlioz himself, attended. Berlioz repeated the concert on 30 December and gave up his plan of going to Germany. Seghers (1801–81) was a Belgian violinist in the Conservatoire

Orchestra. François Habeneck (1781–1849) was a violinist and conductor who founded the Conservatoire Orchestra.

To Joseph d'Ortigue

Paris, 19 January 1833

Never has more intense pain gnawed a man's heart! I am in the seventh circle of hell. I was right, there is no justice in heaven.... Oh! oh! damnation, I could break a red-hot iron between by teeth....*

To Joseph d'Ortigue

Paris, 5 February 1833

I have nothing but happiness to tell you. At this moment the sun shines brilliantly. Henriette and I have been mutually slandered in respect of each other in the most infamous manner. All is cleared up, the strength of her love has been fully revealed. There is formidable opposition. I have written to my father. The dénouement approaches. Come and see me, I beg you, and tell me your news....

To Thomas Gounet

[Paris] 7 February 1833

...I have much to talk to you about. *You have been, we have been strangely deceived* as regards H. Sm..., my good and dear friend, I am intensely happy: until further orders. On my family's side the persecutions are just beginning: on hers they never stop. But she promises me she will be courageous and not give way: as for me, I know I shall not fail in this and we shall conquer our difficulties: *soon*, I hope....

To Humbert Ferrand

Paris, 2 March 1833

...I didn't write to you, for the reason that you have guessed: I am entirely absorbed in the worries and difficulties of my position. My father has refused his consent and has forced me to take legal steps.

In all this Henriette has behaved with irreproachable dignity and calm, her family and friends persecute her even more than mine in their attempts to get her away from me.

* d'Ortigue was a well-known music critic and friend of Berlioz.

To Humbert Ferrand

Paris, 12 June 1833

...It is really too bad of me to cause you anxiety on my account. You know how my life fluctuates. One day fine, calm, full of dreams and poetic fancies : another day, ill with nerves, irritable, snappy and snarly like a dog, vicious as a thousand devils, vomiting up life and ready to end it for nothing, if I didn't have a mad happiness in perspective always coming nearer, good friends, music, and curiosity. My life is a novel which interests me greatly.

You ask how I pass my days? If I am well I read or sleep on the sofa, for I am in comfortable lodgings, or scribble a few well-paid pages for the *Europe Littéraire*. About six I go to see Henriette, who to my sorrow is still ill. I must tell you all about her some day. Your opinion of her is quite wrong : her life too is a strange book, and her outlook on life, her mind, her feelings are by no means the least interesting part of it.

I am still thinking about the opera I asked you to write in a letter from Rome eighteen months ago. As in all this time you have not conquered your laziness sufficiently to do it, don't be angry that I have given it to Deschamps and Saint-Félix. I really *have* been patient!...

To Ferdinand Hiller

Paris, 18 July 1833

...I am going to leave for Grenoble in two days : I must see if I really have lost my father too,* and if I am a pariah to all the family. My father won't give me anything, hoping by this means to stop my marriage. She has nothing, I can do nothing or very little for her : yesterday evening we spent two hours together in tears. I cannot make her accept such money as I dispose of under any pretext whatever. Fortunately I have obtained from the Fund for the Encouragement of Fine Arts a subsidy of 1,000 francs for her, which I will give her shortly. It is the wait for this money, which I want to hand over to her myself, that delays my journey. Immediately afterwards I shall go off to get either from my father, or from my brother-in-law or my friends, or even from money-lenders who know my father's fortune, a few thousand francs which will enable me

* Hiller had just lost his father.

to extricate her as well as myself from the intolerable position we are in.

As I don't know how all this will end, I beg you to keep this letter, so that if any misfortune happens to me you can claim all my music in manuscript, which I bequeath and entrust to you....

To Humbert Ferrand

Paris, 1 August 1833

...I shall perhaps see Henriette this evening for *the last time* : she is so unhappy that my heart bleeds for her : and her timid and irresolute character make it impossible for her to take the least decision. However this must stop : I cannot live like this. This whole story is sad and bathed in tears : but I hope it will only be tears, I have done all that the most devoted heart could do : if her life is not happier or settled, it's her fault....

To Humbert Ferrand

Paris, 30 August 1833

...There have been the beginnings of a marriage process, a civil act which her loathsome sister promptly tore up. Terrible scenes of despair on her part, and reproaches for not loving her, to which I replied with passive resistance by poisoning myself in front of her. Dreadful cries from Henriette (her despair was sublime)—fiendish laughter on my part—desire to live again on seeing her protestations of love—emetics (ipecacuana)— vomiting for two hours, only two grains of opium were left : I was ill for three days but I survived. In her frantic state she offered to do anything I chose, but now she begins to hesitate again. I will wait no more and have written that unless she goes with me to the Mairie on Saturday to be married I leave next Thursday for Berlin. She shall see that I who for so long have languished at her feet can rise, can leave her, can live for those who love and understand me.

To help me to bear this horrible parting a strange chance has thrown in my way a charming girl of eighteen who has fled from a brute who had bought her as a child and kept her locked up for four years like a slave. Rather than go back to him she says she will drown herself, and my idea is to take her to Berlin and through Spontini's influence get her a place in a chorus. If she loves me, I will twist my heart and squeeze out a few drops of love. In the end I will make myself believe I love her. What an absurd story! My passport is ready: I must finish with things here. Henriette will be miserable, but I have nothing to reproach myself with. I would give my life this minute for a month of *perfect love* with her. She must bear the consequences of her unstable character: she will weep and despair at first, then will dry her tears and end by believing me in the wrong....

To Humbert Ferrand

[Paris] Tuesday 3 September 1833

Henriette has come, I am staying. We have made the announcement. In a fortnight all will be over, if human laws will kindly permit it. I am only afraid of their delays. At last!!! Oh! You see, it had to be!

Several of us have made a collection for the fugitive. Jules Janin has taken care of getting her away safely.

To Humbert Ferrand

Vincennes, 11 October 1833

I am married! All opposition has been in vain. Henriette has told me of the hundred and one lies they spread abroad. I was epileptic, I was mad—nothing was too bad. But we have listened to our own hearts and all is well....

How awfully I love my poor Ophelia! When once we can get rid of her troublesome sister life will be hard but happy. We are at Vincennes, where my wife can take advantage of the fine weather to get her strength back by going for long walks in the Park, but I go to Paris every day. Our marriage has caused the devil's own row there....

Berlioz and Harriet Smithson were married at the British Embassy in Paris on 3 October 1833. Liszt was one of the witnesses.

To Humbert Ferrand

Paris, 25 October 1833

...Oh, my dear Humbert, I *believed*, in spite of you all, and my faith has saved me. Henriette is an exquisite creature. She is Ophelia in person—not Juliet, she does not have her passion and fire: she is sweet and gentle, and so different. Sometimes, when we're alone and sitting in silence, her head resting on my shoulder and her hand stroking my forehead, or in one of those charming attitudes such as no painter ever dreamed of, she smiles and weeps at the same time. "What is it, my poor darling?" "Nothing—my heart is so full. I feel you have won me at such a cost, you have suffered everything for my sake. Let me cry, I must." And I listen to her peaceful tears. And then she says: "Sing, Hector, sing something"; and I begin the Ball Scene, which she is so fond of. The Scene in the Country makes her feel too sad, she doesn't want to hear it. She is a deeply sensitive person....

To Humbert Ferrand

Montmartre, 19 March 1834

...I have nearly finished the symphony with viola solo which Paganini asked me for. I was thinking of writing it in only two movements, but a third one came to me and then a fourth, however I hope I shall stop at that....

The symphony was *Harold in Italy*: Berlioz and Harriet had moved to Montmartre, and Harriet was expecting a child.

To Chopin

[Montmartre, early May 1834]

Chopinetto mio, there's a party going out to Montmartre, rue St. Denis No. 10 I hope that Hiller, Liszt, and de Vigny will be accompanied by Chopin. Great idiocy. Too bad! H.B.

To Liszt

[Montmartre, early May 1834]

...I cannot tell you how much this springtime scene moves and saddens me. Besides, yesterday I suffered several wounds in my artistic affections, which make me miserable to the point of tears, and which all my reason (for I have a good deal more reason than you might think) or that of my poor Henriette cannot make me forget or overcome.

Is Vigny coming with you? There is something gentle and affectionate about his mind which always charms me and which to-day I find I almost need. Why aren't you both here now? Perhaps to-morrow I shall feel differently. Are we really playthings of the air? And is Moore right when he says:

"And false the light on glory's plume,
    As fading hues of even : ....
    There's nothing bright but heaven !" ?*

But I do not believe in heaven. It is horrible to confess it. My heaven is the poetic world and there is a slug on each blossom. Look, come and bring Vigny with you. I need you both. Why can I not keep myself from admiring with tenacious passion certain works which are after all so fragile—like ourselves, like everything that exists? ...

To his sister Adèle

Paris, 12 May [1834]
... My friends came to spend half the day with me. We discussed art, poetry, philosophy, music and drama—in a word all that constitutes life—in the presence of this beauty of nature and the Italian sunshine which has favoured us these last few days. My father is well, I gather from the Rocher ladies. Is everyone else well? They tell me you are losing weight? Why? What is wrong? You are so alone, so sad. We shall meet again, I *tell* you, sooner or later. It is impossible otherwise. Farewell, these thoughts sadden me. Farewell, I embrace you with all my affection and that which my good and sweet Henriette bears you.

To Humbert Ferrand

Montmartre, 15 or 16 May 1834
... I am dead with work and trouble, being obliged by my present situation to scrawl at so much a column for these wretched papers which pay me as little as they can....
I have finished the first three movements of my new symphony with viola solo : I am now going to complete the fourth. I think it will be rather good and particularly picturesque in a most unusual way. I intend to dedicate it to one of my friends whom you know, M. Humbert Ferrand, if he will kindly let me. It has a March of Pilgrims singing the evening hymn which will, I hope, make a reputation in December....
My affairs at the Opéra are in the hands of the Bertin family, which has taken over the direction of it. They are going

* The Moore quotation is from the second of his Sacred Songs, which Berlioz had set in Rome as *Méditation Religieuse* : it became No. 1 of *Tristia*.

to give me Shakespeare's *Hamlet* admirably arranged as an opera. We hope that the influence of the *Journal des Débats* will be strong enough to remove the last difficulties which Véron may make. He is in London at the moment: on his return things will be settled one way or another. Meanwhile I have chosen a comic opera in two acts on Benvenuto Cellini, whose curious memoirs you have no doubt read, and whose character provided me with an excellent text from various points of view. Don't talk about this till it is all arranged....

Berlioz was still hoping to get *Les Francs-Juges* put on at the Opéra, but in the end his hopes were disappointed. Armand Bertin was the editor of the powerful *Journal des Débats* and a good patron of Berlioz: his daughter Louise was an amateur composer whom Berlioz was occasionally called in to assist, particularly in her opera *Esméralda*, based on Victor Hugo's *The Hunchback of Notre Dame*.

To Humbert Ferrand

Montmartre, 31 August 1834

You are not forgotten, not the least bit, but you can't know what a slave I am to hard necessity. Had it not been for those confounded newspaper articles I would have written to you a dozen times. I will not write the usual empty phrases on your loss: yet, if anything could soften the blow, it would be that your father's death was as peaceful as one could wish. You speak of my father. He wrote kindly and promptly in reply to my letter announcing the birth of my son. Henriette's confinement was a very bad one, but all ended happily, though only after forty hours of great pain. She thanks you for your messages: she too understands the depth of our friendship. I could write all night, but as I have to tug at my galley-oar all day tomorrow, I must go to sleep....

Berlioz' son Louis was born on 14 August 1834.

To Humbert Ferrand

[Paris] Sunday 30 November 1834

I almost expected a letter from you to-day, and though I am dropping with fatigue I must snatch half an hour to answer it. The *Symphonie Fantastique* is out, and as our poor Liszt has

spent a terrible lot of money over it we arranged with
Schlesinger that not one copy was to be given away. They are
twenty francs. Shall I buy one for you?

I only wish I could send it to you without all this preamble,
but you know we are still very hard up. My wife and I are as
happy as it is possible to be, in spite of our wordly troubles, and
little Louis is the nicest and prettiest child I have ever seen....

Harold in Italy had its first performance on 23 November: it
was a great success and was twice repeated before the end of
the year. Liszt had undertaken the seemingly impossible task of
transcribing the *Symphonie Fantastique* for piano and played
it with success at his concerts.

To Humbert Ferrand

                                    Paris, 10 January 1835
...If I had had the time I should already have begun another
work I am thinking of—a symphony on a new and enlarged plan
—but I am obliged to scribble these wretched ill-paid articles.
Ah! if only art counted for something with our Government, perhaps I should not be reduced to this. Never mind, I must find
time somehow....

To Alfred de Vigny

                                    [Paris, February 1835]
My wife did for a moment think of accepting your gracious
offer [of a box for the premiere of Vigny's play *Chatterton* on
12 February] but all things considered, the thought of the
eclipse in which her talents stand for the time being is too painful to permit her to attend a notable occasion such as the one
to which you have kindly invited us. I shall therefore go alone
to applaud *Chatterton* with all the warmth and affection and
enthusiasm which I feel for its author, and for the cause he
pleads so well....

To Humbert Ferrand

                                    [August or September 1835]
...So you have been to Milan! Not a town I like, but it is
the gateway to Italy. I can't tell you how much, when the
weather is fine, I long for my ancient Campagna and the wild
hills where I went so often....

You ask for news of us. Louis can nearly walk and Henriette is more devoted to him than ever. But I am the only one in our household that he completely approves of. I can't go out of the house without his crying for the next hour. I work like a black for the four papers which give me my daily bread. These are the *Rénovateur*, which pays badly, the *Monde Dramatique* and the *Gazette Musicale*, which pay little, and the *Débats* which pays well. With all this I have to fight the nightmare of my musical position: I cannot find the time to compose. I have begun a gigantic piece of work for seven hundred musicians, in memory of the great men of France. It would soon be done if I had one quiet month, but I dare not give up a single day to it, lest we should go without the necessities of life.

Which concert do you refer to? I have given seven this season and will begin again in November.

At present we sit dumb under the triumph of Musard, who, puffed up by the success of his dancing-den concerts, looks upon himself as a superior Mozart. Mozart never composed anything like the "Pistol-Shot Quadrille", so Mozart died in poverty. Musard is earning twenty thousand francs a year. The other day Ballanche, the immortal author of *Orpheus* and *Antigone*, was nearly thrown into prison because he owed two hundred francs. Think of it, Ferrand: does not madness that way lie? If I were a bachelor, so that my follies would recoil on myself alone, I know what I should do.

Never mind that now though. Love me always, and to please me read de Vigny's *Chatterton*.

The work referred to was never completed as such, but it may have provided the basis for later works, particularly the *Funeral and Triumphal Symphony* of 1840.

To Humbert Ferrand

Montmartre, 16 December 1835

Don't think me a sinner for leaving you so long in silence. You can have no idea how much work I have to do every day and how little leisure I have—but I need not emphasise that. You know how much pleasure I have in writing to you and that I would not easily do without it. I have seen Coste, who is publishing *Great Men of Italy* serially, and he is going to approach you about contributing some articles. Among those already out is a life of Benvenuto Cellini. Read it, if you aren't already familiar with the autobiography of this bandit of genius. . . .

Harold is more successful even than last year : I think it quite outdoes the *Fantastique*. They have accepted my *Cellini* for the Opéra : Alfred de Vigny and Auguste Barbier have written for me a poem full of delightful vivacity and colour. I have not begun to work on the music yet, because I am in the same predicament as my hero Cellini, short of *metal*. Good reports from Germany, thanks to Liszt's piano arrangement of my symphony.

In fact the libretto of *Cellini* was by Barbier and Léon de Wailly: Alfred de Vigny merely revised it.

To Liszt

[Paris] 25 January 1836

. . . You catch me in one of those moments of profound depression that always follow those concentrated rages which gnaw and bite at the heart without being able to cause an explosion . . . you know them unfortunately as well as I do.

The subject of this *heart-quake without eruption* was this : I had been named director of the musical Gymnasium with a salary of six thousand francs plus two free concerts for my benefit and author's rights for each of my compositions : Thiers makes me lose the post by obstinately refusing to allow singing in the Gymnasium. As a result this establishment, to which I was going to add a choral school like that of Choron's, is ruined and has closed down. THEY ARE GIVING DANCES THERE !

To Humbert Ferrand

[Paris] 15 April 1836

. . . I still work frightfully hard at journalism. You know I write articles (concerts only) for the *Débats*, signed "H". They seem to be making a stir. Parisian artists call them epoch-making. In spite of M. Bertin's wish I refused to review either *I Puritani* or that wretched *Juive*. I should have had to find too much wrong with it, and people would have put it down to jealousy.

Then there is the *Rénovateur*, in which I can hardly control my anger over all these "pretty little trifles" : and *Italie Pittoresque* has dragged an article out of me. Then the *Gazette Musicale* plagues me for a résumé of the week's inanities every Sunday. Added to that I have tried every concert room in Paris with the idea of giving a concert, and find none suitable except the Conservatoire, which is not available till after the last of the regular concerts on 3 May....

We often talk of you to Barbier : he is a kindred spirit whom you would love. No one understands better than he the grandeur and nobility of an artist's calling.

Germany still talks of me : Vienna asks for a copy of the score of the *Fantastique*, but I tell them I cannot possibly let them have it, as I propose to give it on tour myself. All the poets in Paris, from Scribe to Victor Hugo, offer me subjects, but those idiotic directors stand in the way. Some day I will put my foot on their necks....

Now I must be off to the *Débats* with my article on Beethoven's C minor. Meyerbeer is coming soon to superintend his *Huguenots*, which I am most anxious to hear. He is the only established musician who has shown a real interest in me. Onslow has been paying me his usual bombastic compliments on the Pilgrim's March. I am glad to think there was not a word of truth in them : I prefer open hatred to honeyed venom....

To his sister Adèle

Montmartre, Friday 1 July 1836

...There are charming choruses which rumour does me the honour of attributing to me, though I have had no hand in them. Unfortunately the individual roles are not nearly so good, not by a long chalk, and the actors go through some cruel grimaces....

This refers to Louise Bertin's opera *Esmeralda*, which was performed at the Opéra on 14 November and hissed off the stage.

To Humbert Ferrand

Montmartre, 2 October 1836

...I am reaching the end of my score : I have only one section, fairly long it is true, of the orchestration to write. At present I have a *written* assurance from the director of the Opéra that it will be put on sooner or later : it is only a question of waiting in patience for the production of works which are to be staged before mine: there are three of them unfortunately! The director Duponchel grows steadily more hostile to the work and distrusts my music more and more every day, though he doesn't know it at all: he is terrified of it. ...

This refers to *Benvenuto Cellini*: Berlioz could not afford to take time off from journalism to write the score without borrowing two thousand francs from his friend Legouvé.

To his sister Adèle

[Paris] 22 December 1836

... If I had anything to do with its success it's in a trifling way. The air really is by Mlle Bertin, but, between ourselves, it ended lamely. My help was limited to suggesting a peroration more worthy of the exordium. That's all. As for my own opera, here is how it stands. I have finished it. I have only to write out the dénouement and orchestrate a large part of the score. According to my contract with Duponchel I am fourth on the list, but it was agreed that I could if necessary be performed earlier. They are now putting on Niedermayer's *Stradella*. Then, if nothing else is ready, I should go on next, but Halévy is straining every nerve and writing his new score at a gallop so as not to lose his turn. Anyhow I'm ready to go into rehearsal, and I'd have been ready with all the music long before if like my hero Cellini I had had the *metal* with which to cast my statue. ...

Quasimodo's aria in *Esmeralda* had made quite a success, and everybody, including Alexandre Dumas, who disliked the Bertins, ascribed it to Berlioz. The reference in the last sentence is to the final scene of *Benvenuto Cellini*, in which the hero runs short of metal in the casting of his Perseus. However Berlioz was now helped by increased honorariums from the Bertins, no doubt because of his services over *Esmeralda*, and also by an unexpected gift from his father, about which he wrote to his sister: "I am afraid my excellent father inconvenienced himself to send me the sum, which I was far from expecting, and this thought bothers me more than I can say. Kiss him and Mama for me."

To Cherubini

[Paris] 24 March 1837

I am very touched by the noble abnegation which leads you not to allow your admirable *Requiem* to be performed at the ceremony at the Invalides; please believe that I am deeply grateful. However, as the determination of the Minister of the Interior is irrevocable, I must ask you firmly not to think of me at all and not to deprive the government and your admirers of a masterpiece which would give so much lustre to this solemn occasion.

I am with profound respect, sir, your devoted servant,

H. Berlioz.

Berlioz had been commissioned to write a *Requiem* for a ceremony at the Invalides on 22 July 1837 : however there had been intrigues surrounding the commission and performance, and Berlioz waited until getting the official signature of the Minister of the Interior before writing to his old enemy Cherubini, who had written a *Requiem* for male voices and orchestra in 1836 and had been hoping that his work would be performed rather than Berlioz'.

To his sister Adèle

[Paris] 17 April [1837]

... This affair, after some diversions created by Cherubini, who wanted to have a new *Requiem* which he had just composed performed at the Invalides, ended in a way which was honourable for him, and for M. de Gasparin, who commissioned me to write the work.

The Minister asked me if I would accept four thousand francs, I didn't think I ought to haggle on this occasion, although the payment is rather niggardly, as the expenses of the performance will be enormous : I asked for five hundred performers and I shall have four hundred and thirty.

The ministerial decree was finally signed about three weeks ago and I have it in my desk : there is no more danger from that quarter. In two months I shall have finished, I hope. I had difficulty in mastering my subject : in the first days this poetry of the Prose of the Dead had intoxicated and exalted me to such an extent that nothing lucid presented itself to my senses, my head was boiling, I felt quite dizzy. Now the eruption is controlled, the lava has hollowed out its bed, and with God's help all will go well. It's an immense affair! I shall doubtless draw on myself the reproach of innovation because I wished to bring this branch of the art back to a truth from which Mozart and Cherubini seem to me to have often departed. Then there are some formidable combinations which happily have not been tried before and which I believe I am the first to have thought of.

Farewell, farewell.

Your affectionate brother,

H. Berlioz.

To Dietsch

[Paris, July 1837]

My dear Dietsch,

I expect you know already that my whole affair has been postponed till further notice by a ministerial decision cancelling the ceremony at the Invalides. I tell you this again in case you have not been informed about it, to save you the trouble of coming from the Conservatoire with your boys to-morrow morning.

You can imagine in what a mental state this infernal mess-up has put me. I am ill in every sense of the term.

I will see you again soon,

Yours ever,

H. Berlioz.

Dietsch was assisting Berlioz in the choral rehearsals of the *Requiem*.

To Bottée de Toulmon*

[Paris] 18 July 1837

... The work exists, it's still there. We will certainly find an occasion for hearing it later. The sectional rehearsals of the vocal parts were going so well! In truth Hell must be involved in it.

A thousand curses!

But as I told you, I defy them to wear me down.

Best wishes.

H. Berlioz.

* Librarian of the Conservatoire.

To Liszt

[Paris] 20 July 1837

...Perhaps you have heard about the latest bludgeon-blow that I have have just received! Fortunately I have a hard head and it would need a special tomahawk to break it. The Council of Ministers, after three days of indecision, has decided to cancel the funeral ceremony at the Invalides.

No question any more of the heroes of July. Woe to the conquered! and woe to the conquerors! As a result, after three sectional rehearsals of the voice parts I learnt by chance—for no one bothered to tell me—that the ceremony would not take place and that my *Requiem* as a result would not be performed. Tell me if that isn't something to blow about like a spermwhale! Everything was going fine, I was sure of everything, the ensemble of four hundred and twenty musicians was arranged and tuned like one of your excellent Erard pianos, nothing could go wrong, and I think that we were going to hear many things for the first time.

Politics has seen to that. I still feel ill. This is what art exposes itself to when it accepts help from a régime as weak and unstable as ours. But as there is nothing else one has to use such support, however unpredictable. O these representative governments, and cheap ones at that, what a farce!

But don't let's talk of that, we won't agree at all, I think. Happily we feel the same about everything else.

Farewell! Farewell! All my friendship, and respects to the ladies.

H. Berlioz.

To his father

[Paris] 29 July 1837

...M. de Montalivert asked how he could compensate me for this muddle, which he says has been caused by politics alone. I replied that in an affair of this kind there was only one kind of compensation possible, and that was the performance of the work.

The *Journal des Débats* is furious, Armand Bertin has written a terrific letter to Montalivet which I saw and sent on myself. Nothing has happened, always the same protestations. It's a decision of the Council of Ministers, etc., and other hypocrisies of the same order.

But this isn't all, I have to be paid for the expenses incurred. M. Montalivet actually consents to recognise them. First of all there are four thousand francs for me, then three thousand eight hundred francs for copying, and in addition the expenses of three sectional rehearsals for the chorus. For I was making preparations, everything was going as I wanted, I should never have had a performance as good as this, and it was marvellous to see how these vocal forces were livening up. Unfortunately I had not got as far as a general rehearsal, so I hadn't yet been able to let the artists hear this immense score which excites their curiosity so strongly. I call such conduct by the government quite simply a theft. My present and my future are being stolen from me, for this performance was of great consequence to me. A minister would not have dared to behave like this under the Empire and if he had I think that Napoleon would have dealt with him : for, I repeat, it's plain theft.

They seek me out, they ask me if I will write this work, I make my (musical) conditions and they accept them : they promise a performance on the 29th July, in writing : I finish my music, everything is ready, and they refuse to go any further. The government wriggles out of the most important clause of the engagement contracted with me : so it's an abuse of confidence, an abuse of power, a filthy trick, a swindle, *a theft*.

At present here I am with, I think, the largest musical work that has ever been written, just like Robinson and his canoe : quite unable to launch it. It needs a vast church and 400 musicians. Never mind ! The *Requiem* exists, and I swear to you, father, that it is something which will make a mark on art : I will certainly contrive to get it heard, sooner or later....

To Alexandre Dumas

[Paris, 23 October 1837]

Ruolz is coming to see you to-morrow Tuesday about a musical affair which you could help to bring off and which interests me deeply. Would you be good enough to give me another leg-up? It's a question of arranging a performance of my unfortunate *Requiem* at a ceremony in honour of the capture of Constantine. If the Duke of Orléans were willing, it would be a simple matter. I will come and see you to tell you more about it. Yours ever,

Hector Berlioz.

Dumas was secretary to the Duke of Orléans. French troops captured Constantine in Algeria on 23 October 1837, but their commander, General Damrémont, was killed in the assault. Henri de Ruolz was the composer of the opera *La Vendetta*, performed in Paris in 1839.

To General Bernard, Minister of War

Paris, 30 October 1837

M. le ministre,

A requiem mass was commissioned from me last March by M. de Gasparin for the funeral ceremonies of July: however my composition was not performed as the ceremony at the Invalides was cancelled.

M. le comte de Montalivet is interested in the performance of my work. The funeral of General Damrémont would be a natural occasion for performing it. Would you be kind enough, M. le Baron, to choose it for this ceremony, and in the event of my request being accepted, let me know fairly soon so that I can make the necessary preparations?

It is a new work, conceived on a vast scale, in consequence it will need several rehearsals.

The expenses of copying and composition have already been met by the Ministry of the Interior.

I am with respect,

M. le ministre,

Your very humble servant,

Hector Berlioz.

To his sister Adèle

[Paris, November 1837]

Louis wishes to thank you for the lovely pair of "touders" that you made for him, he's sending you a work-basket which my uncle will be delivering. I hope you like it. Henriette told me to choose something simple and in good taste. I'm afraid I may not have found one that quite answers to that description, but if not you'll forgive me—I'm not versed in such matters.

Farewell.

Your brother
H. Berlioz.

From the Minister of War to Berlioz

6 December 1837

Sir,

I hasten to inform you of the satisfaction that I felt at the performance of the requiem mass of which you are the author, and which was recently sung at the service in honour of General Damrémont.

The success achieved by this fine and austere composition has worthily matched the solemnity of the occasion : and I congratulate myself on having been able to provide you with this new occasion of displaying a talent which places you in the first rank among our composers of sacred music.

Believe me, sir,

Yours very truly,
Bernard.

Peer of France, Minister and Secretary of State for War.

The *Requiem* was first performed on 5 December 1837 at the Invalides.

To Humbert Ferrand

[Paris] 17 December 1837

...Here are the facts. The *Requiem* was well performed. Its effect on the great majority of the audience was tremendous : the minority, which felt and understood nothing, hardly knew what to say. The newspapers in general have been excellent, apart from the *Constitutionnel*, the *National*, and the *France*, where I have personal enemies. I missed you, my dear Ferrand, you would have been very happy, I think : it is just what you were dreaming of in sacred music. It's a success which has made me popular, that was the real point : the effect on people of the most opposite feelings and habits has been shattering : the curé of the Invalides wept at the altar : a quarter of an hour after the ceremony he embraced me in the sacristy in floods of tears : at the moment of the Last Judgement the terror produced by the five orchestras and the eight pairs of timpani which accompany the *Tuba mirum* can't be described : one of the women singers had a nervous attack. Truly it had a frightening grandeur. You have seen the letter from the Minister of War : I have received I don't know how many others of the kind which you write to me sometimes, minus the friendship and the poetry.

Among others one from Rubini, one from the Marquis de Custine, one from Legouvé, one from Mme Victor Hugo and one from Ortigue—this one is crazy—: then many many more from various artists, painters, musicians, sculptors, architects, prose writers. Perhaps it will be the Opéra next....

To his mother

Paris, 17 December [1837]

That is where I am, dear Mama: as for the *moral*, I have not been paid yet, but the order for payment is ready and will be signed to-morrow, and I know that M. de Montalivet feels himself obliged to add an honorarium of fifteen hundred francs to the four thousand francs promised by M. de Gasparin's decree. At present there is a question of buying my work from me, which would then become national property: the Minister's chief clerks told me so this morning: I don't know anything definite about it, and I also don't know how much they are thinking of offering me for my score or if they want to keep it in manuscript or have it engraved at government expense: whatever may happen, all is going quite well. I sent you about twenty newspapers in two lots: I expect they have all reached you. The English press has also been very good, so we think we can flatter ourselves we have caused a devil of a stir in the four corners of the world. All this is helping to forward my affairs at the Opéra, and I am more or less sure at present of being put into rehearsal when this interminable opera of Halévy, which they have been rehearsing for the last eight months, gets put on. The only chance against it is very unlikely: it would mean Auber, who has a commission prior to mine, writing a five-act opera in four months....

Halévy's opera was *Guido and Ginevra or the Florentine Plague*, performed on 5 March 1838. Auber's new opera, *Le Lac des Fées*, was not put on until 1 April 1839.

To his mother

Paris, 18 January 1838

...I know that my father and you, dear Mama, have been waiting impatiently to know if I have been paid. Well, I have received nothing yet. The Minister of War, an admirable man, has given me the ten thousand francs to cover the costs of the performance of my work, with the result that up to now everybody has been paid *except me*, because unfortunately my dealings are with the Minister of the Interior. Yesterday I went into his offices and made a scene such as has never, I think, been known in such a place. I sent a message to M. de Montalivet by his chief of section that "I should be ashamed to treat my bootmaker as he had behaved to me, and that if I was not paid in the shortest time possible I should make known all the infamous double-dealing I had experienced at the Ministry, so that the Opposition Press would have ample material for a scandal". It seems that before the performance of the Requiem they wanted to CANCEL M. Gasparin's decree and that they have *disposed* of my four thousand francs, or, in plain words, they have stolen them. The honorarium of fifteen hundred francs has disappeared from the memory of the clerks in the Office of Fine Arts, they say at present that it was a *mistake*. I have never seen a more complete collection of scoundrels and thieves. But I will be paid, there is no need to be worried, it's merely a delay, they are too afraid of the Press. They mentioned the possibility of the cross of the Legion of Honour during the Royal Festival in May. We shall see if this is another piece of double-dealing. Anyway it is the least of my worries....

To M. Berlioz, composer   .   .   .   4,000 francs.
    For the price of acquiring the score of the mass which you composed on the occasion of the funeral ceremony at the Invalides in honour of General Damrémont and the other Frenchmen killed in the siege of Constantine.
                    Received, 1 February 1838,
                            Berlioz.

To Maurice Schlesinger
                                [21–26 February 1838]
My dear Maurice,
    I did not get any tickets yesterday either from Monpou or you, and so I haven't seen the new piece: it seems that there is no great harm in my being deprived of it: get someone to do a note on it. I am in the middle of a big article on the Choral Symphony, but it won't be able to appear in the next number, so don't expect it till next week. It would be better to publish it all at once.

Schlesinger was the eldest son of the Berlin publisher Adolf

Schlesinger. Maurice founded a branch of the firm in Paris, and also the periodical *Gazette Musicale*, to which Berlioz contributed from the start. Hippolyte Monpou (1804–41) was a composer of drawing-room songs and comic operas: this one was *Un conte d'autrefois*, produced on 20 February 1838. Berlioz' article on the Ninth Symphony appeared in the *Gazette Musicale* for 4 March.

To Marc Suat

[Paris] 7 March 1838

Your letter made me very happy, and if I haven't answered sooner it's because my present work makes me lose both sleep and sense of reality. I snatch a moment to tell you how enchanted I am to hear of the lively affection you bear my sister. She is an excellent child, who will make you most happy, I know. As for you, I know the goodness of your disposition, and my sister's future strikes me as secure. I may have misread your letter but are you thinking of coming with Adèle to Paris... can you? will you? It would be such happiness for me....

Suat was a solicitor from Vienne, near the Côte-Saint-André, who had become engaged to Berlioz' younger sister Adèle. Berlioz knew him well and liked him.

To his father

Paris, 19 March 1838

...Adèle tells me of testamentary dispositions which our dear mother made in her special favour, and she seems to fear the effect of this on her brothers and sisters. And now you talk of your own intentions, which suggests the deep depression with which you must face the future. In the name of all we hold dear, don't speak like that. We'll talk later, much later of all these money matters which you propose with such sad composure. In any case as regards me whatever you do will always be right.

I wish you would think of travelling: it would be the best thing in the world for you....

Farewell, dear father, don't worry about my future and think more about yourself. The best proof you can give of your affection for your children is to take care of your health and peace of mind.

Berlioz' mother had died in February at the age of fifty-three.

To Legouvé

Paris, 31 July 1838

...There are millions of wrong notes, wrong tempi and especially wrong rhythms. This causes me so much irritation, so much torture of the nerves that it is the sole origin of my present indisposition. But patience! We'll be ready for the first night by 21st or 25th August. The overture, by the way, I think you'll be pleased with. I don't want to count my chickens before they're hatched, but if my score is published you'll give me the pleasure of accepting the dedication, won't you? For after all it's you who provided the *metal* for casting the Perseus and it is to you that poor Benvenuto owes his work of art, such as it is.

See p. 63. *Benvenuto* was eventually produced on 10 September 1838: it was not a success, apart from the overture, and only three performances were given in September.

To Jules Janin

[mid-September 1838]

My dear Janin,

I thank you, but I am so ill that I cannot put two ideas together. I was going out to see you but I had to go to bed. Just give your impressions and that will be fine: be nice to Mme Gras who has been charming and kind throughout the whole affair. The same goes for Mme Stoltz, Massol and Serda. Duprez has made up his mind to give up a part which is unworthy of his grandeur: I have been running round all day without success trying to find a substitute for him, and my performances will be brought to an end through the *goodwill* of the hero of my articles. Duponchel wins his bet, everything is running true to form as you see.

Best regards,

H. Berlioz.

Janin was the most powerful literary critic in Paris, on the staff of the *Journal des Débats*. Mme Gras sang Teresa in *Benvenuto*, Mme Stoltz Ascanio, Massol Fieramosca and Serda the Cardinal. Duprez sang Cellini and behaved in a very unco-operative way, although Berlioz had praised his other performances earlier in his articles. Duponchel was the Director of the Opéra.

To Paganini

[Paris] 18 December 1838

O great and worthy artist.

How can I express my thanks to you ! ! ! I am not rich, but believe me, the approbation of a man of genius like yourself touches me a thousand times more than the royal generosity of your present.

Words fail me, I will rush to embrace you as soon as I can leave my bed, to which I am still confined to-day.

H. Berlioz

Paganini had attended Berlioz' concert on 16 December, at which he had heard *Harold in Italy* for the first time: he had not played the work himself as he complained that there were too many rests in the solo viola part. However, he was so impressed that he sent Berlioz a gift of 20,000 francs, together with a letter which Berlioz reproduced in his *Memoirs*.

To his sister Adèle

[Paris] 20 December 1838

... You know he [Paganini] has lost the use of his voice. When he saw me tears came into his eyes. I confess my own were not far behind my lids. He wept, this man-eater, this murderer of women, this ex-convict, as he has so often been called. Then, wiping his eyes and striking the table with a strange burst of laughter, he started to address me volubly: but as I could not clearly follow his words he went to fetch his little son to serve as interpreter. I gathered that he was "very happy because the insects who write and speak against me won't be quite so bold". What a rumpus the news will make in Germany and England. Such a gesture—and from an Italian—but one must add that he does not compose Italian music. . . .

I think my father will be satisfied. Now I shall be able to make my trip to Germany. It so happens that many German artists are in Paris this winter, and they exhibit a most encouraging fanaticism towards my music. . . .

To Jules Janin

[Paris, January 1839]

... I am very sad to-day. I have just lost my brother, a poor boy of nineteen whom I loved.

Prosper took ill, recovered momentarily and died, just at the time of the fourth and last performance of *Benvenuto* at the Opéra.

To Liszt

[Paris] 22 January 1839

...The revival of *Benvenuto* was a great success: at present it is to be played as often as the ballet arrangements permit. So I depend on the caprices of Fanny Elssler: she is delighted to dance in front of me (stage term), but as the number of ballets that can be given with my opera is very limited, and also as she has not been successful in *La Fille du Danube* nor in the *Sylphide*, how often the opera is performed depends on how long *La Gitane* runs: it is being put on for her at this moment. We shall see.

My fourth performance, which was delayed as you know by Duprez suddenly giving up the part, was very good, theatre full and a lot of applause, except for one number whose length appeared excessive in relation to the weakness of the acting of Dupont, who did not give enough animation to a scene which was already boring and long in itself.

What a world our Opéra world is! What intrigues! All these rivalries! all these hatreds! all these love-affairs! Really it gets more curious from day to day!

You don't say anything to me about Paganini! it was fine though! you would have done that yourself! Really my last concert was magnificent, I have never been performed or understood as on that day. I am ruminating a new symphony, which I would very much like to go and finish near you, at Sorrento or Amalfi—go to Amalfi—but impossible, I am in the breach, I must stay there. I have never led such an agitated life: the musical controversy I have just provoked is of a rare liveliness and even ferocity. My followers send me sheaves of prose and verse and my detractors anonymous abuse. One of them advised me to shoot myself—isn't that delightful? This is a sort of life I enjoy about as much as you do, but by dint of tumbling about among the breakers we'll end by mastering them so that they no longer break over our heads.

And so you're in Rome. M. Ingres will surely welcome you, especially if you will play him our Adagio in C sharp minor of Beethoven and the A flat sonata of Weber. I greatly admire the fanaticism of this great painter's musical passions, and you will heartily forgive him for loathing me when you remember that he adores Gluck and Beethoven. ...

How I enjoy chatting to you to-night! I love you so, Liszt. When are you coming back to us? When are we going to have some more great sessions of talking and smoking, with your long pipes and Turkish tobacco? I have had severe bronchitis, which for a moment made me think of Gluck's ode "Charon calls you". Why am I so gay? Our friends are mostly sad. Legouvé has painful stomach trouble. Schoelcher has just lost his mother. Heine is "not happy". Chopin is ill, in the Balearic Islands. Dumas drags his chain, which feels heavier every day. Mme Sand has a sick child. Hugo alone stands calm and strong.

Now I am furious! They were going to play me to-morrow and now Dupont is ill: they are putting on *La Fille mal Gardée* and the ballet of *Gustave*, with takings of 400 francs!

"Too bad!" as my young Ascanio says, I won't write in the minor key for that.

Please remember me to Mme d'Agoult. I sincerely thank her for her interest in the ups and downs of my life. She does it from affection for you but I am not the less grateful. Farewell. Farewell. I embrace you with my whole soul and wish you a north wind—since you are in Rome. Your friend.

To his sister Adèle

[Paris] 9 April 1839

...He is the most charming and badly brought up child you ever saw. He threatens everyone with his sword and says the most frightful things when crossed. He swears like—like his father. The day before yesterday he made a hole in my bed with the bayonet from my National Guard equipment, which he had taken. And in spite of it all, he is charming. He's enchanted at the idea of picking peaches and strawberries with his grandfather, but I don't know how he will take his parents' absence: he can't be away from them for one evening without tears. Well, you'll see when you come to Paris. ...

Adèle had married Marc Suat in April. Berlioz could not attend the wedding: Adèle suggested that she should come to Paris and take back little Louis with her to the country for a holiday.

To Liszt

Paris, 6 August 1839

... The day before yesterday, as I was smoking a cigar in the Boulevard des Italiens, Batta caught me by the arm. "What are they doing in London?" I asked. "Nothing whatever. They despise music, poetry and drama, everything. They go to the Italian Opera because the Queen goes, and that's all. I feel quite thankful not to have been out of pocket and to have been applauded at two or three concerts. That is all the British hospitality I can boast of. Even Artôt, in spite of his Philharmonic success, was horribly bored." "And Doehler?" "Bored too." "Thalberg?" "Cultivating the provinces." "Benedict?" "Encouraged by the success of his first attempt, is writing an English opera." "Mme Gras?" "Has become fashionable overnight, and beats the Italians at their own game. Wherever she goes she's billed in huge letters as 'The Incomparable Singer'. But I'm told she was hissed at her re-appearance here in *William Tell*." "That's quite true." "But how could that be?" "What about some grog?" "No, I'm off. Come to Hallé's tonight, we'll drink and have some music."*

M. Hallé is a young German pianist—tall, thin and longhaired, who plays magnificently and seems to get music by instinct rather than by reason: that is to say, he is rather like you. Real talent, immense knowledge, perfect execution—we all recognise his gifts. Hallé and Batta played Mendelssohn's B flat sonata, then we had a chorus over our beer: then Beethoven's A major sonata, of which the first movement excited us wildly, and the minuet and finale merely redoubled our musical exaltation, although the bottles of champagne were already in circulation....

Oh, untiring wanderer, when are you coming back to preside over our nights of music again? Between ourselves you always had too many people at your gatherings—too much talk, not enough listening. You alone wasted an amount of inspiration enough to turn a few of us giddy, without all the others. Do you remember that evening at Legouvé's, when the lights were put out and you played the C sharp minor sonata, we five lying in the dark on the floor? My tears and Legouvé's, Schoelcher's

* Batta was a well-known cellist. Benedict and Hallé both settled in England later, the former as a composer: the latter founded the Hallé Orchestra.

wondering respect, Goubeaux' astonishment! Ah! you were sublime indeed that night....

They have just found a means of saving money by not building a theatre for the Italians.* The singers of our big Opéra will be in direct competition with the transalpine singers : they want to bring both troupes together in the rue Le Pelletier. The mixup will be fierce : Lablache against Levasseur, Rubini against Duprez, Tamburini against Dérivis, Grisi against Mlle Naudin and the whole lot against the bass drum. We mean to be there to pick up the dead and dying....

Sometimes when they are at their wits' end they play *Don Giovanni*. If Mozart came back to this world he would tell them, like Molière's president, that he does not wish to be *played*. The other day Ambroise Thomas, Morel and I were saying we would give five hundred francs for a good performance of Spontini's *Vestale* : that set us off—we know it by heart—and we went on singing it till midnight. But we missed you for our accompaniment....

To Humbert Ferrand

[Paris] 22 August 1839

...Spontini is more absurd and embittered than ever. The day before yesterday he sent Emile Deschamps an incredibly ridiculous letter. Now he has gone back to Berlin, leaving all his real admirers saddened and disillusioned. What a strange habitation for genius to choose. True, it moved out a long time ago. But after all, *La Vestale* and *Cortez* are still there....

The French Press had urged the Institute to elect Berlioz a member when a vacancy arose in June on the death of Paër. However Berlioz heard that Spontini was a candidate for the seat and at once withdrew : he also persuaded his friend Emile Deschamps to write a pamphlet on Spontini's behalf, in reply to which Spontini wrote the letter referred to by Berlioz, and had it published. However, he was elected all the same.

To Eugène Scribe

[Paris] 31 August 1839

...I shall not take the liberty of telling you the kind of dramatic ideas that would suit me best : you know perfectly well what they are. However, in seeking a subject which would

* The previous one had been destroyed in a fire.

lend itself to musical development on a large scale and dramatic effects, I perhaps ought to tell you that certain individuals and periods are deeply uncongenial to me—Luther, for example, the Christians of the Lower Empire, and those boorish Druids. I should dearly love an antique subject, but I fear the costumes, and the prosy literalness of our audiences. Perhaps a simple love plot—passionate love—varied with scenes of violent action involving crowds and set either in the Middle Ages or the last century would be most suitable. Of course there is no question of keeping to a heroic or elevated style throughout. On the contrary, I strongly prefer contrasts. . . .

Berlioz approached the reigning librettist Scribe in the hope of getting a really successful libretto for another opera. In the end Scribe produced the first act of *La Nonne Sanglante*, based on an episode in Lewis' *The Monk*: but he did not provide the rest as he was doubtful of Berlioz' commercial success.

To Jules Janin
28 November 1839

I am no longer or not yet at the age where one weeps willingly, but your homage to Paganini made me burst into tears.

Berlioz had used the money given him by Paganini to live on while writing the *Romeo and Juliet* symphony: this was first performed on 24 November 1839 and repeated with great success on 1 and 15 December. Janin's review of the first performance ended with a paragraph in praise of Paganini for having made the composition of the work possible.

To Armand Bertin
12 February 1840

You must be good enough to let me have two days more for my article: I have spent the day in bed trembling like a victim of fever. These infernal nerve troubles have got hold of me again worse than ever, and when I'm in this state it's really very difficult to write anything that makes sense. So don't count on me till Saturday at five. It's safer. I send you our *King Lear* Overture which is published at last, together with the manuscript, which please keep.

The dedication of a piece of music is a commonplace homage

which only has value if the work has merit, but I hope that you will accept it as an expression of the grateful friendship I have long felt for you.

H. Berlioz.

To M. Vatout, Curator of Public Buildings

[Paris] 31 due de Londres, 3 April 1840

Sir,

I have called upon you several times hoping to have the honour of seeing you, in order to learn your decision in respect of the project for a festival in which you have kindly taken an interest. Not having found you in, and as the date set for this musical festival is very near, I take the liberty of writing to you, enclosing a letter from M. de Lavenay which I received the day before yesterday.

Please be kind enough, Sir, to inform me as soon as possible of your ruling in this matter.

I have the honour to be, Sir,

your most humble servant,

H. Berlioz.

Berlioz had been commissioned to write a work, the *Symphonie Funèbre et Triomphale*, for the tenth anniversary of the July Revolution. It was to be performed at an open-air ceremony, at which, as Berlioz knew, the music would not be heard satisfactorily, and he was therefore apparently trying to get the Panthéon for an indoor performance of the work. His request was refused, but he arranged an indoor public rehearsal on 26 July, and two further concert performances took place on 7 and 14 August.

To Victor Hugo

[Paris] 5 May 1840

If to feel is to live, I have lived much to-day. I read your lines this morning. At noon I followed the people to the foot of the column [Place Vendôme], that immortal poem of the other Emperor's. I walked, like Ruy Blas, "lost in my starry meditations". I looked at the monument, and re-read your poem. Now I bow the head in tears and worshipful admiration.*

* On 5 May 1840, the anniversary of Napoleon's death, Victor Hugo published a collection of poems called *Les Rayons et les Ombres*, of which the last poem was called "The Return of the Emperor".

To the Revue des Deux Mondes

Paris, 22 November 1840

...*Iphigeneia* was performed exactly as written: therefore no one can have heard any ophicleides in it. As for Palestrina, "a few sopranos" cannot have been "sufficient for him" as his madrigal is in four parts. The critic must moreover have been strangely preoccupied if he found the work "crushed beneath the weight of instruments", since I performed it, as written, without accompaniment. These are the mis-statements I wish to have corrected, for they libel me in my capacity as an interpreter of the great masters.

Berlioz had given a concert on 1 November 1840, which included, apart from his own works, the first act of Gluck's *Iphigeneia in Tauris*, some Handel and a madrigal by Palestrina. An anonymous critic in the *Revue des Deux Mondes* had tried to discredit Berlioz as conductor of other composers' works. The above is Berlioz' reply, which the paper did not print but merely alluded to jokingly.

To his sister Adèle

[Paris, December 1840]

...Despite the fact that Mozart's Requiem is a masterpiece, it made a poor showing under the dome of the Invalides: it is not written in scale with such a celebration. I had only a few moments of partial satisfaction, and that was with what the gunners did: but even they fired as though it were the baptism of the Count of Paris or some other embryo Prince. I should have liked, instead of these five little wheezing cannons five hundred mortars belching flame as the cortège entered. Nothing of the kind. Everything missed, muffed, even the artillery!...

The remains of Napoleon were buried at the Invalides on 15 December, 1840, and Berlioz had been asked by the government to write a triumphal march for the ceremony: he refused, saying that a suitable work could not be improvised in two weeks. Mozart's Requiem was performed, together with new pieces by Auber, Halévy and Adam.

To Humbert Ferrand

[Paris] 3 October 1841

My dear Humbert,

...I have never led a more active life, or one more pre-occupied even in its inaction. I am writing, as you know perhaps, a grand opera in four acts on a libretto of Scribe called *La Nonne Sanglante*: I think that this time no one could complain about lack of interest in the piece. It is based on the episode in the *Monk* of Lewis which you know. Scribe has drawn from it, it seems to me, a very big part of the famous legend: in addition he has ended the drama with a terrific dénouement borrowed from a work by M. de Kératry, with the greatest dramatic effect. At the moment they are counting on me at the Opéra for next year: but Duprez is in such a state of vocal dilapidation that if I don't have another leading tenor, it would be madness on my part to perform my work. I was and still am in line for Habeneck's post at the Opéra. It would be a musical dictatorship of which I should hope to make much in the interests of art.

...Believe it or not, there has come over me in place of my former artistic fury a kind of cold-blooded poise, a resignation, or contempt if you like in the face of whatever offends me in current musical practices. I am far from being alarmed at this change in myself. On the contrary, the older I get the more I see that this outward indifference saves my strength for the struggle, where passion would cripple me. It's like love again: if you seem to flee, you will be run after.

You have no doubt heard of the *spaventoso* success of my Requiem in St. Petersburg, performed by the combined forces of all the opera houses, the Czar's chapel, and the choruses of the two regiments of the Imperial Guard. Thanks to the munificence of the Russian nobility, the admirable Bomberg, who conducted, made a profit of five thousand francs. When it comes to art, give me a despotic government! In Paris, to put on the whole work, I would have to be mad or prepared to lose what Bomberg made....

...I feel that I am going downhill very fast. The idea that life has an end, I notice, occurs to me frequently. So I find myself snatching rather than culling the flowers on the stony way....

Berlioz' marriage had become more and more difficult: Harriet had become insanely jealous of him and of any woman he mentioned in conversation, she scrutinised his letters, nagged him and finally took to drink. The marriage began to break up in the autumn of 1841, but did not finally end till 1844. Meanwhile Berlioz had begun an affair with the singer Marie Recio, and when he left on his first tour of Belgium in September 1842 she went with him. During 1841 he had composed recitatives for Weber's *Der Freischütz* for the Opéra and had also orchestrated the *Invitation to the Dance* and taken music from *Preciosa* and *Oberon* for the obligatory ballet. When Cherubini died Berlioz thought that Habeneck might succeed him at the Conservatoire and that he might himself succeed Habeneck as conductor at the Opéra: but the Conservatoire went to Auber, and Habeneck stayed where he was. As a result Berlioz embarked on the series of tours which took him all over Europe during the next twenty-five years, beginning with two concerts in Brussels in September 1842, and continuing with an extensive tour of Germany which began at the end of the year. He described this first German tour in ten "open letters" to his Paris friends which now form part of the *Memoirs*.

To Auguste Morel*

Stuttgart, 30 December 1842

I gave my first concert yesterday evening in the Redoutensaal, the King and all the court came to it: the orchestra was excellent and the success very great. After the concert the King sent Baron Rosenhain to congratulate me on his behalf. The Prince of Hohenzollern-Hechingen had a letter sent to me yesterday asking me to perform some pieces in his private concert, I will go there to-morrow....

To Mendelssohn

Weimar, 26 January [1843]

You are wonderfully good and kind, as I was sure you would be. Luck is on my side these days: the concert went well and this morning I received your letter. Yes indeed, I should very much like to give concerts in Leipzig. If it does not depend on someone's special permission, granted as a favour, I should like

---

* A composer who lived in Marseilles and was a friend of both Berlioz and, later, his son Louis.

to give two, as I see that expenses are moderate. Though it irks
me, I shall have to begin with my old stuff, my latest scores
being still in Frankfurt, whence they are being forwarded.
Please thank the directors of the Gewandhaus and tell them that
I shall be happy to present on the 22nd the Finale for three
choruses from my Romeo and Juliet symphony, which will have
arrived by then. But they must be warned that the part of Friar
Laurence needs a first-class bass. . . .

Berlioz had written to Mendelssohn enquiring about the possibility of giving concerts in Leipzig : Mendelssohn replied with a
warm invitation which Berlioz reproduced in the *Memoirs*.

To Ferdinand David* ......

Dresden, 10 February 1843

Please be good enough to send me immediately on receipt of
this note the orchestral parts of my *Romeo and Juliet* symphony.
I am supposed to give four parts of this work in my second
concert here. The first takes place this evening and prospects for
it look splendid. M. de Lüttichau has raised the price of seats by
a third and the whole hall is sold out : we had to have four full
rehearsals, not counting those for the chorus : I am worn out,
but with luck it will go well, I hope.

To Joseph d'Ortigue

Leipzig, 28 February 1843

...Schumann, the taciturn Schumann was electrified by the
Offertorium of my *Requiem* : he opened his mouth, to the great
astonishment of those who know him, in order to say, taking
my hand, "That Offertorium surpasses everything !"

Nothing in fact has produced such an impression on the German public. The Leipzig papers haven't stopped talking about
it for several days and ask for a complete performance of the
Requiem : impossible, because I am leaving for Berlin and they
don't have the forces required for the large-scale numbers in
the work....

To his father

Brunswick, March 1843

I have been wanting to write to you for quite a long time. I
don't know what instinct made me wait until I had a really

* The leader of the Gewandhaus Orchestra in Leipzig.

great success—greater than the rest—to announce. I don't think
I shall ever have another like this recent one. The performance,
first of all, was marvellous. Then they put crowns of laurel on
my scores of *Romeo* and the *Requiem*, on the stage. They encored the Pilgrims' March, and they tried to encore a movement
of *Romeo*, but I had to refuse, it was too long and too hazardous.
After the concert the orchestra came and invited me to a great
supper which they and the chief music lovers of the town had
arranged for me. It was a splendid reunion. I was bombarded
with fresh hurrahs (sung in harmony, as is the custom in this
musical country) and showered with complimentary verses,
toasts and laurel wreaths....

Berlioz conducted a concert at Brunswick on 9 March with
fantastic success: it included *Harold in Italy*, parts of the
Requiem, the *Benvenuto Cellini* overture, parts of *Romeo and
Juliet* and songs with orchestra.

To his sister Adèle
Paris, 8 June 1843
...Your children are, I hope, in good health. Henriette often
speaks to me of your quiet and happy household. She envies
you. Louis has quite grown up and is going to write you a letter.
Henriette is beginning to grieve again because I have had another offer from the London Philharmonic Society to conduct a
concert. But the trip is not yet decided on: they have not replied
to the musical and financial stipulations I have made. We both
send your husband greetings and kisses for your little daughters,
and we kiss you into the bargain.

To Dr. Burck, Leipzig
Paris, 14 September [1843]
...Held in Paris, like Gulliver in Lilliput, by a thousand
invisible bonds, I suffer from lack of air and space, and I cannot even *compose*! No, however strange it may appear, it's only
too true that I haven't the time to be a musician: I have to
waste all my time and work in order to live: because music does
not bring in anything until long after it has been written....

Berlioz was already hoping to arrange another German tour.

To Théophile Gautier

[Paris, November 1843]

...In your article you can joke as much as you like about my journey in Germany, then say that on Sunday the 19th, at the Conservatoire there will be Duprez, Massol, Mme Dorus-Gras singing a big trio of mine; Duprez will sing *L'Absence* by Théophile Gautier, a poet with a great future, with orchestra. I orchestrated this piece at Dresden....

Berlioz returned to Paris at the end of May: on 19 November he conducted a concert at the Conservatoire: apart from *L'Absence*, the programme included the trio from *Benvenuto Cellini* mentioned above, the *Rêverie and Caprice* for violin and orchestra and the Apotheosis from the *Symphonie Funèbre et Triomphale*, which brought the audience to its feet.

To Adolphe Sax

[Late 1843]

...I went to your house recently to ask you to bring Arban to me one of these days with a cornet in B flat and your little trumpet or sax-horn (soprano) in B flat. I want to study the extreme notes of their compass and show you both a table I have just drawn up, a comparative table on the compass of the four instruments, based on the overtones of the tube we were discussing this morning. There must be no uncertainty as to the manner of writing for your little trumpet....

Sax was the inventor of the saxophone: Berlioz persuaded him to demonstrate this new instrument at a concert on 3 February 1844, arranging his early vocal piece *Chant Sacré* for six of Sax' instruments. Arban was a well-known cornet player who often worked with Berlioz. The programme also included the first performance of the *Carnival Romain* overture.

To M. Delessert, Prefect of Police

Paris, March 1844

M. le Préfet,

The cities of England and Germany on certain occasions give musical festivals which always arouse the interest of admirers of art to the highest degree and at the same time provide noble festivities for the people. Some cities in the North of France have followed this example: Paris alone has not yet had a real festival.

An opportunity has arisen to demonstrate the effectiveness and importance of these ceremonies. There is a proposal to hold a great festival at the end of the Exhibition of Industrial Products from 3–6 August, using the vast halls where the exhibition is housed. The festival would be as follows:

On the first day, Saturday, from 2–5 p.m., a concert, consisting of a number of large-scale compositions of a lofty and popular character, to be performed, under the direction of M. Berlioz (one of the signatories of this letter), by a thousand musicians, made up of the sum of the vocal and instrumental resources of Paris, Versailles, Rouen and Orléans, with the addition of delegations from the principal Philharmonic Societies of the provinces. Two days later, Monday, the more well-to-do part of the concert audience would again assemble, for a great ball (also during the daytime); the ball to be conducted by M. Strauss. The price of tickets for the concert would be 10 francs, 5 francs, 3 francs. Seats would be booked in advance from various ticket agencies. Five hundred people only would be admitted, at 20 francs each, to the general rehearsal which would take place on the day before the concert.

Finally a dinner by subscription, presided over by the principal exhibitors, would end the festival....

H. Berlioz.

J. Strauss.

Strauss, unrelated to Johann Strauss of Vienna, was director of the "fashionable balls". The concert took place on 1 August 1844, and was a great success: it included music by Spontini, Gluck, Auber, Beethoven, Rossini, Weber, Mendelssohn, Halévy and Meyerbeer as well as Berlioz' *Hymne à la France*, written specially for the occasion, the march from the *Symphonie Fantastique* and the Apotheosis from the *Symphonie Funèbre et Triomphale*. But the preparations for the concert had exhausted Berlioz, and he had to take a short holiday at Nice, where he wrote the first version of *The Tower of Nice*, later to become the *Corsair* Overture.

To the Queen of France

[Paris] 12 March 1845

Madame,

Allow me to present to your majesty the programme of the third musical festival which I am giving at the Cirque des Champs-Elysées next Sunday. These great artistic ceremonies seem to arouse greater public interest every day, but their success could not be complete unless they succeeded in deserving the notice of your Majesty. Madame, forgive the liberty which I am taking in soliciting the honour of your presence on this occasion. Such a favour would be a powerful encouragement for all the artists and myself....

Berlioz had been engaged by the impressario Franconi to conduct four concerts at his establishment, the Cirque Olympique, early in 1845. Apart from his own works Berlioz introduced music by Félicien David and Glinka, for the first time in Paris.

To Robert Griepenkerl

Paris, [April 1845]

...Since I had your last letter I have undertaken a big musical project: a concert hall which holds five hundred performers, but it is situated almost outside the city. So that at each concert there are new anxieties: for the expenses are immense—6,000 francs. I am giving the fourth one in a few days. The best players of my normal orchestra belong to that of the Conservatoire: now this celebrated society prevents them from taking part in my concerts during the whole of the concert season ...

Griepenkerl was a Brunswick music critic who had become a great admirer of Berlioz on his first visit there in 1843. After the four concerts at the Cirque, Berlioz left for Marseilles, where he gave two concerts in June.

To George Hainl

Avignon, 2 July [1845]

My dear M. Hainl,

I have to come back up the Rhône and as a result cannot arrive in Lyons till Friday: so my letter will arrive before me.

I would only give a concert in Lyons if we could do something out of the ordinary: by raising the price of seats, by putting up posters in the neighbouring towns, such as Châlons, Mâcon, Vienne, Bourgoin, Nantua, Bellay, etc., and also on all the steamers on the Rhône and Saône, to try to take in nine to ten thousand francs. If this is impossible don't let's think about it any more: it's not worth stirring up your whole musical world in Lyons just to get an ordinary result. Besides I am so weary of rehearsals, this profession of drill sergeant has so worn me out at Marseilles that really I would have to make a great effort to get back into it. . . .

I cannot arrange to go to Lyons in August: so I would have to go before or during Rachel's tour and announce that this musical Festival will be the only one that I shall give.

Curiosity ought to be fairly lively among my fellow townsmen—for I am almost a Lyonnais—so that a fairly good house can reasonably be counted on. We must take advantage of this as much as possible and give the concert soon, for I don't have much time at my disposal.

I shall stay at the Hôtel du Parc, next to the Place des Terreaux, where I hope to find a line from you on arrival. My best wishes and sincere thanks.

H. Berlioz.

François Hainl, known as George, was a cellist and conductor of the Grand Theâtre of Lyons: he later conducted the Paris Opéra and Conservatoire orchestras. Berlioz describes himself as "almost a Lyonnais" as the Côte-Saint André is only thirty miles from Lyon. The great actress Rachel was touring the provinces at that time. Berlioz gave two concerts in Lyons in July and then returned to Paris for a week, before leaving for Bonn in August for the celebrations in connection with the unveiling of the Beethoven statue.

To George Hainl

41 rue de Provence, 2 August 1845

My dear George,

You will shortly receive two copies of my *Musical Travels in Germany and Italy*: one is for you and the other for Isidore Flachéron—I would be grateful if you could see that it reaches him. I was hoping to hear from you yesterday about the little cameo brooch which Marie left at the hotel and which I asked you to enquire about, but I expect it hasn't been found. I am getting ready to leave for Bonn, where everybody is going. It's a regular exodus of artists, men of letters and the inquisitive. I don't know where we shall be able to stay. I expect they will have to put up tents on the banks of the Rhine and sleep in the barges.

Have you no news of Bordeaux?

Marie and I send regards to Mme George and kisses to your two charming little girls.

As for you—what can I say? I esteem you for many reasons, and what I think and feel is easy to guess.

H. Berlioz.

Berlioz intended to give concerts in Bordeaux. The Beethoven Festival is described by him in *Evenings in the Orchestra*, 2nd Epilogue. The *Musical Travels* contains accounts of his first German tour and his student days in Italy which were eventually incorporated in the *Memoirs*.*

To George Hainl

26 September [1845]

...I am going to Vienna about the 10th of next month, so don't lose any time. I have two works in progress which we must perform in Lyons some day. Meanwhile we have enough other ones, and you know that I want nothing so much as to contribute as much as I can to the success of your annual concert. Only, because of the difficulties of performance I don't think we should insist on doing the large extracts from *Benvenuto* which you spoke to me about. Here at any rate it would be difficult to put them on well in a concert.

The two works are probably *The Damnation of Faust*, which Berlioz was expanding from his early *Eight Scenes from Faust*, and *La Nonne Sanglante*, on which he was still working spasmodically. He left for Vienna on 22 October.

To the Society of the Friends of Music, Vienna

Vienna, 6 December 1845

...The magnificence of your ensemble, the power of your tutti in the superb rendering of the three great German masters

* Flachéron, a painter, was Berlioz' fellow-student in Rome.

[Mozart, Haydn, Beethoven] were profoundly impressive; at the same time one was vividly aware of the vitality and confidence of each individual orchestral or choral section, and of the musicianship which led them easily through the most formidable difficulties. This marvellous performance, largely the work of amateurs, would alone be enough to assure Vienna's musical pre-eminence over all other European cities.

To Desmarest

Vienna, 16 December 1845

...There was one piece, the *Carnaval* overture, in a concert which I did not conduct myself, which the audience insisted on hearing three times in succession. There have been banquets, speeches, portraits, wreaths, a conductor's baton in silver gilt presented by the 40 principal artists and music lovers of Vienna, in fact astounding success. And all this is due almost exclusively to our poor old *Symphonie Fantastique*: the Scene in the Country and the March to the Scaffold turned the Austrian entrails inside out: as for the *Carnaval* and the *Pilgrim's March*, they are popular pieces. They are now naming pâtés after me. I have excellent musicians: a young orchestra, half Czech and half Viennese which I trained, for it has only been in existence for two months, and now it goes like a lion. This morning I rehearsed in addition the Kärntnertor Orchestra, the leading one in the Germanies, for my concert to-morrow. On the 30th I shall have the chorus and orchestra of the Vienna Theatre, doubled in numbers, for *Romeo and Juliet* complete. For Friar Laurence I have Staudigl, who is a fine strong bass. And what a musician! Marie is radiant with pleasure at all this success. I am going to bed a little tired from rehearsing....

Desmarest was a leading French cellist of the time. Berlioz described his second tour in six further open letters which are included in the *Memoirs*. He gave five concerts in Vienna with great success. The banquet was given to him on the eve of his birthday, on 10 December, and the baton was presented to him on this occasion.

To J. Hoven

Prague, 21 January [1846]

...Nothing is easier, when you are writing to distant friends, than to say: "I'm having the most incredible success here":

you know that for the time being at least they can't refute it, and even then, as with slander, some impression of it always remains. But in this case, without being at all starry-eyed about it I can only say that it appears that it is generally held that the consensus of opinion seems to be that on the whole, all things considered, one might venture to state that the verdict of the public is virtually unanimous that—

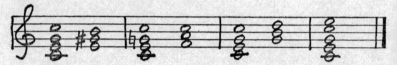

Seriously, my first concert was an exceptional success. All the Praguers whom I know assure me that their city has never been in such a state of musical excitement. They encored three pieces: Dr. Ambros and Kittl say that this never happens for instrumental music here. The Scene in the Country and the March to the Scaffold especially made an extraordinary effect. I thought the performance quite remarkable, the orchestra, composed of a combination of players from the theatre and the senior pupils of the Conservatoire, astonished me by the quickness of its reaction and the skill of most of the players. It's perhaps gratitude which makes me say this: for the greater part of the musicians treat me like a Fetish, a Manitou, a Great Lama. Kittl comes to the rehearsals at the head of a crowd of students from the Conservatoire, whom he brings to study how to break new ground and the art of making one's way through the undergrowth. As for Dr. Ambros, his happiness is so complete that he is positively contagious: it would be a pleasure to come to Prague merely to see his delight. Tomaschek has made his pronouncement: he is a third for, two-thirds against. He says that I am not entirely mad, but not far from it. On my arrival I was also told of the opposition of a musical labourer who knows nothing about music, called Got or God, who fell foul of the *King Lear* overture which he heard a year ago, and takes pride in proving that no one can possibly understand anything of what I am doing. I am still waiting to hear what effect my concert has had on his opinion: meanwhile I'm managing to sleep. Nearly all the nobility of Prague came to the performance. The ladies did not spare their aristocratic hands. In fact all is well: there's only one insect I wish I could rid myself of but can't,

who devours me as much as he can: it's the director of the
theatre. His privilege allows him to take twelve per cent of the
receipts of concerts, and when these are considerable, as they
were last Monday, the tithe becomes crushing. What can I do?
As usual, render to Caesar what pertaineth not to Caesar. Sic
vos nos vobis, etc. Next Sunday, l'ultima academia, and the
day after partiremo per Vienna. Till I have the pleasure of seeing you again, please remember me respectfully to Madame
Vesque and give my regards to all your aviary of little angels,
Cherubim, and Seraphim, especially not forgetting Mlle Félicie,
whose pretty hand I kiss with the courtesy of a Knight of the
Round Table.

Naturally my wife joins me in this and wishes to be remem-
bered to you.

Farewell, farewell, with the most perfect cadences, usual and
unusual.

H. Berlioz.

J. Hoven was the pseudonym of Vesque de Puttlingen, a Polish-
born Belgian who was imperial counsellor in the Austrian State
Chancellery and a composer and pianist. Ambros was a Czech
civil servant and musicologist, author of a well-known History of
Music. Kittl was Director of the Prague Conservatoire. Tomaschek was the doyen of Czech composers. Berlioz gave another
concert in Vienna, then went to Budapest, where he gave the first
performance of his newly written version of the Rákóczy March.

To Joseph d'Ortigue

Prague, 27 January 1846
...I arrived here expecting to fall into the middle of a popu-
lation of antiquarians and pedants who would admit nothing
but Mozart, and were ready to spit upon any modern composer,
instead of which I have found artists who are devoted, attentive and of a rare intelligence, and do four-hour rehearsals without complaining, and at the end of the second rehearsal get more
excited about my music than I had dared to hope....

To Robert Griepenkerl

Breslau, 10 March 1846
My dear Mr. Griepenkerl,
I only received Mr. Zinkeisen's letter the day before yesterday

and I answer you only to-night because I had to conclude my arrangements with Prague. So I thank you with all my heart, you and Messrs. Müller and those of your friends who are interested in my concerts, for the trouble you are kindly taking in organising a musical session for me in a hall outside the theatre, and I authorise and indeed beg you to prepare everything for the middle of April, the 17th or 18th at the latest, for I absolutely must leave for Paris on the 20th.

I only have to give one concert here, and then I shall go to Prague, where they are putting on *Romeo and Juliet* at the end of the month. After the three concerts I gave there last month I had to go back at short notice to Vienna and Budapest, though I definitely promised to return to Prague before leaving Germany: those excellent Czechs gave me such a welcome that it would be very ungrateful of me not to keep my word. According to my calculations I shall leave Prague on the 10th at the latest and I could arrive in Brunswick on the 13th: we could have the rehearsals on the 15th, 16th and 17th, the concert on the 18th or the 19th and I could leave you on the 20th by the train from Hanover. I rely on the kind care of Messrs. Müller to arrange the same orchestra for me that I have already had the honour of conducting once: I could not wish for a better one.

... I have worked very hard this year, if not in composing, at least in the public production of several works which were already more or less finished. I am worn out, exhausted, and I feel more and more depressed: the cold grips my heart. It's the beginning of the end... I have suffered too much, I have felt too much not to be burnt out soon: yet I feel I have never been so much a master of my musical faculties as I am now. But I haven't the time to compose....

Griepenkerl: see p. 88. Zinkeisen and the Müllers were Brunswick musicians. The concert at Brunswick eventually took place on 21 April. Berlioz was in fact working on *The Damnation of Faust* during his travels, but he had to write "in postchaises, in railway trains, on the Danube steamers".

To Joseph d'Ortigue

Breslau, 13 March 1846
...I have made a curious discovery: that I am so deeply attached to Paris—Paris, that is to say you, my friends, the

intelligent people there, the whirlwind of ideas in which one
moves—that at the mere thought of being excluded from it I
literally felt my heart fail and I understood the torture of
deportation. I am working furiously on *Faust* and it will soon
be finished....

There had been a question of offering Berlioz the post of
Imperial Kapellmeister in Vienna, but he declined. He was back
in Paris at the beginning of May.

To J. Hoven

Paris, 2 July 1846

...I was so pressed for time that I had to spend three whole
nights working on it. I was fêted and serenaded in every way.
The town of Lille is the most musical in France.

Now I am quieter and have taken up my work on *The
Damnation of Faust* again in good order : it goes on, but is still
far from being finished. I shall have some difficulties in getting
it performed, very probably, because of the war without mercy
or truce which I have declared against the Opéra in my articles
and especially on the management of that imbecile theatre. I
am arch-embroiled with Pillet and Mme Stoltz, whom I shook
up in a somewhat violent fashion. As for the other director, the
one at the Opéra-Comique, I am on the best of terms with
him....

Berlioz had been commissioned to write a cantata, *Chant des
Chemins de Fer*, for the opening of the Northern Railway at
Lille on 14 June, to a text by Jules Janin. With it Berlioz per-
formed the Apotheosis of the *Symphonie Funèbre et Triom-
phale*. Pillet was the new Director of the Opéra, but Rosina
Stoltz held the reins.

To George Hainl

Paris, 21 or 23 July 1846

My dear George,

Habeneck stands fast and will not get off his podium. I am
deeply embroiled with the Pillet-Stoltz administration and can
make no move. In any case they don't want a conductor but a
kind of butler who will carry out the wishes of the Directress
and admire everything she does or gets done. Think whether

such an opening appeals to you and above all don't be embarrassed on my account.

H. Berlioz.

Remember me to Mme George and the two pretty young ladies.

To his father

[Paris] 16 September [1846]

...This will interrupt you in the middle of the vintage. I too am working strenuously, on a large work which is nearly done and which I want to put on in Paris towards the end of November. I have had to be poet and musician at the same time: my score, begun and pursued across country, in Bavaria, Austria, Hungary, Bohemia and Silesia, was going faster than my versifiers in Paris and I was thus compelled to do without them. It quite surprised me how easily I was able to....

The work was *The Damnation of Faust*: Berlioz wrote the libretti himself for most of his later dramatic works. He completed the score on 19 October, and gave two concert performances of it at the Opéra-Comique on 6 and 20 December, which involved him in disastrous financial losses.

On 14 February 1847 Berlioz left for Russia, accepting Balzac's offer to lend him his fur coat for the trip. He gave concerts in St. Petersburg and Moscow and returned to St. Petersburg for a performance of *Romeo*, which was repeated on 30 April.

To Liszt

St. Petersburg, 27 April/19 May [1847]

...I think a great deal about you, and there are many opportunities of talking about you here, for people love and admire you as much as I do. Don't you think you and I travel around a great deal? Just now I am sad, sad enough to die of it. I am having one of my bouts of isolation: and it is the playing of *Romeo and Juliet* that brought it on. In the middle of the Adagio I felt my heart contract, and here I am, caught by the evil for God knows how long. My wretched temperament!

But enough of this, I have played a great deal of music here. Now the King of Prussia has had me notified by Count Roeden that the Berlin Opera is at my disposal to put on *Faust* complete. So I'm going to Prussia, but my heart is not in it. Will

I recover it? There I go lamenting again. What a misery to be
an electric machine that can be electrified! The Princess tells
me you are writing a great deal. When is your *Sardanapale* due
in Vienna?...

Farewell. I embrace you. I should like to see you. The sun
shines as it does in Italy—34 degrees of heat [93.2F.]—a torture. Come hither ice, fog, insensibility! Farewell again, don't
laugh at me: if you do I shall know it wherever you are.

The Princess was Carolyne Sayn-Wittgenstein, Liszt's mistress
for the rest of his life. They had met for the first time at Kiev
the previous February. Berlioz met her in Russia in April and
entrusted her with this letter to take to Liszt. *Sardanapale*, an
Italian opera after Byron, was begun by Liszt about 1846 but
only exists in the form of sketches.

To Leopold Ganz

Berlin, 24 June 1847

I leave tomorrow, and having been unable to say good-bye to
you to-day I must write you a few lines to thank you personally
and ask you to transmit my thanks to the artists of the Chapel
Royal for the admirable way in which they performed my work
The Damnation of Faust. Be so kind as to tell Mr. Elssler how
grateful I am for the trouble he took with the chorus and that
the results which he obtained were the most satisfying that a
composer could wish for. I am enclosing a copy of my letters on
Germany: you can see and let the artists of the orchestra see (on
page 155) in what terms I have spoken of them and whether
the small observations I have made on matters of detail are
likely to hurt them or to be taken in bad part.

Farewell, my dear friend, my best regards to your brother
and believe in my sincere devotion.

H. Berlioz.

Ganz was the leader of the Berlin Royal Opera Orchestra. His
brother Moritz was a cellist in the same orchestra and Elssler
was the chorus master. The letters referred to are Berlioz'
Musical Travels in Germany and Italy: see p. 90. Berlioz also
published several letters on his present Russian and German
visits which were later incorporated in the *Memoirs*. He reached
Paris on 7 July.

To Léon Escudier

Paris, 20 August 1847

As I promised verbally to you, I undertake during the period of my service as conductor of the Royal Academy of London to pay you the sum of a thousand francs for each ten thousand francs which I shall receive as salary for this appointment: in addition you will be entitled to a thousand francs payable in instalments of ten per cent of the sums paid to me by M. Jullien up to the sum of ten thousand francs, as a result of the contract in respect of the opera in three acts which I am to compose for him.

Sincerely,

H. Berlioz.

Escudier, the director of *France Musicale*, had arranged for Berlioz to become the conductor of a new opera company at Drury Lane which was to be opened by Antoine Jullien, a French impresario married to an English wife. Berlioz had now given up all hope of the conductorship of the Paris Opéra.

To Joseph d'Ortigue

Paris, 26 August August 1847

...You see that there was nothing to make me hesitate, and that I have definitely had to give up fair France for perfidious Albion.

I am going to write one more letter for the *Débats* and then I will go to the Côte. The first one on Vienna appeared the day before yesterday. I will address the one on Russia to you: it's agreed.

Berlioz took the thirteen-year-old Louis to the Côte-Saint-André to visit Berlioz' father, who was in very frail health. He returned to Paris in October and left for London on 2 November, arriving there on the 5th.

To Tajan-Rogé

London, 10 November 1847

Your letter would have been answered sooner had it not been for the thousand and one worries which overwhelmed me the moment I set foot in Paris. You can have no idea of my existence in that infernal city which thinks itself the home of Art.

Thank heaven I have escaped to England and am more independent financially than I dared to hope. Jullien, the manager here, is a most intrepid person and knows London and the English better than anybody: he has made his fortune and is going to make mine, he says. I let him have his own way since he does nothing unworthy of art and good taste—but I have my doubts....

This winter during my stay in London I will publish the continuation of my letters on my musical excursions. Perhaps you have seen the first three on Vienna and Budapest. I have now to write the ones on Prague and Russia.

I have come *alone* to London: you may guess my reasons. I badly need a little freedom, which so far I have never been able to get. Not one coup d'état but a whole series was necessary before I succeeded in shaking off my bonds. Yet now, while I'm waiting for full rehearsals to begin, my solitariness is going to seem very strange.

Since I am in a confidential mood, will you believe that I had a queer little love affair in St. Petersburg—now don't laugh like a full orchestra in C major—a poetic, heart-rending and perfectly innocent affair with a young (not too young) girl, one of your chorus singers, who said: "I shall write", and in speaking of her mother's obsession with her marrying, added: "What a bore!" Oh, our walks! oh, the tears I shed when, like Faust's Marguerite, she said: "What can you see in me—a poor girl so far beneath you?" I thought I would die of despair when I left St. Petersburg, and was really ill when I found no letter from her in Berlin. She did promise she should write: but in Paris, again no letter. What a bore! Probably by now she is married. I can picture it all again—the banks of the Neva, the setting sun. In a maze of passion I crushed her arm against my breast and I sang to her the melody of the adagio in *Romeo and Juliet*. Ah me! not two lines since I left her. I am not even sure it was she who waved farewell in the distance just as I got into the coach. Farewell: you at least shall write to me....

Tajan-Rogé, the cellist, was a friend of Berlioz who was in St. Peterbsurg at the time. The girl was a corsetière who sang in the chorus at a theatre. She was engaged, but her fiancé, to whom she was not greatly attached, was away. She did write to Berlioz, but the letter went astray. Berlioz later wrote to Tajan-Rogé

enclosing a letter which he asked him to deliver to her personally, and he transmitted her reply to Berlioz. Her fiancé had
now returned to St. Petersburg and she had gone back to him,
though she assured Berlioz that she would always be grateful to
him for his affection.

To Auguste Morel
           76 Harley Street, London, 31 (*sic*) November [1847]
     Jullien asks me confidentially to get your report on the success
of Verdi's new opera.* We begin next week with *Lucia di
Lammermoor*, which can hardly help going well with Mme
Gras and Reeves. He has a beautiful voice, and sings as well as
this awful English language will allow. I had a warm reception
at one of Jullien's concerts, but will not begin my own till
January.
     Your friend M. Grimblot has given me the entrée to his club,
but heaven alone knows what amusement is to be found in an
English club. Macready gave a magnificent dinner in my
honour last week : he is charming and unassuming at home,
though they say he is terrible at rehearsals. I have seen him in
a new tragedy, *Philip van Artevelde* : he is superb, and has put
the piece on splendidly. No one here understands the handling
and grouping of a crowd as he does. It is masterly.

To Gaetano Belloni†
                                    London, 19 December 1847
     ...As to *Faust*, it is not engraved, and it is developing even
at this moment at a frightful rate. For Scribe is arranging it as
a grand opera for our next London season. It will be given here
towards the end of December 1848. This is *between ourselves* :
nobody in Paris except Scribe knows about these preparations,
and I have reasons for keeping them secret....

To Auguste Morel
                                    London, 8 December [1847]
     ...The opening of our season was a tremendous success.
Madame Gras and Reeves were recalled frantically four or five
times and they both deserved it. Reeves is a priceless discovery

---

     * *Jerusalem*, revision of *I Lombardi*.
     † Liszt's secretary and also an impresario.

for Jullien: his voice is delightful in quality, he is a good
musician, has an expressive face, and acts with a characteristi-
cally Irish verve....

To Auguste Morel
> London, 14 January 1848

...You have no doubt already heard of the horrible position
that Jullien has got into and dragged us in with him. However,
as we must ruin his credit in Paris as little as possible, don't talk
to anyone about what I am going to tell you. It wasn't the
Drury Lane enterprise which destroyed his fortune: this was
already destroyed at the beginning, and he had no doubt counted
on good receipts to restore it. Jullien is still the same lunatic that
you knew: he hasn't the least idea of what an opera house
needs, nor even of the most obvious requisites for a good musical
performance. He only had one score when he opened the theatre.
We've been surviving on the good will of Lumley's* agents, who
have been lending us the orchestral parts of the operas we're
doing. At the moment Jullien is touring the provinces, taking a
lot of money with his promenade concerts: the theatre here has
quite respectable takings every evening, and, to be brief, after
having made us consent to the reduction of our salaries by a
third, *we are not paid at all*.

If Jullien does not pay me on his return, I will try to make
arrangements with Lumley and give concerts at the Queen's
Theatre. For now there is a good opening for me here, a place
left vacant by poor Mendelssohn's death. Everyone keeps telling
me. So I have reason to believe that it's *here* that I could make
a position for myself....

So France is wiped off my musical map, and I have decided
to turn my eyes and my thoughts from there as much as possible. To-day I am not at all in a melancholy frame of mind, I
have no spleen: I speak to you with the greatest sang-froid, the
most complete lucidity of spirit. I see things as they are....

To General Lvov, St. Petersburg
> London, 29 January 1848

...I have just heard Mendelssohn's last oratorio *Elijah*. It is
magnificently great and of an indescribable harmonic rich-
ness....

* Director of Covent Garden.

Oh! Russia! and its cordial hospitality, and its literary and artistic climate, and the organisation of its theatres and its imperial chapel, a precise, clean and inflexible organisation without which, in music as in many other things, one can do nothing good or beautiful—who will give them back to me? You are extremely good to have spoken of me to His Majesty and to allow me still to hope that I may establish myself with you some day. I am not counting too much on this idea: everything depends on the Emperor. If he wanted it, in six years we would make Petersburg the centre of the musical world. . . .

To Auguste Morel

London, Saturday 12 February 1848

. . . My music has taken with the English like fire to gunpowder. The *Rákóczy* and *Danse des Sylphes* were encored. Everyone of musical importance was at Drury Lane for my concert and most of the artists came to congratulate me afterwards. They had expected something diabolical, involved, incomprehensible. Now we shall see how they agree with our Paris critics. Davison himself wrote the *Times* notice: they cut half of it from lack of space, but still the rest has had its effect. Old Hogarth of the *Daily News* was really comic: "My blood is on fire", he said to me: "never have I been excited like this by music."

Now I am trying to see how I can give my second concert: Jullien is not paying his instrumentalists or choral singers any more, and I don't dare expose myself to the danger of seeing them fail me at the last moment. Last night, after *Figaro*, the defection began. The horns told me they wouldn't be coming any more. . . .

Berlioz gave a concert on 7 February at Drury Lane, including the *Carnaval Romain* and *Benvenuto Cellini* overtures, *Harold in Italy*, and extracts from *Faust*, the *Requiem* and the *Symphonie Funèbre*. The press was excellent, but Jullien appropriated the receipts without paying anyone anything.

To Joseph d'Ortigue

76 Harley Street, London, 15 March 1848

. . . For my musical career I can only think of England or Russia. I had taken my leave of France a long time ago: the recent revolution makes my decision stronger and more inevitable....

The republican revolution of February 1848 had more or less stopped cultural activity in France, and Berlioz' patron, Armand Bertin, who was an Orléanist, had gone into hiding. In these circumstances Berlioz began to compile his memoirs.

To Charles Hallé

London, March 1848

I am very *sorry* to have the pleasure of seeing you : nevertheless I thank you for coming to the house immediately after your shipwreck on the coasts of England. If you are at home tonight we'll commiserate together while *fuming*. I will come to you about ten....

Hallé had had to leave Paris because of the Revolution : "fuming" is a play on the word "fumant".

To H. D. Leslie

London, Sunday morning 7 May 1848

Dear Sir,

I was ill all day yesterday, which prevented me having the honour of seeing you. I wanted to ask you to present my excuses to the Committee of the Amateur Music Society in connection with my overture.

I have not heard it for fifteen years and I do not think it worthy of appearing on your programme. It would not make an effect and could harm me greatly, especially at the moment when I am only just beginning to be known in London. So please be kind enough to replace it at the next concert with some piece which the orchestra knows already, which should not be difficult, and believe that I very much regret having to disappoint you.

Yours faithfully,

H. Berlioz.

P.S. Please return the music to 72 New Bond Street.

Leslie was a composer and co-founder of the Amateur Music Society, 1847. The Overture was probably that to *Waverley*, which had first been performed in London in 1840.

To Pierre Duc

[London] 26 May [1848]

Our piece, the *Apothéose*, has come out at last. It was thought necessary to tamper with my sub-title. I had written "Composed for the inauguration of the Bastille Column", and further down : "Dedicated to M. Duc, architect of the Bastille Column". This made it clear why the column came into it at all and why the dedication was appropriate. But since the last Chartists' agitation the London bourgeois has a deep fear of anything remotely or nearly related to revolutions, and as a result my publisher refused to consider any mention on the title page either of your monument or of those to whom it was put up.

I have sought in vain to send you the scores together with the Scottish airs you asked for. Instead I send you the *Apothéose* by itself, for a parcel of the kind you want would cost a great deal. The Hungarian March for four hands has also been published by Beale, and the Chorus of Sylphs will appear shortly. Our piece would, I think, be quite impressive if sung by a large chorus and orchestrated. I may have it performed in Paris if it becomes possible to give music there. Meanwhile you'll have to be content with the piano score.

Speaking of Paris, the reproaches my friends make about my absence are scarcely valid if they think that my staying away is doing me harm. A man must have a tricolour flag over his eyes not to be able to see that music in France is dead and that it is the last of the arts our rulers are going to take any notice of. They tell me I'm holding aloof from my country. I don't hold aloof from it : I flee from it as one flees from a barbaric shore when one is looking for civilisation, and I have done so not only since the Revolution. For long now I have stifled my love of France and uprooted from my heart the foolish habit of centring all my thoughts on her. During the last seven years I have lived entirely on what my works and concerts have earned me in foreign countries. Without Germany, Bohemia, Hungary and especially Russia I should have starved in France over and over again. Friends write to me of "positions" to take, of "posts to apply for". What position, what posts? There aren't any. Isn't Auber at the Conservatoire, Carafa at the Gymnase, Girard at the Opéra? What else is there? Nothing. And the love of mediocrity—has that been purged from the French mentality

by the Revolution? Possibly, but only to have been replaced by
the love of something worse, if indeed there is anything worse
than mediocrity.

No, I have nothing to do in France, except cultivate the
friendships which are dear to me. For my career I have tried
enough, suffered enough, waited enough. I shall not fulfil it
there. In France I have experienced nothing but frustration in
greater or lesser degree. I have found only stupid opposition, because the national mentality is stupid where serious matters of
art and literature are concerned. I have an invincible and ever-
growing contempt for those "French ideas" which are quite unknown to other nations. Under the previous government I
found nothing but scorn and indifference: I shall now find
preoccupation with other and weightier questions added to
scorn and indifference. I wrote three times to Louis-Philippe
when he was King requesting an audience. I did not even receive a *reply*. I wrote to Ledru-Rollin recently and he was as
polite as the King. There is only one opera house in Paris, the
Opéra, which is managed by a nitwit and is closed to me. Do
you suppose that if Duponchel is dismissed they won't find
twenty others like him? Some day perhaps I shall be approached
when I am very old, very tired and no longer good for
anything; but I may not have lost my memory, and such
belated confidence in me, *if it comes*, will only be the more
painful.

I therefore have nothing better to do than what I am doing
now. Like a savage I go my own way, I hold on to my freedom,
I keep moving as long as the earth will bear me, as long as
the woods have moose and deer: and if I am often weary
and sleepless and suffer from cold, hunger and the ravages
of the pale-faces, at least I can dream alone above the waterfall and in the silent forest, worshipping the grandeur of
nature and thanking God that He has left me a feeling for her
beauty.

I saw *Hamlet* recently. The new Hamlet, Brooke, is superb,
much better than Macready or Kemble. What a world is that
masterpiece, and what havoc that fellow makes in one's heart
and soul! Shakespeare meant to depict the nothingness of life,
the vanity of human designs, the tyranny of chance and the
indifference of Fate or God towards what we call virtue, wicked-
ness, beauty, ugliness, love, hate, genius and folly. And he has

cruelly succeeded. In the performance this time they had deigned to give us *Hamlet* as written, and almost uncut—an unusual thing in this country where one finds so many people who are superior to Shakespeare. For that matter they do the same to music : Costa has orchestrated and corrected for Covent Garden Rossini's *Barber of Seville* and Mozart's *Figaro* and *Don Giovanni*. The bass drum runs riot.

The two Italian theatres are locked in a mortal combat of prima donnas. Lumley hurls Jenny Lind into the breach, Delafield ripostes with Viardot-Garcia. *La Sonnambula* is on at both theatres, and there are concerts composed of thirty seven Italian items, flanked for form's sake by the overture to *Euryanthe* or a Beethoven concerto. And the public takes it all stoically, while wishing it could have something better—for London has a serious public for music. . . .

Let me tell you, by way of stopping all this verbiage, that I am preparing a concert at the Hanover Square Rooms, and the musicians, hearing of Jullien's bankruptcy and the loss it has involved me in, are insisting on playing for nothing. I'm looking forward to having a magnificent orchestra, made up of the elite of the Queen's Theatre and Covent Garden. I shall still have about £60 (1500 francs) of expenses to pay. It's on the 29th of June. That is all my news. I must say I miss our delightfully easy, unpretentious conversations at Mme Vanderkelle's, and the fine wit and cultivated taste with which M. de Montville flavours them, and your own leaps and exclamations of enthusiasm at whatever is beautiful, and the way you deliver your admiring verdicts through puffs of tobacco (I mean smoke), and the recumbent posture of the ladies while we discuss.

Only one thing has always shocked me in those gatherings—a coarse and prosaic thing which Mme Vanderkelle does her best to conceal and yet fails to, a thing unworthy of a house like hers, and one that offends all decent company—I mean her upright piano. No, madame, in a house appointed like yours it is not permissible to sport such a wardrobe : it is not permissible in a choice circle such as yours to allow an instrument of this nature to be heard. It is a crime of lèse-art. On this pun I shake you all by the hand and beg you—what was I going to beg you? Ah yes, beg you on no account to let Duc sing the Apothéose any more. My warmest greetings.

H. Berlioz.

Pierre Duc, the architect, was an old companion of Berlioz from the Villa Medici in Rome. The *Apothéose* was that of the *Symphonie Funèbre et Triomphale*. *Lêse-Art* is a pun on *lézard* and *les arts*. Berlioz' concert took place on 29 June and was a great success artistically, though not so financially. The programme included, among other items, the first three movements of *Harold*, the *Carnaval Romain*, excerpts from *Faust*, *La Captive* and "Ah, non giunge" from *La Sonnambula* sung by Pauline Viardot, *Zaïde* sung by Mme Sabatier, and two movements of a Mendelssohn piano concerto.

To the Editor of the Morning Post

London, 10 July 1848

Sir,

Allow me to avail myself of your paper to express in a few words my spontaneous feelings at the welcome which has been given to me in London. I am on the point of returning to the country which is still called France, and which after all is my country. I am going to see how an artist can live there or how long it will take him to die among the ruins under which the flower of art is crushed and buried. But however long may be the ordeal which awaits me there, I shall retain to the end the most grateful remembrance of your splendid and skilful artists, your intelligent and attentive public and of my colleagues of the Press who have given me such generous and unwavering support. I am doubly happy to have been able to admire their excellent qualities of warmth and responsiveness, combined with real honesty in criticism. These are clear evidence of a genuine love of music and a guarantee for the future to all admirers of the art, for they can rest assured that you will not allow it to perish. The personal aspect is strictly secondary here : for, believe me, I love music itself far more than *my* music—and I only wish that I had had more opportunities to prove it to you.

Yes, our Muse, alarmed by the horrid clamour which echoes from one end of the Continent to another, seems at least assured of an asylum in England. The hospitality will be all the finer if the host never forgets that one of its sons was the greatest of all poets, that music is one of the forms of poetry, and that on the same freedom which is characteristic of Shakespeare's immortal conceptions depends the development of the music of the future.

Farewell then, all of you who have treated me so cordially, I

am desolate at leaving you, and I repeat involuntarily the sad
and solemn words of Hamlet's father, "Farewell, farewell, remember me".

Hector Berlioz.

To the Minister of the Interior

[Paris] 18 July 1848

...It was not my doing if the Conservatoire failed to use my
services more actively: the musical opinions of the previous
Director [Cherubini] always kept me at arms' length. I would
in fact be happy to assist in the teaching. I could, for instance,
hold a chair of Orchestration. This modern branch of the composer's studies is not taught anywhere, and opinion has it that
I possess the requisite knowledge and that I have even made
contributions to it. I have moreover written a treatise on the
subject which has been translated into the chief European
languages.*...

To Liszt

[Paris] Sunday 23 July 1848

...France at the present time is like a forest inhabited by
anxious men and raging wolves, both seeking means of destroy-
ing each other....

In fact I miss London very much, especially since I have been
here. When I arrived I found ten jokers sitting in committee
at the Conservatoire working out a scheme which contained
among other compliments to me the cancelling of my position
as librarian. If the Minister approves, as is almost certain, I
shall have nothing left except occasional articles which the editors now pay for at half-price—when they pay....

To J. W. Davison†

[Paris] 26 July 1848

...I am very sadly affected by the deplorable state in which
I have found the music and musicians of Paris after my long
absence. All the theatres closed, all the artists ruined, all the
professors idle, all the students in flight, poor pianists playing
sonatas in the public squares, historical painters sweeping streets,

---

* The Treatise on Modern Instrumentation and Orchestration had
been published in 1844.

† Music critic of The Times.

architects employed in mixing mortar on public building sites, etc. ...

Berlioz had returned to Paris on 14 July 1848: on 28 July his father died, but he was not able to go to the Côte-Saint-André till 8 August. Meanwhile the new Director of Fine Arts, Charles Blanc, saved Berlioz' position as Librarian of the Conservatoire. While in the country he thought again of his childhood love Estelle, now Mme Fornier, and wrote to her but received no reply: this visit is described in the *Memoirs*. He returned to Paris on 10 September. In the middle of October Harriet suffered another stroke, while Berlioz and Louis were with her. Later Berlioz took Louis back to his school in Rouen.

To his son Louis

[Paris, 21 October 1848]

Your mother is a little better, but she is still in bed and under orders not to talk. The least emotion too would be fatal to her, so please don't write her a letter like your last one to me. Nothing is more distressing than to see you giving yourself up to moping and idleness: you will be eighteen in four years without having any career to go into. You keep telling me that you want to be a sailor: you must want pretty badly to leave me, because once you are at sea God knows when I shall see you again. If I were free and independent I would leave with you and we would seek our fortunes in India or elsewhere, but even to travel one must have a certain affluence, and my career as a composer keeps me in Europe. I would have to give it up completely if I left the Old World for the New. I write to you as I would to a grown boy. You must think over what I say and you will understand. For no matter what happens I shall always be your best friend, the only one entirely devoted to you and full of unchangeable affection for you. I know you love me and this will make up to me for everything. But it would indeed be sad if at twenty you were still a boy without any use to yourself or to society. I enclose some envelopes so that you can write to your aunt. Tell me again about your teeth: have you cleaned them properly? Farewell, dear child, I embrace you with all my soul.

To Count Wielhorsky

Paris, 28 November [1848]

... Meyerbeer has begun rehearsing his *Prophète*: he is a

courageous man to risk launching a work of such dimensions at
a time when riots or a change of government can cut him short,
however great his eloquence. Halévy has just won a great success with his *Val d'Andorre* at the Opéra-Comique. It is really
good. There are some charming melodies in his score and real
feeling. I said what I thought when I wrote about it in the
paper. Clapisson's *Jeanne la Folle* is quite the opposite: no
ideas, no style, it's simply gross, dull and flat. You will wonder
how grossness can combine with flatness: I don't know how
the composer did it—it's one of his trade secrets....

To Liszt

[Paris] end of March 1849

Belloni told me of all the troubles you have been having. I
was very upset, as you can well imagine. But I know how
energetic and decisive you are in times of crisis. Still your project for a tour of the United States seems violent to me—to cross
the Atlantic to make music for Yankees who just now are only
thinking of Californian gold! You are the best judge of the
advisability of such a trip. As for what can be done here beforehand, I really don't know: it changes from day to day with
the riot-meter....

The Italian Theatre flaps only one wing: the Opéra never
had any, but they say *Le Prophète* will supply the lack of them.
Concerts, except at the Conservatoire, bring in nothing. When
the crowds who are coming to the Industrial Exhibition are in
Paris, when the new Chamber is elected and seated, when the
emotion caused by the premières of *Le Prophète* has calmed
down, perhaps you can try something. We are all impatient to
see you....

Liszt was about to settle in Weimar with Princess Sayn-Wittgenstein, and was unsure of his position at the time. Meyerbeer
had invited Berlioz to a private rehearsal of *Le Prophète*. Berlioz
had begun the *Te Deum*, which he finished this year, together
with the Funeral March for the Last Scene of *Hamlet* and the
first part of the *Memoirs*. On 15 April 1849 two excerpts from
The Damnation of Faust were given at one of the Conservatoire
concerts, a society which had not performed any music of his
for sixteen years: the performance was a success.

To Jules Janin

[Paris] Saturday, 21 April 1849

...It was the overturning of a barrier. If the other Great Walls of China which still hem me in could likewise collapse, perhaps the music I have composed might receive the same welcome here as in the rest of Europe and I might be quite forgiven for being alive and French. Perhaps I might also produce new works, more important than those I have been engaged on up till now. If I have lived during the last six years, I owe it solely to Germany and Russia; and you can't imagine with what heaviness of heart I sit down to work, knowing as I do that I can only expect my music to be well received abroad....

To his sister Adèle

[Paris, 25 August 1849]

...When doctors send a patient to a watering place it is generally because they don't have anything else to prescribe. If it weren't for Henriette's grave condition, I would come to the Côte next month. But any moment a fresh attack could come....
I need not tell you, dear sister, what sad and deep thoughts bind us three in all that is associated with memory of our wonderful and excellent father. The thought of the sad anniversary has revived it with painful force. I have his book, as you know, annotated by him, and I have just read it. His pencillings showed him pondering and correcting with great care, and I was struck afresh by the fine integrity with which he practised medicine, and by the clarity and breadth of his mind, which should have shone in a wider circle. But his ineffable goodness and the care he lavished on us as children are far deeper reasons for regret. I should like to see you both : please give me at once some absolutely truthful news about Nanci. I will write to her soon.

I have only lately got back to work—music, I mean. I am finishing, concluding, completing my score. I am seized by a sort of feverish impatience to become once more involved in musical projects. And I want to set them down as soon as possible. This ardent occupation is the only one that could help me suppress the longing for travel which grips me increasingly. Do you know, I dream only of ships, seas, distant isles, hazardous explorations. My musical travels through Europe have merely developed this instinct, which has always been dormant in me. I can see its futility, its childishness, but can do nothing about it. South America, New Zealand and the Pacific Isles are not practical, but were it not for my obligations here I would begin exploring the terra firma of our old Europe again, and take a chance on giving some productive concerts in those parts of the north where I haven't yet been, Sweden and Denmark, or revisit Russia, where I was so well received. Perhaps I may be able to go to Holland this winter : it's only a few steps away now, thanks to the railway. Travel on land is so easy and cheap nowadays. ...

His sister Nanci had developed an undiagnosed illness which later turned out to be cancer of the breast. Berlioz' father's book was entitled "Mémoire sur les maladies chroniques, les évacuations sanguines et l'acupuncture." Berlioz' *Te Deum* was finished in October of this year. In January 1850 he founded the Philharmonic Society in Paris, which occupied a good deal of his time for the next year and a half. Apart from the classics, the Society performed Berlioz' *Requiem*, two of his symphonies, parts of *The Damnation of Faust* and several smaller choral works, including a new one, *The Shepherd's Farewell*, which later became part of *The Childhood of Christ*.

To his sister Nanci

Paris, 3 April [1850]

...Hugo's salon is full of monstrous old women, ugly enough to make a dog bark, and malicious and pretentious in the highest degree. The other day, if Mme Janin hadn't brought a bit of contrast, I'd have imagined myself in a coven of witches. But the great thing about these soirées is that no music is played. Dumas was there, amusing himself by tossing mots right and left at the company as he strolled about. He had his daughter on his arm, a young person of nineteen, too like her father to be pretty, but with a kind of quadroon air about her that is rather attractive; the originality of her appearance was heightened by a gold sequin headdress, which made her look like a Madagascan odalisque. Farewell, my poor sister, God grant that you have been able to read this letter to the end, and that it may have helped you to forget your pain for a few minutes. ...

Berlioz had at last learnt the truth about Nanci's illness and was trying to keep up her spirits with Parisian gossip. She died the following month.

To his sister Adèle

[Paris] Monday 13 May [1850]

Give me at least some news of yourself. Your silence worries me. I fear your grief, though you must have suffered a thousand times more while watching over the agony of our poor dear just delivered. Are you ill? In that case let Suat write to me. Farewell, I kiss you. Poor sister! Now there are only two of us.

To Balzac

[Paris] 12 June 1850

...Since the eve of my trip to Russia I have not seen you once, which makes three enormous years. Have you ever thought of the anguish that would be felt by certain passionate beings at seeing the features of their idol only in mirrors thrice removed? That is the way I feel, not having seen you. In less roundabout fashion, let me ask you when I can go and shake your hand and beg you to introduce to Mme Balzac one of her most devoted servants.

Balzac had just returned from his second Russian trip and was married to his long-courted love Mme Hanska: he died only two months later.

To Brandus

[Paris, March 1851]

I will never consent to accept on behalf of the artists whom I direct what I would not accept for myself if the business concerned me alone. Material loss is far less damaging than the effect created in the musical world and the public mind when a serious enterprise is reduced to the level of a fashionable vulgarity: and it would be a libel on our players to impute to them feelings any different from mine. If the matter comes up again, say that you *did not dare* propose it to me.

The Philharmonic Society had been getting into financial difficulties, and eventually closed down on 25 March 1851: Brandus, the music publisher, had evidently made some proposal to improve its financial position at the cost of its artistic integrity. A few weeks later the Minister of Commerce appointed Berlioz to the jury which was to judge musical instruments at the Great Exhibition in London of 1851.

*To Camille Pal**

Paris, 15 April 1851

...It will be no sinecure. I am very much afraid there's going to be a stormy contest between the instrument makers of Paris and those of Berlin. All are friends of mine and I shall be caught between hammer and anvil. But I am resolved to be a Minos worthy of such assizes and not to render injustice. The Lord knows—or rather I'm sure he hasn't the least idea—where I shall find lodgings. The Minister cannot say whether the English management has thought of keeping a kennel for us in the Crystal Palace or anywhere else. But then the Minister is very young—only four days old.

To The Minister of Commerce

Paris, 20 April 1851

...I shall do my best to respond in a worthy manner to your confidence in me by defending the French exhibitors as far as the interests of art and the justice of their cause will allow me.

Berlioz left for London on 9 May: his report on the Exhibition is reprinted in *Les Grotesques de la Musique*.

To Joseph d'Ortigue

27 Queen Anne Street, Cavendish Square, London,
21 June 1851

...It's France which comes out ahead of the whole of Europe, without any possible comparison: Erard, Sax and Vuillaume. All the rest is in the class of pots, pans and penny whistles....

Tell M. Arnaud† I shall be happy to set a series of his poems on Joan of Arc, if I too hear a *voice from heaven*. He should try to write short verses: long lines and elaborate couplets are fatal to melody; and it would be necessary to make it into a popular legend, very simple but dignified, divided into a lot of different songs or sections....

To Liszt

Paris, 19 rue de Boursault, 6 August 1851

I have just returned from London, and hear from Belloni that you intend to produce *Benvenuto* in Weimar. I thank you a

* Berlioz's brother-in-law, husband of Nanci.
† A canon of Poitiers.

thousand times for having thought of it. It will be a great pleasure for me to see this poor work reborn or rather born under your direction. I have sent the score to my copyist who is repairing it and making a few necessary changes. ...

To Liszt

Paris, 29 August 1851

However childish my joy may seem, I shan't pretend otherwise with you. Yes, I am full of joy at the thought of having the work presented to an unprejudiced public, and presented by you. I have just looked at it carefully after thirteen years of oblivion, and I swear I'll never again find such verve and Cellinian impetuosity, nor such a variety of ideas. But this only makes it the harder to perform : theatre people, singers especially, are so devoid of humour. But I count on you to Pygmalionise all those statues.

To Count Lvov

Paris, 21 January 1852

...It is impossible to do anything in Paris, so next month I shall go back to England, where at least the desire to love music is real and persistent.

The feeling for truth in art is as extinct as the feeling for rightness in morals, and were it not for the energy of the President of the Republic we would now be in the position of seeing ourselves assassinated in our own houses. ...

If I can be of the least use to you in my newspaper articles command me, dear master. It will be a pleasure to tell our few serious French readers of the great and good things that are being done in Russia. It is a debt I shall gladly pay, since I shall never forget the warmth of my reception and the kindness of your Empress and your great Emperor's family. What a pity he himself doesn't like music ! ...

To Liszt

19 rue de Boursault, Paris, 4 February [1852]

...As you can guess, Marie, who has never heard *Benvenuto*, wants to join me, so don't press us, I beg you, but be good enough to reserve a small suite for us at the Hotel de Russie or elsewhere. My arrangements with Beale are now concluded, and I have to be back in Paris by the 24th at the latest.

Liszt had invited Berlioz to stay with him and Princess Sayn-Wittgenstein at the Altenburg in Weimar for the first perform-ance of *Benvenuto*, due to take place on 16 February. However it was postponed because the leading tenor and a group of his followers were obstructing the work by pretending that it would ruin their voices. The première eventually took place in March, by which time Berlioz had left for London to conduct for the New Philharmonic Society.

To M. Mocquard
                    19 rue de Boursault, Paris, 26 February 1852

I do not have the honour of being known to you personally except through some polyglot puns which we exchanged at a cheerful supper three months ago. I am afraid that at this moment a pun in action may be presenting me in an essentially false light to the Prince-president.

I am told that people are hoping to make him interpret some purely musical criticisms which I have published recently in the *Journal des Débats* as some sort of absurd and thinly disguised political opposition.

If this is so, please be kind enough, when you find an oppor-tunity, to tell the Prince the truth, which is this : my position as an honest critic has made me a host of enemies in Paris : the contempt which I do not conceal for the insolent mediocrities with which our artistic world is encumbered, has made me many more. As for my attitude to the Prince who has dragged France and civilisation out of the horrible morass in which they were drowning, it can be summed up as one of grateful admiration, and I beg him to believe this. This is not of course of any great importance to him, but you will understand that I cannot allow myself to be slandered to him in this connection. My devotion to the Prince is entirely unconnected with any personal interest. I am only concerned with my art. I have no other ambition than that it too should be safe from the insane and deplorable doc-trines which tend to inhibit its growth. In any case I cannot practise it on a large scale except outside France, but I have had my share of frequent and protracted exiles to which I have been thus condemned, and it is at the moment of leaving for Eng-land, where I have been summoned for an important musical enterprise, that I have thought it necessary to address these lines

to you, Sir, so that in addition to the sins of absence I shall not
be charged with others which I shall never be guilty of.

Your devoted servant

Hector Berlioz.

Mocquard was the private secretary of Prince Louis-Napoleon,
later Emperor Napoleon III, who had seized power by a coup
d'état in December 1851. An article by Berlioz voicing the
grievances of his fellow-musicians had appeared in the *Journal
de Débats*, which was in opposition to the new government, and
Berlioz, as a convinced supporter of Napoleonism, was afraid
that his remarks might be misinterpreted politically. However
his letter won him no advantage with the government.

To Liszt

Paris, 2 March [1852]

...It surprised me greatly that some such thing had not yet
occurred. The worst thing about this tenor is that his ill-will is
accompanied by incompetence, and I fear his partisans, or at
least our opponents, may form a cabal on the first night. But I
shall say nothing to discourage you further. I am behind you in
exact proportion to your noble persistence. Act as if I were not
involved, and be as bold as you wish. If the tenor wrecks his
rôle perhaps the audience will realise his inadequacy : besides if
the rest comes through I'll be more than content.

Farewell. No need to recommend Joachim to me : I know him
of old and esteem him highly. I leave for London in a few hours.
The Paris papers must have given you details of the New Philharmonic Society. It has stirred up London devilishly, and as
soon as I arrive I shall have on my neck all of old England in a
fury. Anderson, Costa and the rest are the angriest. But if Beale
lets me have the necessary amount of rehearsal I snap my
fingers at their opposition. Farewell, dear Liszt—write to me in
London—the truth as always : I have faith only in you....

Joachim was the leader of Liszt's orchestra in Weimar at the
time : he had previously played for Berlioz in Leipzig and
Vienna and had been engaged by him as a soloist in the Paris
Philharmonic Society concerts. Costa, the conductor both of the
opera and the Philharmonic Society in London, was annoyed
at Berlioz being brought in to conduct for a new musical society
backed by the music publisher Beale.

To his sister Adèle

London, 17 March 1852

...I have an excellent orchestra, and a fine chorus, so that everything has so far gone perfectly. Only the soloists defy all efforts to animate them : they sing like marble monuments....

Your ideas about England—cockfighting and other such things—you'll allow me not to answer seriously : they are opinions that date back to the Empire....

To Liszt

[London, March 1852]

My dear, good, wonderful friend, I am overjoyed to have this new proof of your friendship for me. I embrace you with all my heart and say "Thank you" without making phrases. Don't forget to transmit my gratitude to the artists of the Weimar theatre for the zeal and talent and skill with which they have supported your efforts, and you can add some words of apology for the difficulties which my score contains. Tell them that in performing as they have done such mercurial and fiery music they have given the greatest proof of musicianship that anyone could ask of artists to-day....

This refers to Liszt's production of *Benvenuto Cellini* in March. Berlioz' first London concert took place on 24 March.

To Joseph d'Ortigue

[London] 25 March [1852]

Just a line to tell you of my colossal success. Recalled I don't know how many times, acclaimed and everything, as composer and as conductor. This morning I read in *The Times*, the *Morning Post*, the *Morning Herald*, the *Advertiser* and others, panegyrics such as have never been written about me. I have just written to M. Bertin so that our friend Raymond of the *Journal des Débats* can make a pot-pourri of all these articles and at least the gist of the matter will be known about. Beale is wild with joy, for it really is an event in the musical world....

To Joseph d'Ortigue

London, 30 April 1852

...The orchestra at times surpassed all that I have ever heard in verve, delicacy and power. All the papers praise me, except the *Daily News* which is edited by Hogarth, a splendid old man who used to be one of my staunch supporters, but who is now secretary of the old Philharmonic Society. I'm now preparing Beethoven's Choral Symphony, which so far has been sadly mutilated here.

Can you believe that all the critics are against *La Vestale*, of which we performed the first part yesterday? I confess I am utterly cast down at this *lapsus judicii* and am almost ashamed at having succeeded at such a cost—as if I did not know that the good, the beautiful, the true, the false, the ugly, are not the same to everyone, and that the appreciation of certain works of genius is necessarily denied to whole nations....

Berlioz performed large sections of *La Vestale* at his third concert, as well as the first four parts of his *Romeo and Juliet*, repeated by request from his first concert. At the same concert Mme Pleyel, the former Camille Moke, played the solo part in Weber's *Konzertstück*, with Berlioz conducting.

To his son Louis

London, Monday 3 May [1852]

You say you are going mad! You must actually *be* mad to write me such letters: in the midst of the strenuous fatigue of my present life, it's the last straw. In your last letter from Havana you said you would arrive home with a hundred francs. Now you say you owe forty. Who told you to pay fifteen francs' duty on a box of cigars? Couldn't you have thrown them in the sea?...Here is half of a hundred franc bank note: you will have the other half as soon as you acknowledge the receipt of this. You can then stick them together and a money changer will give you the money. It's a usual procedure when sending money through the post....You chose your own profession—a hard one, I grant you, but the hardest part is over. Only five more months at sea, and you will be in port for six months' study, after which you will be able to earn your own living. I am putting aside money for your expenses during those six months. I can do no more....

What is all this about torn shirts? Six weeks in Havana and all your clothes ruined! At that rate you will want dozens of shirts every five months. You must be laughing at me.

Please weigh your language when you write to me. I don't

like your present style. Life is not a bed of roses, and I can give
you no career except the one you chose yourself. It's too late to
alter that now....

Louis had suddenly decided to give up the sea, and expressed
his wish somewhat impudently to Berlioz. Louis was in Paris
when his father returned, doing nothing at all, and Berlioz had
to support him. He was finally persuaded to continue in the
merchant navy and re-embarked in August.

To Joseph d'Ortigue

London, 5 May [1852]

...Short stories, short histories, tales, romances, whip-cracks,
criticism and discussions (in which music is treated only incidentally and not theoretically), biographies, all carried on in the
form of conversations or read and told by the musicians of an
anonymous orchestra, *during the performance of bad operas*.
They don't take their parts seriously unless a masterpiece is
being performed. The work is divided into *evenings*: most of
the evenings are purely literary and begin with these words:
"they are performing a very dull French or Italian or German
opera: the percussion players carry on with their business while
the rest of the orchestra listens to such-and-such a reader or
speaker", etc.

When an evening begins with these words: "They are performing *Don Giovanni* or *Iphigeneia in Tauris* or *The Barber*
or *La Vestale*, the orchestra full of zeal does its duty and nobody
reads or speaks", the evening merely contains a few words on
the performance of the masterpiece. You will appreciate that
those evenings are rare, and that the rest give rise to innumerable biting comments and ironies, not counting the stories whose
interest is purely fictional....

During his stay in London Berlioz had compiled his book *Evenings in the Orchestra*, and was now looking for a publisher for
it. It was published in September 1852 by Michel Lévy, and
was such a success that a second enlarged edition appeared the
following year.

To Joseph d'Ortigue

London, 22 May 1852

...You speak of the expenses of our concerts: they are

enormous. Every impresario in London is expected to lose this year. In fact Beale, in the programme of the last concert, actually told the public that rehearsals for the Choral Symphony had absorbed more than a third of the subscription....

To Joseph d'Ortigue

London, Saturday 12 June [1852]

I was going to leave yesterday and then to-morrow. However, I am staying a few days more unless I can get rid more quickly than I expect of final business, visits, dinners, letters of thanks, etc. How I shall miss my glorious chorus and orchestra! Those beautiful women's voices! If only you had been here to hear our second performance of the Choral Symphony. The effect in that enormous Exeter Hall was tremendous....

A naïve Birmingham amateur was heard the other day regretting that I had not been engaged for the Birmingham Festival. "For I hear", said he, "that Berlioz is even better than Costa!!!"...

Berlioz spent the summer in Paris, but in November went to Weimar, where he saw two performances of *Benvenuto Cellini* and himself conducted the first two parts of *The Damnation of Faust* and the first four parts of *Romeo and Juliet*. Liszt also intended to perform Berlioz' *Te Deum*, but Berlioz was unwilling to let him have the score at that moment.

To Liszt

[Paris] 1 January 1853

...I could need it suddenly. I have it all ready, chorus and orchestral parts, and for a large number of performers. It lasts an hour....

Berlioz had hoped that his *Te Deum* might be performed at the wedding of Napoleon III on 29 January 1853, but instead Auber got the commission to arrange the music. The Weimar performance did not materialise either, but meanwhile Covent Garden decided to put on *Benvenuto*.

To Liszt

Paris, 4 March 1853

...They seem, as usual, to want to put it on straight away, in double quick time, without drawing breath....

Berlioz arrived in London on 14 May: while there he conducted for the old Philharmonic Society a concert of his works, including *Harold*, the *Carnaval Romain*, and, for the first time, *The Repose of the Holy Family*, which later became part of *The Childhood of Christ*.

To Brandus
> 17 Old Cavendish Street [London], 1 June 1853

...This little scene, very well sung by Gardoni, was encored: it's one of the best things I have written....

To Armand Bertin
> [London, 27 June 1853]

My dear M. Armand,

Benvenuto failed last night at Covent Garden, just as in Paris. Only, the opposition showed itself in advance and in such a way that its plan was disclosed. See the article in *The Times*, which is not an analysis of the work but a fairly accurate account of the evening. I withdrew the work the same night....

To Liszt
> Paris, 10 July 1853

...A cabal of Italians, determined, enraged and virulent, had been organised to stop the performances of *Cellini*. These curious characters, helped by some Frenchmen who had come over from Paris, booed from the first scene to the last, and even whistled during the performance of the *Carnaval Romain*, which had been applauded a fortnight before at Hanover Square. They had decided to go the whole hog, and the presence of the Queen, and the Royal Family of Hanover, who were at the performance, the applause of the vast majority of the public, nothing could stop them. They were going to do it again at the later performances and so I withdrew my score the next day. There were even Italian singers *in the wings*. However I didn't lose control for a moment and I didn't make the slightest mistake while conducting, which does not often happen with me. With about one exception my actors were excellent and the performance of the chorus and orchestra can count among the most brilliant.

To Franz Dingelstedt

Frankfurt am Main, 16 August 1853

Dear Sir,

I have been in Germany for some weeks and my engagements will keep me in Frankfurt for another ten days. Allow me to ask you if before returning to Paris it would be possible for me to make a journey to Munich with any advantage. This capital is the only one in Germany which I have not yet visited, and the high position it occupies in the world of the arts make me very keen to make some of my recent compositions known there, among them my dramatic legend *The Damnation of Faust* which I have just performed at the Baden musical festival and which is being rehearsed at the moment at the Frankfurt Theatre.

Please tell me if it would be possible, with your support, to organise a concert of this kind in Munich, and what would be its financial and musical conditions.

I shall decide according to the advice which you kindly give me : but whatever my decision may be, believe me that I should be very grateful if you would be so kind as to write me a few lines on this subject.

Dingelstedt was manager of the court theatre in Munich at this time. The Munich visit did not come off, and after this short trip to Germany Berlioz returned to Paris, where, however, he found an invitation to visit North Germany in October, beginning with concerts at Brunswick and Hanover.

To his sister Adèle

Hanover, 17 November 1853

...I was given a banquet attended by the whole of musical and literary Brunswick, and presented with a silver and gold baton set with garnets : they have founded a charitable institution for artists and their widows and called it the Berlioz Fund, on account of a concert whose proceeds I donated to it. One Sunday in the public gardens I was acclaimed by the crowd, and the band played fanfares when they saw me. In short, the whole town is gripped by a tremendous revival of interest in my music. It's been the same excitement here, only here for the first time : eleven years ago the public and the musicians were pretty unenthusiastic. Our ambassador cannot contain his astonish-

ment. "You've brought the dead to life," he exclaimed. "Hanover audiences are the most frigid in the world." My chief
claqueur is the king himself. He and the queen have insisted on
coming to all my rehearsals. "I cannot see you conducting, but
I can sense it," he said. The poor young man has been blind
since the age of fifteen. When he goes out, the queen acts as his
Antigone. You should have seen him in his box at the concert
the other evening, getting really worked up, and his officers
and courtiers, who understand nothing of music, dutifully
imitating him....

Berlioz then went to Bremen, where he conducted *Harold*, with
Joachim as the viola soloist: on 1 and 10 December he conducted in Leipzig.

To Joseph Joachim
[Leipzig, 11 December 1853]
...The concert the day before yesterday was stunning. In
the *Tageblatt* this morning there is a superb article which I
will bring you to-morrow. The students came after the concert
to serenade me. Everyone is happy and so am I. I'll be delighted
to go to your concert on 1 April....

Berlioz returned at the end of the year to Paris, where he found
that a certain Count Tysczkiewicz had sued the manager of the
Opéra on the ground that he had bought a ticket for Weber's
Freischütz, whereas the work he heard there was a cut and
travestied version of the score. The lawyer for the Opéra put
the blame on Berlioz, who had superintended a production of
the work there twelve years before.

To the Editor of the Gazette Musicale
Paris, 30 December 1853
...On reading this I felt for a moment divided between
anger and hilarity: but how could one not finish by laughing
at such an accusation hurled against me, whose profession of
faith in such matters has been shown in so many ways and in
so many different circumstances?
Me. Celliez must have had great confidence in the historian
he consulted to use such documents in support of his case and
insert them in his plea. However, supposing myself above

suspicion in this respect, and knowing the profound indifference of the public to such questions, I would have made no protest against this imputation of musical malpractices, were it not that, as I now learn, the musical journals of the Lower Rhine credit it—they must really *want* to believe me guilty!—and berate me with a violence which does them honour. One of them quite simply calls me a brigand. Now here is the truth.

The cuts, suppressions, mutilations of which M. Tysczkiewicz has rightly complained were made in Weber's score at a time when I was not even in France: I only knew of them a long time later, at a performance at which the masterpiece was disfigured as he claims, and my surprise then was at least as great as the astonishment I feel to-day at seeing them attributed to me. . . .

To Ferdinand David

Paris, 7 January 1854

. . . This absurd business vexes and outrages me as you can readily understand: I have spent fifteen years of my life as a critic fighting against correctors and mutilators. When *Freischütz* was put on at the Opéra I prevented its being shorn of a single note: I managed to have it performed in full, for the first time in France, and now I am accused of having mutilated it myself, though the cuts were made during my absence from the country, without my being informed, and by a Director [Roqueplan] with whom I am not on speaking terms. . . .

To Joseph d'Ortigue

Paris, 17 January 1854

Yes, dear d'Ortigue, you are right. It is my ungovernable passion for Art which is the cause of all my trouble, all my real suffering. Forgive me for letting you read so easily between the lines. I knew it would hurt you, and yet I could not restrain the words that were burning my lips, although I might have known that your opinions on Art would be in accordance with your religious beliefs. When it is a question of a judgment against something that concerns me directly, e.g. my own works, I am so used to opposition that I take it, as I should, silently and even resignedly. But as soon as the opposition threatens my idols, the blood goes to my head and my heart begins to pound and

I get so distressed that it has all the appearance of anger, and the people I'm talking to take offence.

You know well that I love the beautiful and the true, but I have another love quite as ardent and insatiable—the love of love. And when some theory would rob the objects of my affection of the qualities for which I love them, and would thus seek to prevent me from loving them, or to persuade me to love them less, then something inside me snaps and I cry like a child with a broken toy. I know it's puerile, but it's true, although I do my best to cure myself. Like a true Christian you have punished me by returning good for evil. . . .

Your notes are capital, and I think I shall be able to use them, though I have never felt less like writing. This article is one of the great number which I don't know how to begin. And I feel so sad to the core. Life slips away. I would like to *work* so much and I am compelled to *drudge* in order to live! But what does anything matter!

To the Editor of the Gazette Musicale

Paris, 22 January 1854

Several Paris newspapers have announced that I shall soon be moving to Germany, where one of the cities is about to nominate me musical director. I realise how deeply my final departure from France would be bound to distress a large number of people, and how difficult it must have been for them to accept such grave news and give it currency.

So it would be agreeable to me to be able to deny it just by saying, like the hero of a well-known drama: "I stay with you, beloved France, reassure yourself!" My regard for the truth obliges me, however, to correct it in one particular. The fact is I must leave France in a few years' time, but the court orchestra of which I have been entrusted with the conductorship is not in Germany at all.* And since everything gets known sooner or later in this terrible Paris, I might as well say now where my future residence is to be: I am director-general of private concerts to the Queen of the Ovas in Madagascar. The orchestra of Her Majesty Ova is composed of distinguished Malayan artists and a few outstanding Madagascans. It is true that they do not like white people, and I could in consequence expect to

* There had been a question of Berlioz obtaining the conductorship in Dresden, a position occupied by Wagner till the revolution of 1849.

suffer much during my first days on foreign soil, if so many people in Europe had not taken it upon themselves to blacken me. I therefore hope to arrive among them ready bronzed against suspicion. Meanwhile kindly inform your readers that I shall continue to live in Paris as much as I can, and go to the theatre as little as I can : nevertheless I shall still go and fulfil my functions as a critic, with even greater zeal than before. I wish to have one last fling—there are no newspapers in Madagascar.

To Liszt

Paris, 24 January 1854

... I am afraid that you may have thought me guilty of an indiscretion regarding the Dresden affair which you told me about. I haven't said a word to anybody : I think it is Belloni whom the Escudiers heard murmur something about it. It is they who have reported the affair in *France Musicale* : hence the stupid rumour in the other Paris papers which made me write the letter to the *Gazette Musicale* yesterday which perhaps you have seen....

Berlioz was working on the score which eventually became *The Childhood of Christ*. On 3 March Harriet died, after a long illness. Louis had been able to see her shortly before she died.

To his sister Adèle

Montmartre, Monday 6 March 1854

... Louis had been spending four days with us and had gone back to Calais the previous Wednesday. Fortunately she saw him again. I had left her a few hours beforehand, and returned ten minutes after she breathed her last—no longer in pain, and without any movement. Her condition was dreadful. Paralysis was complicated by erisypelas and she had great difficulty in breathing. She had become a formless mass of flesh—and beside her was that radiant portrait which I had given her last year, where she looks as she was, with her great inspired eyes. Nothing left. My friends have stood by me. A large number, with Baron Taylor leading, followed her to the cemetery.

And the dazzling sun, the great view over the plain of Saint-Denis. I couldn't follow. I stayed in the garden. I had gone through too much the previous day trying to find the Pastor, M. Haussmann, who lives in the Fauborg Saint-Germain: by one of those cruel chances that are so common, my cab had to go past the Odéon where I saw her for the first time 27 years ago, when she had the intellectual elite of Paris at her feet. The Odéon, where I suffered so much—we could neither live together nor leave each other, and we have spent the last ten years resolving this grim dilemma. We each suffered so much at each others' hands. I have just come from her grave. She rests on the side of the hill, facing north, towards England, to which she never wanted to return.

I wrote to poor Louis yesterday. I will write to him again. How horrible life is! Everything comes back to me together, the bitter memories and the happy—her great qualities, her cruel demands, her injustice, and then her genius and her miseries. She made me understand Shakespeare and true dramatic art. She suffered hardship with me: she never hesitated when we had to risk our livelihood for a musical undertaking. Yet, as against this courage, she always opposed my leaving Paris, she didn't want to let me travel. If I had not taken drastic steps I should still be virtually unknown in Europe. And her jealousy, *without cause*, which ended by altering my whole life....

I have no taste for anything. I care about music and the rest about as much as—I have kept her hair. I am here alone in the large living room next to her empty bedroom. Buds are coming out in the garden. Oh! to forget, to forget! We all live so long—and now there is Louis so tall, he is no longer like that dear child I used to see running down these garden paths. There is his daguerrotype portrait, made when he was twelve. It seems to me that I have lost that child, and the big one whom I kissed six days ago does not console me for the loss of the other.

Don't be surprised if I sound strange. What a deadly faculty it is to remember the past! There is the reason why I have so cruelly succeeded in arousing similar feelings in some of my works. Yet everyone says we must be glad her sufferings have come to an end. It was a dreadful life: I have nothing but praise for the three women who looked after her.... Farewell. Fortunately there is Time which keeps moving and crushing, which kills everything, sorrows and all.

To his son Louis

[Paris] Monday 6 March 1854

My poor dear Louis,

You know all. I am alone and writing to you in the large sitting-room next to her deserted bedroom. I have just been to the cemetery where I laid two wreaths on her grave, one for you and one for myself. The servants are still here and are arranging things for the sale : I want to realise as much as possible for you. I have kept her hair. . . .

You will never know how much we made each other suffer : our very suffering bound us to each other. I could not live with her nor without her. . . .

Alexis and I talked about you yesterday. How I wish you were more rational ! It would make me so happy to feel that you were sure of yourself. I shall be able to do more for you now than has been possible before, but I shall take every precaution to prevent you squandering money. At present I am penniless and shall be for at least six months : I must pay for the doctor and the sale which will not bring in much. The King of Saxony's director wishes me to be in Dresden next month and I shall have to borrow money for the journey. . . .

To Liszt

11 March 1854

. . . I have just seen my poor Henriette die : in spite of everything she was always so dear to me. For the last twelve years we have not been able either to live together or to part. These very tortures we suffered have made the last and final separation more painful for me. She has been delivered from an appalling existence and from the frightful pain which she endured for the last three years. My son came to spend four days here and was able to see his mother again before she died. Luckily I was not away. It would have been terrible for me to hear from a distance of her death, in isolation. Enough of this. It's an event which I had to talk to you about. I have finished. Farewell.

Liszt to Berlioz

[Weimar, 1854]

She inspired you, you loved her and sang your love, her mission was fulfilled. . . .

To his sister Adèle

[Paris] Saturday 11 March 1854

Dear, admirable sister,

...You are right to say that I should feel thankful at having been near her. I can't face the thought that she might have died alone. At least she saw her son, who might not have come had I been away, and she saw me a few hours before her death, and knew I was near. I go to the cemetery every morning: it hurts me less than if I kept away....

Yes, of course there was a marriage contract. I have just re-read it. What use can it be to Louis? Against whom? Not against me, presumably. We were married under the law of community property, with the following conditions: I was not held responsible in any way for the debts incurred by my wife before our marriage, though I acknowledged them and they were paid long ago. The survivor is entitled to property up to the value of a thousand francs from the estate. I shall take nothing. I give everything to Louis absolutely. I tell you all this without quite understanding the point you raise in your letter.* Unfortunately Louis is still such a child that I am forced to give him only a little at a time and have myself to buy some of the things he needs. I had a letter from his commanding officer yesterday which pleased me: he says he is very satisfied with him....

To his son Louis

[Paris] 23 March 1854

Your letter is an unexpected pleasure, dear boy. With seventy francs a month you should be able to save, if you can learn to plan and give up the habit of squandering money. Tell me whether you can get back the watch you pawned at Le Havre. My father gave it to you. If you can't I will buy you another. I have had a watch chain made for you of your mother's hair: keep it carefully. I also had a bracelet made for my sister: the rest of the hair I shall keep....

Did you see Jules Janin's touching words about your poor mother and his exquisite reference to my *Romeo*—"Strew flowers"? I hope for another letter from you before Saturday.

God grant that my German trip may bring in something. The

* Adèle had apparently been wondering whether Berlioz would now legalise his relationship with Marie.

Montmartre apartment is not let and I may have to pay rent there for another year....

Berlioz left for Germany at the end of March.

To Roquemont

Hanover, 1 April 1854

...The King of Hanover, learning of my arrival, put off the musicians, singers and others who were due to take part in the last programme of the Philharmonic Society, and expressed a wish that the programme should be recast so as to contain nothing but my music. The Queen begged me to include at least two pieces from *Romeo*, the Adagio and *Queen Mab*. She came to the rehearsal yesterday, and after the Adagio from *Romeo* which she likes so much she had me summoned to her to compliment me, and she added: "Now I know this wonderful piece by heart, and I shall not forget it." I leave to-morrow for Brunswick where I have to prepare a concert which I am giving on Tuesday....

Roquemont was Berlioz' music librarian. After Brunswick Berlioz went to Dresden, where he gave four concerts. He had had hopes of being appointed musical director there, but this did not materialise.

To Henry F. Chorley

Dresden, 14 April [1854]

My dear Chorley,

Allow me to introduce to you Mr. Rosenhain, a pianist and composer of the right kind, who wants to appear in London this spring, and so will certainly need your support. He is a very fine musician who understands everything, and I think you will be happy to make his acquaintance.

Where is our *Faust*? I sent Beale a copy of the complete piano score. I imagine it has been in your hands for some weeks. It still contains a fairly large number of mistakes, and I ask you to be kind enough to see that I am sent the final proof of the English edition so that I can go over it before it is printed.

I have finished the oratorio *The Arrival at Saïs*, with the exception of a short piece which hasn't come to me yet. Now I am trying to realise your idea for the first part of the Trilogy and I think I shall manage it. This appeals to me very much, and I shall begin to write it in the train on the way back to Paris.

We are giving *Faust* in the theatre here next Tuesday. The orchestra and chorus are admirable and I have a first-class Mephistopheles. My second concert will be on Saturday of next week, with *Romeo and Juliet, The Flight into Egypt* and the *King Lear* Overture.

I gave a concert at Hanover a fortnight ago, the programme of which had been requested by the King: the performance was marvellous.

It contained : the overture to *King Lear*

> *Absence*, a song from my *Summer Nights*, sung by Mme Nottès
>
> *Tendresse et Caprice*, Romance for violin and orchestra, admirably played by Joachim
>
> *Queen Mab* and Love Scene from *Romeo and Juliet*
>
> *Le Jeune Pâtre Breton*, song for tenor and orchestra
>
> And my *Symphonie Fantastique*.

The King and Queen were charming to me and even came to the rehearsals.

After the concert M. von Platen came to tell me that the King was awarding me his Order of Guelfs, a rare decoration which Marschner alone among musicians has been given. I haven't received it yet . . . I wait.

Chorley was the music critic of the *Athenaeum* : though friendly with Berlioz, he did not understand his music to any great extent. This English edition of *Faust* has never been found.

To Liszt

Dresden, 14 April 1854

. . . I am adding a third part to the work at the suggestion of the English publisher Beale, who is going to publish an English edition of this "Biblical Trilogy". This third part, which he came to Paris to ask me for, will in fact be the first part, and its subject will be the Massacre of the Innocents. So the whole thing would go like this :

1.   The Massacre of the Innocents.

2. The Flight into Egypt.
3. The Arrival at Saïs.
This would last an hour and a half.

The Massacre of the Innocents was later replaced by "Herod's Dream". On his return to Paris in May Berlioz completed *The Childhood of Christ*. He was worried about Louis, who was now a naval officer on board the *Phlegethon*, and was afraid he might get involved in the war against Russia.

To his sister Adèle

[Paris] 15 May 1854

...Louis wrote to me that the *Phlegethon* is assigned to carrying despatches only. Even so at night I get terrible spasms of the heart. But he is very pleased with his position. He has been put in charge of a wardroom of midshipmen who are all three or four years older than he is. ...

In August the ship took part in the bombardment of Bomarsund.

To his sister Adèle

Paris, Sunday 27 August 1854

I have been in torment these last few days. He tells me nothing of his impressions but I can imagine what the poor child who has never even seen a skirmish must have felt in the middle of that hell which is called a naval battle. I had gone to spend a week at the seaside when I read in a local paper that the *Phlegethon* was soon to be in action. I came back to Paris at once in the hope of getting some news. ...

What intoxicating air I breathed a week ago, stretched out on the cliffs of St. Valéry, with the calm sea softly swishing three hundred feet below my green bank. What marvellous sunsets, what peace and pure air on those heights! Only such passionate encounters with nature can make me forget for an instant the griefs of my unsatisfied love of art. But these very sights revive them again more keenly than before: all is linked together. ...

Berlioz had been invited to go to Munich to conduct one of the concerts given in connection with the Industrial Exhibition there: but he did not go.

To Hans von Bülow

[Paris] 1 September 1854

...At the moment of leaving, a place became vacant in the Academy of Fine Arts of our Institute, and I stayed in Paris to make the calls which are necessary for the candidates. I resigned myself quite frankly to those terrible visits, the letters, to everything which the Academy inflicts on those who wish *intrare in suo docto corpore* (Molière's Latin): and they elected Clapisson. . . .

I have just spent a week at the seaside, in a little-known Norman village: in a few days I shall leave for the South, where I am expected by my sister and my uncles for a family reunion.

I don't expect to be back in Germany till the winter. . . .

Clapisson was a violinist and composer of light operas.

After a short visit to the Côte-Saint-André Berlioz returned to Paris in October.

To Gounod

Paris, 11 October 1854

My dear Gounod,

For the last four or five years I had definitely given up any ideas about the *Nun,* and I am astonished that you have felt even a moment's embarrassment about her and me. You should have told me about it sooner, you could have rid your mind at once of this unnecessary anxiety.

So I assure you, and you must believe me, that I feel no regrets and no left-over bitterness, and my most sincere wishes for the success of your new work have long been yours.

Don't forget that I owe you a debt of gratitude for the profound and noble emotions which your *Sappho* aroused in me, and it's a debt I want to repay! We are artists, after all!

I am not sure if I shall be free on Saturday night: however if you will send me two seats for the dress rehearsal and don't give me disagreeable neighbours I will do my best to attend, in spite of my aversion to the ridiculous way these important occasions are always handled at the Opéra.

Farewell, courage and don't doubt your devoted

Hector Berlioz.

Gounod had set Scribe's libretto of *La Nonne Sanglante* which had originally been written for Berlioz: see p. 79. *Sappho* was Gounod's first opera.

To his son Louis

Paris, 26 October 1854

I was sad this morning, dear Louis. I dreamt that we were walking, you and I, in the little garden at the Côte, and not knowing where you are my dream has affected me deeply....

I have some news which will not surprise you, I think. I have married again. This liaison by its duration had become indissoluble, you well understand: I could neither live alone nor abandon the person who had been living with me for fourteen years. My uncle, on his last visit to Paris, approved of this himself, it was he who raised the subject. All my friends think the same. Your interests are safeguarded of course. If I die first my wife will only have a quarter of my small fortune and even that I know she intends to leave to you. My situation is more fitting thus, being more regular. I do not doubt that if you harbour in your mind any painful memories or unfriendly feelings for Mlle Recio you will keep them entirely to yourself out of affection for me. We were married very quietly without fuss or mystery. If you mention this in your letters write nothing that I cannot show to my wife: I would hate there to be any cloud over my domestic life. But your own heart will tell you what to do.

Admiral Cécile tells me he has received your letter. He says you cannot enter the Marines till the end of your three years' service, but after that you will have the right to if you wish.

I am deep in all the business of preparing for the first performance of my new work, *The Childhood of Christ*....

To Liszt

Paris, 14 November 1854

...The first performance of *The Childhood of Christ* will take place on 10 December next: I expect to lose about eight or nine hundred francs on this concert. But it will, I hope, be *useful for Germany*. And I am weak enough to want a few hundred people in Paris to hear it whose support, if I get it, will be valuable to me, and also several dozen toads whose bellies are likely to swell because of it. I am told that the German translation has been very well done and I ask you to give special thanks to my exact and lively translator [Cornelius]....

I have had my son here for a few days : he brought me his *trophies from Bomarsund*. Now he has been baptised ... and the baptism luckily has not been fatal for him. He is leaving again this evening for the Crimea. *My wife* sends her best wishes.

To Princess Sayn-Wittgenstein

Paris, 16 December 1854

... It was received like a Messiah, the Magi nearly appeared and offered it frankincense and myrrh. The French public is like that. I am told that I have reformed, that I have changed my manner ... and similar nonsense. It reminds me of what the Academicians said when I was in Rome in 1830. The regulations obliged me to compose a piece of religious music which, at the end of the first year of my exile, was to be judged in public session at the Institute. But, as I could not compose in Italy— I don't know why—I had a fair copy made of the Credo from a Mass of mine which had already been performed twice in Paris before my departure for Rome, and sent it to my judges, who declared that the piece "already revealed the beneficial influence of my stay in Italy" and showed unmistakable evidence that I had "completely abandoned my unfortunate musical tendencies". ...

All the Press up to now, except the review of our friend Scudo, treats me magnificently. I have received a pile of extremely enthusiastic letters : when reading them I often felt like saying, as did Salvator Rosa, who got impatient when his small canvases were always praised : *sempre piccoli paesi* ! Its success is an insult to its elder brothers. ...

To Alfred de Vigny

[Paris] Tuesday 19 [December 1854]

Dear de Vigny,

Do come next Sunday at two o'clock to hear the second performance of my oratorio *The Childhood of Christ* : it would give me great pleasure. It lasts no more than an hour and a half, and judging from the experiment carried out *in anima publica* it's nothing to be afraid of. You won't have time to fall asleep. Farewell, dear invisible poet, believe in the sincere, faithful and affectionate admiration of your devoted H. Berlioz.

The work was repeated on 24 December and 28 January and

there were two further performances on 7 and 23 April 1855.
Berlioz visited Hanover in February 1855, where the work was
also given, and then went on to Weimar for another performance, where he also conducted the *Symphonie Fantastique* and
Lélio together, and in another concert extracts from *Romeo*,
Faust and *Cellini*, and *La Captive* : Liszt played his new E flat
concerto in the same concert, with Berlioz conducting. In March
he went to Brussels for three performances of *The Childhood of
Christ*.

To Daussoigne-Méhul

Brussels, 22 March 1855

...I have just received a letter from London telling me that
the concerts of the New Philharmonic Society which I am to
conduct are arranged for 25 May and 13 June.

After Berlioz had agreed to conduct these two concerts he heard
that Costa had resigned from the old Philharmonic Society, who
wished to offer the post to Berlioz. However Wylde, the director
of the New Philharmonic Society, who was jealous of Berlioz,
refused to release him from his contract with them. The Philharmonic Society turned to Spohr instead, and later to
Wagner.

To George Hainl

19 rue de Boursault, Paris, 14 April [1855]

My dear George,

Would you be good enough to insert the enclosed notice
wherever you can—in the Lyons papers? You will be doing me
a great favour. It's a big undertaking and this must be drummed
into the heads of the exhibitors or I shall be in a very hazardous
position. It will cost seven thousand francs. I have no performers without fees except the five hundred children who sing the
chorale. Do what you can.

Well! so you have been boring the silk weavers with my
Flight into Egypt! Somebody I don't know wrote me a very nice
letter from Lyons in which he told me that the public gave the
appearance of not knowing what the devil it meant.

Some friends of Berlioz had agreed to put up the money for the
first performance of his *Te Deum* in the church of St. Eustache

on the day before the opening of the Universal Exhibition, 30 April 1855.

To Marc Suat

[Paris, 20 April 1855]

My dear Suat

I haven't a minute, I'm running about all day preparing my *Te Deum*, which will be performed by nine hundred musicians at Saint Eustache on the 30th of this month. Yesterday I saw the Archbishop, the clergy of St. Eustache, and the mayor of the 3rd arrondisement. All are most gracious, I have got the necessary permissions. We are having an organist from London :* on that day the new chapels of the church with their decorations and new paint are to be unveiled to the public. At my suggestion the Curé will bless the flags and banners of the Catholic exhibitors while we play a movement of the *Te Deum* composed for the purpose. The whole thing is being arranged with the heads of the delegations from Austria, Bavaria, Saxony, Ireland, Italy, Spain, France, Canada and America, all Catholics. We are hoping for an enormous crowd at St. Eustache. I shall have to have two rehearsals a day. So you see I have no time to dawdle. . . .

To Liszt

[Paris] Monday 30 April [1855]

Dear Friend,

I write three lines to tell you that the *Te Deum* was performed to-day with the most magnificent exactness. It was colossal, Babylonian, Ninevean. The splendid church was full. The children sang like one artist, and the artists—as I had hoped and as I had the right to expect considering how carefully I had chosen them. No mistakes, no waverings. I had a young man who came from Brussels who conducted the organist from a distance and made it all work in spite of the space separating the organ from the rest of the performers. . . .

My God, why weren't you there? I assure you that it's a formidable work : the *Judex* surpasses all the enormities I have ever been guilty of before. You are the first person I am writing to (harassed as I am) because I know well that there is not a man in Europe who is so interested in this *event* as you are. Yes, the

* Henry Smart.

Requiem has a brother, a brother who has come into the world
with teeth, like Richard III (minus the humpback) and I tell
you he has bitten the public to the heart to-day. And what an
immense public! We were 950 performers. And not a mistake:
I can't get over it.

Some friends from Marseilles came to me, Lecourt, Remusat,
etc. Lecourt was in a state: he streamed with tears like a river!
Farewell, I am going to bed. What a pity I am the author—I
would write an interesting article! We shall see what my colleagues *sing* about it. This time there is no question of *piccoli
paesi*, it's a scene from the Apocalypse.

Laugh at me if you like: I don't mind anything to-day. Please
shake with your hand, *colla tua possente mano*, the hands of
Cornelius, Raff, Pohl, all our friends.

I am not adding anything to the Princess, I have a long letter
to write to her.

Farewell, Farewell, Farewell!

H. Berlioz.

To Auguste Morel

Paris, 2 June 1855

... You ask me to describe my *Te Deum*, but I find it very
difficult. I can only say that its effect both on the performers and
myself was stupendous. Its immense grandeur and breadth of
style struck everyone, and you can understand that the *Tibi
omnes* and *Judex* would have even more effect in a less large
and resonant building than the church of St. Eustache.

I start for England on Friday. Wagner, who is conductor for
the old London Philharmonic Society—a post which I was compelled to refuse, being engaged by the other society—is buried
beneath the vituperations of the whole British press. He remains
calm, for he says that in fifty years' time he will be master of the
musical world. Verdi too is embroiled with all the Opéra people.
He made a tremendous scene at the dress rehearsal yesterday.*
It saddens me—I know what he is going through. Verdi is a
fine and serious artist. Rossini is here and holds mock court on
the boulevard every evening; he looks like a superannuated
satire.

Berlioz arrived in London on 9 June: while there he had a long
evening conversation with Wagner—the only one of its kind.

* *I Vespri Siciliani.*

To Liszt

London, 25 June 1855

...We spoke a great deal about you with Wagner recently, and you can imagine with what affection, for on my word of honour I think he loves you as much as I love you myself.

He will no doubt tell you about his stay in London, and about all he has had to suffer from hostility and prejudice. He is superb in his ardour and warmth of heart, and I confess that even his violence delights me. It seems that Fate prevents me from hearing any of his recent compositions! The day when he conducted his *Tannhaüser* overture (at the request of Prince Albert) in the Hanover Square Rooms, I was obliged to attend a ghastly rehearsal of the chorus for my concert with the New Philharmonic two days later. We were doing the first four parts of *Romeo*; but it was so appalling that I had to put a stop to such horrors and remove the voices altogether, against the advice of Dr. Wylde, who thought it was all going splendidly...

Wagner finishes to-morrow at Hanover Square and is going to make his escape the day after. We're dining together before the concert. There is something singularly attractive about him, and if we both have asperities of character, at least our asperities dovetail   explain this to Cornelius....

Meyerbeer has arrived. His *Star* is rising at Covent Garden, but it's taking its time....

To Theodore Ritter

London, Tuesday morning [3 July] 1855

...Yesterday a terrible rehearsal at Exeter Hall. Glover's cantata, very piquant in style, but difficult: it made me sweat enough to fill the gutter in the Strand: and the finale of *Harold*, and a fierce concerto by Henselt played by M. Klindworth in a free style which kept me dancing on a slack wire for an hour, with Cooper our first violin, not being able to stand it, shouting "Sempre tempo rubato!" and the cornets who couldn't come because of the military bandwagon of *l'Etoile du Nord* which kept them at Covent Garden... always *l'Etoile du Nord*, evening party at Glover's to which Meyerbeer was supposed to come, excuses from the great man saying he had a terrible colic,... then Meyerbeer finally arriving when everyone had stopped bemoaning his absence, congratulations on the end of his colic, wanderings through the London streets by moonlight, I go to rejoin my wife at the Ernsts', Mme Ernst asks me if I like Molière, yes, by God! I'm going to recite or declaim something of his: a scene from *Le Misanthrope*, after which they bring in the chessboard and Ernst sits down with M. Louis Blanc and there they are wrestling with these stupid combinations till three in the morning.... Wagner leaving after good old Mr Hogarth had introduced him to Meyerbeer, asking these two lions if they "knew each other", Wagner's joy at leaving London, recrudescence of fury against him among all the critics after the last concert at Hanover Square, indeed he conducts in a free style, as Klindworth plays the piano, but he is very winning in his ideas and conversation, we go and drink punch with him after the concert, he renews his friendship for me, he embraces me with passion, saying that he had had a lot of prejudices against me, he weeps, he jumps, he has hardly left when the *Musical World* publishes the passage from his book where he slates me in the most amusing and witty fashion, delirious joy of Davison while translating this to me, "All the world's a stage", as Shakespeare and Cervantes have said: Ella presents me with a superb volume, the complete works of this same Shakespeare, Poet, as they took the precaution to inform visitors to the Crystal Palace: W. Shakespeare, Poet—kind of you to let me know— and I shake you all by the hand....

Ritter was a pianist and violinist who made the piano score of *The Childhood of Christ*. Glover was an Irish composer who also wrote criticism: his cantata was *Tam O'Shanter*, and was well received. Klindworth, a pianist and violinist, was a pupil of Liszt: he made the piano transcription of Wagner's *Ring*. Meyerbeer's *L'Etoile du Nord* was being staged at Covent Garden at the time: it required a military band on stage. Ernst was a violinist, who lived first in Paris and later in London. Wagner had attacked Meyerbeer five years before in *Judaism in Music*. Ella was a violinist: Berlioz dedicated *The Flight into Egypt* to him.

To Auguste Morel

Paris, 21 July 1855

My trip to London, where each time I feel more at home, was

a brilliant success. I mean to go back next winter after a prospective tour through Austria and Bohemia—provided we are not at war with Austria.

I do nothing but correct proofs from morning to night and see, hear, know nothing.*

Meyerbeer ought to be pleased with the reception of *l'Etoile du Nord* at Covent Garden. They threw him bouquets as if he were a prima donna. ...

To the Grand Duchess Maria Pavlovna of Saxe-Weimar

[Paris?, 12 September 1855]

My *Benvenuto Cellini*, assassinated in France several years ago, has recovered a spark of life thanks to the ministrations of a celebrated Doctor, your court conductor in Weimar [Liszt]. A German publisher [Litolff] has been found who wants to give the patient the fresh air of a little publicity, and I make bold to ask Your Imperial Highness to continue your patronage of the convalescent by accepting the dedication of this work.†

To Richard Wagner

Paris, 10 September 1855

Your letter has given me real pleasure. You are right to deplore my ignorance of German, and I have often told myself that, as you say, this ignorance makes it impossible for me to appreciate your works. Expression wilts almost always under the weight of translation, no matter how delicately it is handled. In true music there are accents which belong to special words and words which have their special accents. To separate the one from the other, or to give them mere rough equivalents, is like having a goat suckle a puppy and vice versa. But what can I do? I find it so devilishly hard to learn languages: a few words of English and Italian are all I can manage.

So you are melting the glaciers as you work on your *Nibelungen*. It must be splendid to compose in the presence of the glories of Nature. That is another joy I am deprived of: beautiful scenery, high peaks and the splendours of the sea absorb me entirely instead of stimulating me. At such times I can only

---

* The *Te Deum, The Childhood of Christ* and *Lélio* were all being published simultaneously.

† The Grand Duchess, sister of Czar Nicholas I of Russia, was a fervent supporter of Liszt and Berlioz.

feel and not express. I can only draw the moon from her reflection at the bottom of a well.

I should like to be able to send you the scores you so kindly ask for. Unfortunately my publishers no longer give me any copies of them. But there are two, or rather three—the *Te Deum*, *The Childhood of Christ* and *Lélio,* a lyric monodrama, which are coming out in a few weeks, and these at least I can send you. I have your *Lohengrin* : if you could let me have your *Tannhäuser* it would give me great pleasure.

The meeting you suggest would be a treat for me : but I must not let myself think about it. I have to travel in order to earn my living, as Paris only produces dust and ashes for me. Oh well. If we could live another hundred years we might get the better of many men and many things. Old Demiurge must laugh in his beard at the continual success of his well-worn, oft-repeated farce. But I will not speak evil of him, since he is a friend of yours and you have become his champion. . . .

To Princess Sayn-Wittgenstein

Paris, 6 November [1855]

. . . Yesterday I began my rehearsals, my battles with architects, copyists and so on. I have nine days to go, baton in hand from nine to four. The whole of Paris wants to sing, blow and scrape, and one has somehow to tune all these voices, all those instruments and all these pretensions. . . .

Berlioz had to organise a monster festival beginning on 15 November in connection with the prize-giving at the end of the Paris Exhibition : he had been put in charge of this by the Emperor, who was present at the first concert.

To Liszt

Paris, 17 November 1855

. . . The giant orchestra worked like a quartet. Yesterday especially : we moved the orchestra down into the great nave, the sonority was doubled in power, and the effect was immense. There was an apocalyptic audience, I thought I was in the Valley of Jehoshaphat : and the takings came to six thousand and several hundred francs ! On the day of the official ceremony the orchestra caused a scandal. After my Apotheosis piece, in spite of protocol my boys sent up a barrage of hurrahs and

applause and threw their hats into the air as if they had been at
a rehearsal....

The orchestra and chorus consisted of 900 performers : the first
concert, which contained Berlioz' new cantata *L'Impériale*, the
Tibi omnes from the *Te Deum* and the Apotheosis from the
Symphonie Funèbre, went less well because of official inattention
and bad acoustics, but all this was set right at the second concert on the following day.

To Princess Sayn-Wittgenstein
                         [Paris] Sunday 6 December 1855
   So the Berlin pedants are off on their pseudo-religious hobby-
horses again ! Materialist music—dramatic—passionate—
worldly ! They want the Christian to pray as a statue would if
it could speak. And these great babies, who find modern sacred
music wrong in being so expressive, make no objection at all to
the nonsense contained in the innumerable dramatic farragos
with which Europe is flooded.... Raphael and Michelangelo
committed a crime against religious expression when they used
colour : they should have painted only in black and white : in
any case, the faces of their Madonnas are so expressive and
meaningful !...
   The Gotha concert will definitely take place on 6 February. I
have another at Liège on 29 January and one here in Paris on
the 23rd. I'll send you a list of the ladies who are killed or
injured.

Liszt's setting of Psalm 13 had been performed in Berlin and
had aroused a certain amount of adverse criticism as being too
"theatrical".
   After another performance of *The Childhood of Christ* on 25
January 1856 in Paris, Berlioz left for Gotha and Weimar, where
Liszt had organised another Berlioz Week (including *Benvenuto*
and *The Damnation of Faust*), and Berlioz told the Princess of
his plan to write an opera on the Aeneid. He also heard *Lohengrin*, and admired much of it, while rejecting Wagnerism.

To Liszt
                               [Paris] 12 April 1856
   ...I have employed my time since my return from Weimar

in orchestrating the six pieces of my *Nuits d'Eté* and generally revising all my music so as to correct printing mistakes. I have started working out the main lines of the great dramatic machine which the Princess takes so much interest in. It's beginning to take shape : but it's huge and therefore dangerous. I need plenty of peace of mind, which is precisely what I haven't got. Perhaps it will come. Meanwhile I ruminate, and gather my strength like a cat before a desperate spring. I am trying above all to resign myself to the sorrows which this work cannot fail to bring me. ...

To Princess Sayn-Wittgenstein

Paris, 17 May 1856

The day before yesterday I finished the poem of the first act. It will be the longest and it took me ten days to write it—the first ten I have had free since my return from Weimar. I have been a dozen times on the point of throwing everything into the fire and giving myself over to the contemplative life. But now I am sure not to lack the courage to reach the end. The work has got hold of me. Besides I reread your letter from time to time to spur myself on. Usually I feel discouraged at night but come back into the breach in the morning—the youth of the day. Now I can hardly sleep : I think of nothing else and if I had my time to myself, in two months the whole mosaic would be complete. But how to get it? Always these infernal articles to write : recitals by beginners of both sexes, revivals of antiquated operas, first performances of antiquated operas ... As for the music, I shall need a good year and a half, I guess (American expression), to construct it. It will be a very big construction : let us hope it is built of bricks baked in the fire and not of unbaked bricks like the palaces of Nineveh. ...

Farewell, Princess, you too will have to answer to the shade of Virgil for the outrages I am committing in my verses against his beautiful poetry—especially if my palace is of unbaked bricks and my hanging gardens are planted with only willows and wild damsons.

P.S. There will be a barcarolle for the serpents of Laocoon.

To Theodore Ritter

17 rue Vintimille [Paris] 23 May 1856

My dear Theodore,

You haven't given news of your overture. You must have heard it now : what do you think of it? ...

My trip to Bordeaux fell through, that to Ghent also, as the King of the Netherlands drew up another programme with his own hand. You know this dilettante king who only recognises two composers, Donizetti and Thomas. The Baden scheme still holds good. I haven't yet begun my calls for the Institute. I have finished the second act of the poem of my great devil of an opera. I am thoroughly ill: I sleep in the streets. I don't know what the matter is. They are playing *Richard Coeur-de-Lion* at the Opéra-Comique, and there's another, a rival production to-night at the Théâtre-Lyrique. It's delicious! The Romance moves the whole house. The whole thing has a finesse, a truth, an inspiration and a judgment which are ravishing. And no boorishness in the orchestra. I much prefer these little orchestras with holes in the elbows of their jackets and even in their trousers to those great shouting barkers in their tawdry brass finery, bawling from their soap-boxes: "come in, gentlemen, standing room only!"

I have no news from Litolff nor, as a result, of the publication of *Cellini*. Nobody replies to me from Germany, except Princess Wittgenstein who writes me long letters encouraging me to work at the vast score.

I had a great sorrow lately, my excellent friend and former anatomy teacher Amussat died, worn out after 30 years of effort and bitter struggle. You know that poor young Fumagalli also died, in Florence.

Everyone is dying. I'm never out of the cemetery. Sax lost a child first and three days later his sister. The good Lord is mowing us down. . . .

I am about to go over my second act again.

Louis has come back from Toulon: he went to Athens and called at Tenedos! At Tenedos! it's strange for me to hear someone talking about this island, whose name I wrote several times in my first act. . . .

Ritter's overture was first performed by the Philharmonic Orchestra of Nancy: Berlioz performed it in Paris the following year. Adolphe Adam had died and there was again a vacancy for the Institute, for which Berlioz was standing. *Richard Coeur-de-lion* is an opera by Grétry: the romance is "O Richard, O mon roi". Fumagalli was a composer and a pupil of Liszt.

To Toussaint Bennet and Theodore Ritter

[Paris, May 1856]

Good! good! the news at last! The overture went well, let the world stop now, it's the least of my worries....

I am going to spend the day touring the academic strong-points. Believe it or not M. Ingres himself unbends and promises me his vote...on the second ballot, if his Benjamin, Gounod, is not elected on the first.

The musicians of the fine arts section are very much on my side, including Halévy, in spite of my recent article on his *Valentine*. Auber is as always unruffled and determined to side with the big battalions, like the good Lord and other scoundrels. As for Carafa, he's as immovable as a block-head....

Offenbach has invented an opera by Mozart, the *Impresario*, of which all the Press are singing praises. I haven't seen it and am glad, for if I had I would probably find it ridiculous, and I adore Mozart.

Here I am hung up in my work, at the most interesting moment, by a review. For two days I've made vain efforts to begin it and for two days I've done nothing, either in prose or verse....

P.S. Between ourselves, now that I have written two acts the music torments me, it wants to come, it makes me lose patience —but I resist, I must finish the poem. However, I'm jotting down ideas. My ladies send you affectionate greetings and I kiss Paul.

Berlioz was elected to the Academy on the fourth ballot. Offenbach had made a rearrangement of Mozart's *Impresario* for the Bouffes-Parisiens. "My ladies" means Marie and her mother, who was living with the Berlioz'. Toussaint Bennet was Theodore Ritter's father.

To Princess Sayn-Wittgenstein

[Paris] 24 June [1856]

A thousand apologies, Princess, for not replying till now to your last two letters. As you will have guessed, the *Aeneid* and the Academy were the cause of the delay, but the *Aeneid* much more than the Academy. Every morning I got into my cab, visiting book in hand, and all the way along my pilgrimage I thought not of what I was going to say to the next Immortal on my list but of what I was going to make my characters say. And now this double preoccupation is at an end. The Academy has elected me, as you know; and the libretto is nearly finished. I'm at the last scene of the fifth act. I grow more impassioned about the subject than I should, but I am resisting urgent appeals to attention from the music. I want to finish it all properly before I start the score. Yet last week it simply wasn't possible not to write the Shakespearean duet:

> In such a night as this
> When the sweet wind did gently kiss the trees, etc.

So the music of this litany of love is done. But I shall need another fortnight to file down, carve, polish, twist and untwist the verses such as they are. I still have twenty-four colleagues to call on and thank. I saw fifteen this morning, and I was forced to bear the embraces of those who voted against me. So there you are: I have become respectable, no longer a vagabond or a Bohemian. What a comedy—I don't despair of being Pope one day!... Forgive the triviality and coldness of this letter: could it be that already I—? No! My Institute uniform is not even ordered.

Seriously though, the music section has behaved admirably to me, and apart from Carafa I owe a lot to my colleagues. I should never have thought that public opinion would attach such importance to this nomination. I even knew that you had drunk a toast in the Altenburg to my candidature: I thank Liszt and you and our friends for it.

At the next academic dinner—for we are going to have some —I shall raise a toast to the Altenburg and the spirits that haunt it. I forgot to tell you that it gives me an income of fifteen hundred francs a year—fifteen fewer articles to write!

To Madame Bennet

[Paris] Tuesday 1 July [1856]

Please give us the pleasure of coming to dine at our house next Thursday at half-past six: you will find at dinner a really extraordinary young man called Ritter, who plays the piano in a way that makes mad with despair those who have not heard him, and who composes in a way that makes mad with joy those who have been able to hear his works.* He has a father, a bit

* Theodore Ritter was of course Madame Bennet's son.

eccentric, between ourselves, who has a mania for playing the bassoon at meals and at weddings, and would play it even at funerals if he was allowed to. But I have had a solid plug inserted into the tube of his instrument, and you can rest easy, the bassoon will make no sound.

To Princess Sayn-Wittgenstein

[Paris, July 1856]

...The provisional title of the work is *The Trojans*. But that is not important, it is the music that matters now : and you will see what an enormous score this libretto presupposes.... Would you believe it—I have fallen in love, but utterly in love, with the Queen of Carthage. I adore her, this beautiful Dido!...

In August Berlioz went to Baden for what now became more or less an annual concert. He had sent the Princess his libretto for her comments.

To Princess Sayn-Wittgenstein

Baden, 12 August 1856

...What an analysis! That is what I call entering into the author's intentions! But you wanted to cheer me along and I shall not be deluded by your words. You go so far as to credit me with the beauty of Virgil's poetry and praise me for my thefts from Shakespeare! Do not fear : I have the courage to carry on to the end : it was not necessary to try and lure me on with eulogies that I do not deserve—it is beautiful because it is Virgil : it is striking because it is Shakespeare. I know it. I am only an interloper : I have ransacked the gardens of two geniuses, and cut a swathe of flowers to make a couch for music, where God grant she may not perish overcome by the fragrance.

Once I am back in Paris I am going to emancipate myself as much as I can from all other business, and start on my musical task. It will be a hard task. May all Virgil's gods come to my aid, or I am lost. The great difficulty throughout is to find the musical form—that form without which music does not exist, or exists only as the abject slave of the word. There lies Wagner's crime : he wants to dethrone music and reduce it to expressive accents. This is to outdo the system of Gluck, who most fortunately did not succeed in following his own impious theory.

I am for that kind of music which you yourself call "free"— free, imperious, all-conquering. I want it to seize everything, to assimilate everything, and for there to be for it no Alps or Pyrenees. But when it makes its conquests it must fight in person, not through its lieutenants. Let there be fine verses ranged in battle array, but let music fight like Napoleon, in the van, and march at the head of its phalanx like Alexander. Music is so powerful that in certain instances it can triumph alone, and it has a thousand times earned the right to say like Medea: "Myself, which is enough". To want to take music back to the old recitation of the antique chorus is surely the most incredible folly (as well as being, fortunately, the most futile) in the history of art.

To find the means of being expressive, and truthful, without ceasing to be a musician: rather, to endow music with new means of action—that is the problem. Another hurdle in my path is that the feelings to be expressed move me too much. That is bad. One must try to do coolly the things that are most fiery. This is what held me up so long in the *Romeo and Juliet* Adagio and the Finale of the Reconciliation. I thought I should never see my way. Time! Time! He is the great master. Unfortunately he is like Ugolino, he eats his children....

Your grateful and devoted Iopas.

To Princess Sayn-Wittgenstein

Paris, 3 September 1856

...I am quite transported by some words of Old Nestor in Shakespeare's *Troilus and Cressida*. I have just re-read this amazing parody of the *Iliad*, where nevertheless Shakespeare makes Hector even greater than Homer did. Nestor says that Hector raising his sword aloft to spare the trembling Greeks as he sped through battle in his chariot made him think:

Lo, Jupiter is yonder, dealing life!

What a picture I would make of that if I were a painter! God in heaven but it's beautiful. I feel my heart will burst when I come across lines like that....

At Plombières, musing in the woods, I wrote two important pieces, the chorus of the Trojan mob at the beginning of the first act and the aria of Cassandra....

Berlioz had stopped at the watering place of Plombières on his way back to Paris.

To Princess Sayn-Wittgenstein
4 rue de Calais, Paris, 14 November [1856]
...I only interrupt my Phrygian task for a few reviews in which I discuss conceptions worthy of the society of Bushmen and Hottentots of the Cape of Good Hope....

To Toussaint Bennet
4 rue de Calais [Paris] Sunday morning [late 1856]
My dear Bennet,

I am reassured at last. I thought you were annoyed with me —I didn't know why. You left without a peep, without leaving me your address. You stayed in Germany without giving me a sign of life—all was mysterious. But I see that on the contrary you are in good humour. All the better. Theodore's letter is charming and I thank him for it. Let him work, let him do counterpoint, let him hear horrors and masterpieces! That's good. Let him wallow in music, dive into it, float on it, submerge himself in it, it's the only way to learn to be a good swimmer.

I am still ill with my intestinal neuralgia: it makes me very cross and morose. Nevertheless I am working at my score which advances slowly. But I am interrupted at every moment by articles, pests and bores of every kind...and I am still revising the poem. Since I saw you I have made fifty corrections and changes.

The Parisian has not become more stupid than before, that would be impossible. On the contrary he seems to begin to perceive his stupidity. But how he is bamboozled! What live toads he is made to swallow!...

To Toussaint Bennet
Paris, 26 or 27 January [1857]
...I have behind me an act and a half of score finished. With time, the rest of the stalactite will perhaps form itself well, if the roof of the grotto does not cave in....

To Toussaint Bennet
Paris, 5 or 6 February 1857
...A few days ago I was in a state of ecstasy: I had just played my first act through mentally from one end to the other. Now, there is nothing so foolish as an author who, imitating the good Lord, considers his work on the seventh day and finds it

good. But just imagine: apart from two or three passages, I had forgotten the whole thing. The result was that in reading it through I actually made discoveries—hence delight, joy! The only part I had left was the mime scene for Andromache: its importance daunted me. Now it is done, and of all the act I think it is the piece which comes off best. I shall get Leroy to try it through soon (it's a clarinet solo, with chorus). I've wept buckets over it: imitating the good Lord again, you will observe —though a lively sensibility wasn't his strong suit, if one is to believe that appalling old rogue Moses....

To Princess Sayn-Wittgenstein

4 rue de Calais [Paris] 13 February 1857

...The first act is completely finished. It's the longest: it lasts an hour and ten minutes. All the rest must be as compact as possible so as to keep the whole within reasonable proportions.

As for my impressions on the subject of this music, they vary with my mood, according to whether the sun shines or it rains, whether I have a headache or not. The same piece which caused me transports of joy when I read it yesterday leaves me cold and disgusted today. I can only console myself for these variations with the thought that it has been the same all my life with everything I have done.

The other day, as I was finishing the mime scene for Andromache, an instrumental piece with chorus, I had a visit from the cornettist Arban, a man with the keenest sense of melodic expression. He began to sing the clarinet solo, admirably, and there I was in the seventeenth heaven. Two days later I got the clarinettist at the Opéra, Leroy, a first class virtuoso, but cold, to come and try it out. My piano was a little low in pitch, the two instruments weren't quite in tune, the virtuoso phrased it "approximately": he found it very "pretty"—and there I was in hell, at odds with Andromache and Astyanax, ready to throw the whole thing into the fire. What a curse is this "approximately" in musical performance. However I think the young man will end by understanding his solo if I make him study it bar by bar: but for the moment it's beside the point. The last piece I have written, which I hope you will like, is the ensemble which comes before the love duet in the 4th Act...It seems to me that there is something new in the expression of this happiness at *seeing the night* and *hearing the silence*, and

in finding sublime utterance for the sound of the sleeping sea.
And this ensemble links on to the duet in an unexpected way—
which came about by pure chance, for it had not occurred to
me while writing each piece separately....

Berlioz conducted a concert for Ritter in Paris in April. In
August he again went to Baden to conduct a concert of his own
works, consisting of the *Francs-Juges* overture, the *Judex
crederis* from the *Te Deum*, extracts from *The Flight into Egypt*,
La Spectre de la Rose, sung by Mme Videmann, and the
Rákóczy March. He returned to Paris in September and the
third act of *The Trojans* was written between then and the end
of November.

To Princess Sayn-Wittgenstein
                              Paris, 30 November 1857
...I am being pushed against my will into the conservative
position : but it's so easy to abstain from certain arguments and
there are so many other points on which I have the good fortune
to agree with you that I hope in future not to be drawn into such
sanguinary debates....

No great credit to me if I turned down the American offer [a
five months' concert tour]. Should I not stay here and stick to
my task? And I would have been in a fine mess now if I had
accepted. They talk in America of nothing but bankruptcies :
their theatres and concert halls are rushing towards the Niagara
Falls. Ours are in no such danger : there's no cataract because
there's no current. We paddle about on a placid swamp, full of
frogs and toads, enlivened by the songs of a few ducks.... But I
live in my score, like La Fontaine's rat in his cheese, if you will
pardon the comparison....

I go at it with a concentrated passion which seems to increase
the more I satisfy it...Never shall I forget, Princess, that it is
to you and to you alone that I owe the delights that this work
has brought me. No indeed, without your encouragement, without your affectionate reproaches, I would never have undertaken
such a thing....

The influence of Wagner was on the increase, and his supporters
were claiming a kind of monopoly of modern music for him,
which Berlioz naturally resisted : Liszt was becoming an

increasingly ardent supporter. The Princess, however, was jealous of Wagner's influence on Liszt.

To Adolphe Samuel, Brussels*

Paris, 26 December 1857

...You give lessons: we receive them here, from every Tom, Dick and Harry. I should have answered you at once, but I was feverishly gripped by an impassioned scene in my fifth act, which I really could not tear myself away from. I finished it this morning and breathe a little easier.

I wonder what I am about to undergo in the way of burning regrets and vexations when I have finished this huge musical and dramatic construction. The time is near. In two months it will be done. Where shall I then find the theatrical manager, conductor and singers that I need? The new opera will lie there like Robinson Crusoe's canoe until the sea comes up to set it afloat—if there is such a thing as the sea for works of this nature. I am beginning to think that the sea is only a dream of shipbuilders.

To Auguste Morel

Paris, 21 December 1857

...Nothing will keep the public from going to the Opéra—whence a complacent negligence on the part of the management which is beyond belief. You should hear the music that is occasionally played at Court. And now the poor King of Prussia has lost his mind: I don't know whether his brother shares his feeling for art. The small German courts where music is really prized are not very wealthy, and Russia—like England—is monopolised by the Italians. There remains Queen Pomaré, but Tahiti is rather far away....

The last sentence refers to an extravaganza which Berlioz had written after the Exhibition of 1855 in the form of a letter to the Tahitian Queen.

To his son Louis

Paris, 24 January 1858

...The young man is one of the most fervent disciples of the

* Composer, critic, and professor of harmony at the Brussels Conservatoire.

extravagant school known in Germany as the music of the future. They will not give up their determination that I should be their leader and standard bearer. I say nothing, write nothing and let them have their way. Sensible people will know what to make of it all.

Hans von Bülow, who was now Liszt's son-in-law, together with Liszt had been doing all he could to promote Berlioz' music in Germany and make him a kind of head of the avant-garde, a position which Berlioz did not really relish. Meanwhile Wagner had come to Paris to try to arrange for the production of one of his operas there. Towards the end of February Berlioz for the second time gave a reading of the poem of *The Trojans* to a group of friends at his house.

To his son Louis

Paris, 9 February 1858

... I'm working as hard as I can to finish my score, and gradually it's getting done. At the moment I am at Dido's final monologue ("Je vais mourir"). I am more pleased with what I have just written than with anything I've done so far. I believe that the music of these terrible scenes of the fifth act will carry heartrending conviction. Once again I have altered this act: I have made a large cut, and added a character piece which is intended to contrast with the epic, passionate style of the rest. It's a sailor's song: I thought of you, dear Louis, when I wrote it, and I send you the words. It is night, the Trojan ships lie at anchor in the port. Hylas, a young Phrygian sailor, sings as he rocks at the masthead....

To Princess Sayn-Wittgenstein

Paris, 20 February 1858

... You know my Pyrrhonism. I believe in nothing: that is to say I believe that I believe in nothing. Therefore I believe in something. Just see what words are good for and where logic takes you! Nothing is real but feelings and passions. I am talking more nonsense! What about pain, and death, and fools—and a thousand other too real realities? Would you kindly ask Liszt to compliment Mme Milde for me on the way she played *Alceste*? I believe you when you tell me how good she was....

To Adolphe Samuel

Paris, 26 February 1858

I have worked at the poem with extreme patience, and will not have to make major changes. Why should we not have patience? I was reading yesterday in a life of Virgil that he took eleven years to write the *Aeneid*, yet to him it seemed so unfinished that on his death-bed he ordered his heirs to burn it....

I think you will be satisfied with my score. You can easily guess what the scenes of passion, of tenderness or of nature, whether calm or stormy, must be like: but there are other scenes of which you cannot as yet have an idea. It no longer matters to me what happens to the work—whether it is produced or not produced. My musical and Virgilian passion has been sated. Farewell, dear friend, Patience and Perseverance! I may even add Indifference: what does anything matter?

To Richard Pohl

[Paris] April 1858

Are you going to the Prague Festival? Count Nostiz has invited me. Are you going to the Cologne Festival? The committee and our good friend Hiller have invited me. I have refused both invitations. I am too absorbed in my great affair to leave Paris.

I am in the middle of reducing for piano my score of *The Trojans*, which has been completely finished, as you no doubt know, for a month.* This labour has made me see a lot of little faults which the most assiduous reading of the work hadn't made clear: and I'm correcting them as best I can. If later God wills that I can let you hear it, I hope you will be pleased with it. In any case I can do no better, and I am putting all my efforts and all my concentration into removing the blemishes which I find. What I can promise you is that there is great truth of expression and that the work is music. If a Cassandra or a Dido or an order from the Emperor come my way I can produce the work.

But there is another person who could well come first, that is Death.

---

* Pohl, a music critic living in Weimar, was an ardent supporter of Berlioz, Liszt and Wagner and translated Berlioz' libretti and other writings. Berlioz finished the score of *The Trojans* on 7 April 1858.

Farewell: until that horrible hag presents herself, let us live and always frankly love what is beautiful, it's the only way of laughing at her....

In August he returned to Baden and there conducted one of the finest concerts of his lifetime—Beethoven, Mozart, Weber, a Litolff piano concerto played by the composer, and four parts of *Romeo*.

Berlioz knew that his one chance of getting a proper performance of his opera was to obtain an Imperial edict ordering one of the national theatres to put it on. Back in Paris he had an audience with the Emperor, with forty others, and presented the text of *The Trojans* to him.

To Liszt

Paris, 28 September 1858

...Napoleon had his 25 below zero look, and he took my manuscript with the assurance that he would read it if he had the leisure—since when I have heard nothing more. The trick was neatly done. It's as old as the hills: I'm sure King Priam did it in just the same way....

To Humbert Ferrand

Paris, 26 November 1858

I have nothing to tell you, I simply want to write. I am ill, miserable—how many I's to each line! Always I and me! One's friends are for oneself, it ought to be oneself for one's friends....

My dejection melts away as I write. Please don't let us leave so many years without writing, as we have done....

Last night I dreamt of music, this morning I recalled it all and mentally performed the adagio of Beethoven's B flat symphony just as we did it three years ago at Baden, so that little by little I fell into one of those unearthly ecstasies and wept my eyes out at the sound of that tonal radiance which emanates from angels alone. Believe me, dear friend, the being who wrote such a marvel of inspiration was more than a man. Thus sings the archangel Michael, as he dreamily contemplates the spheres... And not to have an orchestra now which would sing that seraphic poem for me! Down to earth now! Someone is coming in.

Vulgar, commonplace, stupid life! No more orchestra. O that I had a hundred cannon to fire all at once!

Farewell. I feel better. Forgive me!

To Princess Sayn-Wittgenstein

Paris, 7 January 1859

I thank you a hundred times for your wonderfully sympathetic letter. Allow me to kiss the hand (*la man pietosa*—we don't have the adjective in our language) that wrote it. I am in such pain, and any sympathy is precious to me, yours especially. The doctors say I have a general inflammation of the nervous system, and that I must live like an oyster, not think and not feel (it would be more honest to say die). Do you know that I have days when I am as hysterical as a young girl? At such moments the slightest accidents can cause strange results. The day before yesterday I was talking quietly with some friends by my fireside when someone brought in a newspaper in which I saw announced a new biography of Christopher Columbus. At once the whole life of that great man appears to me in a flash. I see it all in one glance, like a painting, and my heart contracts at the thought of that memorable epic. I fall into a fit of indescribable despair, to the astonishment of those present. The incident was attributed to my disease, and I was not going to expose myself to mockery by admitting that the name of Columbus alone had brought on the fit. My trouble is an entanglement of causes and effects in which the wisest physiologists and psychologists would lose their way and their Latin.

But enough of the sick man and his illness. Your letter (*pietosa* as always), the one from Liszt which preceded it, and Mme Viardot, whom I have been seeing recently, have pretty well brought me up to date with your life at Weimar. I can see you all at the Altenburg, and hear your interesting conversations in the evenings . . . I think about it (despite my doctor's orders) and admire the warmth of heart and the intelligence which shines out from your little corner of the world . . . How I would love to listen, and drink in your words and Liszt's (who is so magnificent when he talks about subjects that move him). They would like to send me to Cannes to get some southern sun—but if I were free it is to Weimar that I would go . . . But so many voices cry: "Stay" that, like the Wandering Jew, I obey. . . .

Nothing new from the ancient world. Cassandra is agitated

and her great black eyes keep flinging forth lightnings : Dido
still languishes : the beautiful Anna Soror seems to divine the
tragic fate of Carthage : Aeneas with a groan obeys his gods—
sorry, I have just written a line of blank verse. Many friendly
voices repeat : "Stat Roma !" But it's untrue : Rome does not
exist yet. . . .

To Princess Sayn-Wittgenstein

Paris, 22 January 1859

. . . This city is a cemetery dotted with memorial stones. I live
only in the past. Everywhere I find reminders of friends or enemies who are no more : here I met Balzac for the last time :
there I walked with Paganini : in another spot I accompanied
the Duchesse d'Abrantès, a silly good woman : this is the house
where Madame de Girardin lived, a clever woman who thought
me a lunatic : this is the pavement where I talked to Adolphe
Nourrit : that empty house over there is Rachel's : and so on,
and so on. They are all dead. So many people dead ! Why
aren't we dead yet?

Paris was being radically reconstructed by Baron Haussmann.
The Duchesse d'Abrantès was Balzac's mistress at one time :
Nourrit was the leading tenor at the Opéra, who wanted to
commit suicide after hearing Duprez' début—Berlioz and Os-
borne talked him out of it, but two years later he killed himself
by jumping out of a window. Rachel, the famous actress, had
died the previous year, aged 38.

In spite of Berlioz' efforts at Court there was still no definite
news of a production of *The Trojans*. On 23 April he conducted
The Childhood of Christ in Paris in what he regarded as the
best performance yet.

To Humbert Ferrand

Paris, 28 April 1859

. . . What pleased me most was that the mystical chorus at
the end of the work, "O my soul", was for the first time sung
with the right expression and nuance. In that vocal peroration
the whole work is summed up, for it seems to me that a feeling
of the infinite, of divine love is in that passage. . . . No, I have
made no move about *The Trojans*. However, people are talking
about it more and more . . . I let them talk and do as they will,

and stay still like the mountain waiting for Mahomet to come to it. A fortnight ago I was at the Tuileries. The Emperor saw me and shook my hand as he passed. He is so well disposed towards me! But he has so many other battalions to lead: one must realise that the Greeks, Trojans, Carthaginians and Numidians can hardly occupy his attention. In any case, my sang-froid is easy to understand... The actor-singers at the Opéra could not be further from possessing the necessary qualities for some of the roles. There is no Priameïa virgo, no Cassandra. The Dido would be quite inadequate, and I would rather be stabbed ten times in the breast with a rusty old kitchen knife than hear them massacre the final monologue of the Queen of Carthage, "Je vais mourir". Shakespeare has said it: "Oh, it offends me to the soul to hear a passion torn in tatters, to very rags". And passion abounds in *The Trojans*. Even the utterances of the dead have a sadness about them which seems still to belong a little to life. The young Phrygian sailor cradled high on the mast of a ship in the port of Carthage is prey to an intense nostalgia. He remembers with longing the great forests on Mount Didymus. He loves...

To Princess Sayn-Wittgenstein
                                            Paris, 20 June [1859]
...As for the principal object of the work, the musical rendering of the characters and the expression of their feelings and passions, this was from the beginning the easiest part of my task. I have passed my life with this race of demi-gods; it seems to me that they must have known me, so well do I know them....

In February selected chapters from his *Memoirs* had begun appearing in the *Monde Illustré*. In August he again went to Baden, where he conducted *Romeo*, the Choroebus scene from Act I of *The Trojans*, and the love duet from Act IV.

To Richard Pohl
                                    Paris, Wednesday 17 August 1859
My dear Pohl,
    I leave tomorrow evening for Baden, eager to shake your hand and talk with you a little.
    I am very anxious about the two extracts from *The Trojans*

which we are performing at the concert. It's a little coup d'état. Have a look at the programme which appeared in the *Journal des Débats* to-day. These two scenes, for which Mme Viardot has developed a passion, were performed with piano only before an audience of about twenty a fortnight ago, and the effect they produced has led me, in fear and trembling, to risk performing them at the concert. The first is very difficult for the orchestra, and we shan't have many rehearsals.*

Thank you for all you have done and prepared for the *Grotesques*.† You will give me news of Weimar.

I have been quite ill, I have had a lot of worries and heart-breaks of all kinds. I really need to see understanding friends such as you. I have been a bit better, though, for the last two days: the thought of this music dominates and intoxicates me and gives me my strength back....

To his son Louis

[Paris] Friday evening, 23 September 1859

...Carvalho is very enthusiastic about the poem of *The Trojans* He wants to stage it at his theatre. But how? He has no tenor for Aeneas. Mme Viardot suggests that she plays both Cassandra and Dido. The public might, I believe, accept this anomaly, which incidentally is not without precedent. And so my two rôles would be played in the grand style by this great artist....

Tonight I finished putting the first act of *Orpheus* in order....

Carvalho was putting on Gluck's *Orpheus* at the Théâtre-Lyrique, and put Berlioz in charge of establishing a correct score: both the versions so far used in Paris had been cor-rupted by "rearrangement".

The Princess, who came to Paris about this time, urged Berlioz to compose an *Antony and Cleopatra*.

To Princess Sayn-Wittgenstein

[Paris] 28 October 1859

...So you wish to tempt me with Cleopatra. Ah yes, indeed, with such a subject I think one could do something grand, but

---

* The scenes were sung by Pauline Viardot and Jules Lefort, and made a great impression.

† Berlioz' *Les Grotesques de la Musique* had been published in March.

very bitter. I know no instance of a love more poisoned than Antony's for the Queen of Egypt. I don't suppose any man was ever so unfortunate as that unfortunate man after the defeat of Actium and the flight and base defection of his infernal mistress, the serpent of old Nile. The prospect of that great ocean of woe frightens me. All the same, if I get some of my strength back, I will try....

I see they have announced a revival of Flotow's *Soul in Pain* at the Opéra. There was an irrepressible need for us all to hear some Flotow. Farewell: a thousand greetings to Liszt, and to you all my—no, not all, but a great deal. Come, this is foolish. I must take my cup of whatever it is with ten drops of laudanum and forget things till to-morrow. "Gods of oblivion"—I really wish you could have heard that chorus, but it couldn't be managed.

Soul in Pain was a ballet, known in Germany as *Der Förster.* "Gods of oblivion" is a reference to the final scene of *The Trojans.* All that Berlioz' doctor could prescribe for his gastric ailments was laudanum.

To Princess Sayn-Wittgenstein
                    Paris, Monday evening 5 November 1859
...Of all the subjects that could inspire me, this one [*Antony and Cleopatra*] is the least accessible to French taste and therefore the most dangerous. Do you think I would have the impertinence to disfigure Shakespeare's creation by fashioning an academic Cleopatra?...Oh no! It's just because that blazing, mercurial Egyptian lass is the very antithesis of such clods that she would captivate me. I adore the giddy creature—insisting on Julius Caesar sleeping with her wearing his sword, and tormenting the wretched Antony again and again in the cruellest manner, yet refusing to survive him and not surviving him: the imperial grisette, who plays hop-scotch in the streets of Alexandria, whose mood changes twenty times in a quarter of an hour at the will of fantasy, who brazenly questions Mardian the eunuch about his sexual predilections: and finally the silly, weak woman, fleeing the battle of Actium without knowing why. What a character for musical fantasy! But for whom would I write such a work? Of course—for you, by God! (Forgive me.) But first I must fulfil my contract and do the opera for Bénazet....

Berlioz had been commissioned by Bénazet, the director of the
Baden theatre, to compose an opera on a theme from the Thirty
Years' War. Meanwhile he was writing the ballet music for
The Trojans. Orpheus opened on 18 November and created a
furore.

To Princess Sayn-Wittgenstein
> Paris, Friday 2 December 1859

... I'm in the middle of composing the ballets for *The Trojans*.
I write dance tunes everywhere, in the streets, in the café, at my
friends' houses. The immense success of *Orpheus* at Carvalho's
theatre has seriously shaken Royer, the director of the Opéra.
There is talk of replacing him with Prince Poniatowski. The
prince loudly proclaims—too loudly—that he will put on *The
Trojans* if appointed. The prince has a work in rehearsal, which
the author of *The Trojans* will have to review : there you are—
the familiar game....

Berlioz tried to get Liszt elected as Corresponding Member of
the Institute. " 'Is it as a composer or as a virtuoso that you are
presenting M. Liszt?'—'As everything', I answered, 'Does that
suit you?' Wagner was not even brought up—such are academic bodies." But the committee nominated Verdi and Conti.

To Princess Sayn-Wittgenstein
> Paris, 13 December 1859

... Flattering for Verdi, isn't it? But he had nothing to do with
it and must be greatly surprised. For I may tell you that Verdi is
a true gentleman, very proud and unyielding, who knows how
to put the little dogs and great donkeys in their place when they
get out of hand : he is as far from Rossini's ranting, buffooning
and joking—sometimes stupid joking—as he is from the snake-
like flexibility of Meyerbeer. He has on many occasions rudely
rebuked the people at the Opéra and the Ministry of Fine Arts
for their sins of omission. You must grant him your esteem at
least for that.

We'll do better for Liszt at the next vacancy. Delacroix and
a few others have acted rather unworthily.* As for Liszt, I'm

* Delacroix had apparently voted for Verdi, though keeping up
friendly relations with Liszt and the Princess.

sorry that he ascribed to this election an importance which it does not have for him. It was important for us, for us alone. The Institute should attach people of stature to itself instead of taking to its bosom with a protective air so many dwarfs who are not even worth drowning in the irrigations of Gulliver....

Your letters disturb me terribly. Your ideas, your visions react on me like gunpowder on flames. If I were twenty years younger, you would make something out of me. But what can I do? I don't have the freedom or the peace of mind or the health necessary to tackle it and carry it through. If you knew how I waste my time! I am hardly able to spend one hour in forty on something artistic. A good twenty are spent in pain of one sort or another, at least twelve in sleep, and seven in making ends meet and fulfilling the foolish duties which keep me alive.

The other day, as I was entering Mme Viardot's salon (where there was some music going on), the distant sounds gave me a kind of shock followed by a flash of perception, and I seemed to glimpse our Cleopatra standing in a circle of dazzling light. Oh yes, I think I could make a fascinating creature out of that sting ray. It would be quite different from anything I have done. There would be such scope for the strange, the unexpected, the untrammelled! I feel that I would limit myself to borrowing a few details from Shakespeare, and that I would do better to give free rein to my fantasy. I would have to have the interior of a pyramid, the priests of Isis, their mysteries and mumbo-jumbo: for Cleopatra, some grosser audacities, the scene with Cydnus, a secret orgy for Mardian and the women, as a counterpart to the public orgy of the triumvirs on the young Pompey's galley. Perhaps there could be some way of bringing the frigid Octavia and the wild Cleopatra face to face. What a confrontation that would make. Yes, it would be curious—but one needs time, and life. I am thankful that I have been able to complete, and go over for more than a year, my Trojan score: it's a favour from providence that I appreciate only too well...Besides, it's so disheartening to see the probable fate of these great musical machines. On all sides are great donkeys and little dogs, not to mention the pigs that shove their snouts in where the artist has sown. To what purpose the cultivation of pineapples, sugar-cane and the noble palm tree?...

To Franz Erkel

4 rue de Calais, Paris, 25 January 1860

My dear M. Erkel,

Thank you for your letter and the information you have given me. Indeed I have not given anyone in Germany the right to publish my instrumental arrangement of the *Rákóczy March*, and I give you full legal authority to obtain redress for the strange fraud which you tell me about. Do everything that you think proper: I rely entirely on your sagacity and loyalty.*

The publication of a piano reduction based on the manuscript I left in Budapest is all the more annoying as this manuscript differs from the March which I inserted into *The Damnation of Faust* after my visit to Hungary. I added a rather more developed coda than the one in the first version, which greatly increases the effect of the peroration. If I knew how to get a copy of the score to you I would send it, so that the work could be heard in Budapest in its proper form. But I think the Austrian police will not let my parcel reach you. The two copies you said you sent me have not arrived.

I await a few words from you, meanwhile I shake your hand and ask you to be kind enough to remember me to the artists of the National Theatre.

To Pauline Viardot

Paris, 25 January 1860

... I got up not feeling at all well, perhaps I shall be stronger this evening for Wagner's concert. He has sent four tickets.

Wagner was giving a series of three concerts in Paris, all with the same programme, consisting of the *Flying Dutchman* and *Tannhäuser* overtures, the preludes to *Lohengrin* and *Tristan*, and six other extracts from *Tannhäuser* and *Lohengrin*. Berlioz attended the first two concerts and after the second one published a review in the *Journal des Débats* which was full of praise: however he made some general criticisms of the harmonic style, in particular of that of the *Tristan* prelude, and in the final paragraph he set out his own musical creed, favouring freedom, innovation and expressiveness. Wagner replied with an open letter to the paper which implied that Berlioz' criticisms

* Erkel was a Hungarian nationalist composer and the conductor at the National Theatre in Budapest.

were made out of jealousy because of the non-performance of *The Trojans*. This began the rift between the two men, though for the moment relations remained friendly.

Berlioz' sister Adèle was suddenly stricken by illness and died on 2 March. This blow put him in a state of torpor from which he was only aroused by Carvalho's production of *Fidelio* in May.

To Charles Hallé

4 rue de Calais, Paris, 4 April 1860

My dear Hallé,

I congratulate you on the resounding success of your attempt to reveal Gluck to the English. So it is true that sooner or later the flame shines out, however thick the layer of dirt that seemed to have extinguished it. This success is prodigious if one considers how difficult it is to appreciate *Iphigeneia* in concert form and how much Gluck's work in general really belongs to the stage. All lovers of what is eternally beautiful owe you and Chorley the liveliest gratitude.

There are no other orchestral parts of *Armide* except those at the Opéra, and I am sure the Opéra would not lend them to you. Besides they contain a mass of alterations made some time ago by Gardel and others, and instruments added by I don't know whom, which you would certainly not want to make use of. Since your intention is to produce Gluck as he is, you will have to copy the parts from the score, which as it happens is one of the least faulty and confused that Gluck has left us. The composer, no one knows why, never used trombones in it: the same applies to *Iphigeneia in Aulis*. In *Orpheus*, *Alceste* and *Iphigeneia in Tauris*, on the other hand, the instrument plays a very important part.

In *Iphigeneia in Aulis* Gluck has made some alterations in some passages and also written some ballet music which can only be found in the manuscript score of the opera. You won't be able to make your English edition really accurate without coming to Paris. But if it is only a piano score, the harm will be less great. I don't think there was ever a composer so negligent as Gluck or one who took less care of his works, for all the pride he seemed to take in them. They are all in the most complete disarray and disorder imaginable.

I have not been attacked by Wagner so far as I know, he merely replied to my article in the *Débats* by what purported to be an explanatory letter but which no one could understand. This rambling and turgid effusion did him more harm than good. I did not reply one word.

Farewell, dear Hallé. Please remember me to Madame Hallé and give my best regards to Chorley when you see him.

Berlioz wrote two articles on *Fidelio* which elicited a friendly letter of congratulation and fellow-feeling from Wagner on his birthday, 22 May.

To Richard Wagner

Paris, 23 May 1860

I am very glad that you liked my articles on *Fidelio*. I worked on them with care, but without any hope that they would be of the least use to anybody. I don't really believe any longer in the education of the public through criticism: or at least I think that it takes a very long time for criticism to bear fruit. I do not know if you still have illusions: for my part, for many years now I have seen things as they are. You at least are full of ardour and ready for the struggle: I am only ready to sleep and to die. All the same I still feel a kind of feverish joy whenever my love for the beautiful finds an answering echo, and I hear in the distance, above the noise of the crowd, a friendly and approving voice. So I thank you for your letter: it has done me good. Since we last saw one another I have been ill, wretched, plagued in a thousand different ways. When you write to me why do you call me "Dear Master", like people who stand on ceremony? Between us it's out of place.

So it was your birthday yesterday? You Germans are very punctilious about such occasions. Quite rightly: it's the opportunity for a display of family affection and for the reunion of friends. But look at me: I have a family, I have excellent friends, and yet I could have thirty birthdays a year and nobody would venture to celebrate a single one—they know my aversion to it. Don't laugh, I'm so ill. Farewell, good day, courage, and don't call me "dear master" any more: it annoys me. Kindest regards.

In August Berlioz conducted his annual concert at Baden, consisting of the *Francs-Juge*s overture, extracts from *Faust* and Gluck's *Orpheus*, and Berlioz' new orchestration of Schubert's

Erl-King. He returned to Paris in September, having persuaded Bénazet to release him from the Thirty Years' War and accept instead a comic opera on Shakespeare's *Much Ado about Nothing*.

To his son Louis

Paris, 21 November 1860

Here is a hundred-franc note. Be sure to acknowledge it. I am thankful you are better. Your stomach aches were worrying me. It looks as if my disease too were wearing itself out. I feel stronger since I no longer take medicines, and I have been working so hard that the occupation itself helps to cure me. I can scarcely keep up with the music of my little opera, so rapidly do the pieces come to me. Each wants precedence and sometimes I begin a new one before the old one is finished....

You ask how I manage to reduce Shakespeare's five acts to one. I have only taken one theme from the play (the rest is of my own devising)—that in which Beatrice and Benedict, who detest each other, are mutually persuaded of each other's love, whereby they are inspired with true passion. The idea is really comic....

To his son Louis

Paris, 14 February 1861

...It worries me to hear of your state of mind. I can't imagine what these dreams are that are making your present life so impossible. All I can say is that at your age I was far from being as fortunate as you are. What is more, I never dared to hope that you would find a berth so soon after getting your captain's certificate. It is natural that you should wish to get on, but sometimes the chances of one year bring more change into a man's life than ten years of struggle. How can I teach you patience? Your mania for marriage would make me smile if I were not saddened at the sight of you aspiring to the heaviest of all chains and the sordid vexations of domestic life— the most hopeless and exasperating of all lives. You are twenty-six, and have eighteen hundred francs a year, with a prospect of rapid promotion. When I married your mother I was thirty and had only three hundred francs in the world, lent me by my friend Gounet, and the balance of my Prix de Rome scholarship, which had a year and a half to run. Then there were your mother's

debts, nearly fourteen thousand francs, which I paid off gradually, and the necessity of sending money to her mother in England, besides which I had quarrelled with my family, who cast
me off, and I was trying hard to make my first small mark in the
musical world.

Compare my hardships with your present discontent! Even
now do you think it's much fun for me to be tied to this infernal
galley-oar of journalism which affects every aspect of my career?
I am so ill that I can hardly hold my pen, yet I am forced to
write for my miserable hundred francs, while my brain teems
with projects and plans which I cannot carry out thanks to my
slavery. You are well and strong while I writhe in ceaseless,
incurable pain. For the last month I have not had a single day
to work at my score of *Beatrice*: fortunately I have plenty of
time to finish it. I read the piece to Bénazet, who was delighted.
So this opera will be performed, in the new theatre at Baden.
The fate of *The Trojans* is still undecided. A week ago I had a
long conversation with the Minister of State about it: I told
him all the shabby behaviour I have had to put up with. He
asked to see my poem. I took it to him the following day, since
when I have heard nothing. Public opinion is getting increasingly
indignant at my exclusion from the Opéra, when Wagner can
get in so easily under the aegis of the Austrian ambassador's
wife. . . .

Marie thanks you for your kind messages. She too is ill. Dear
boy! you have at least a father, friend, devoted brother who
loves you more than you seem to think, but who longs to see
your character become firmer, your mind more decided. . . .

To his son Louis

Paris, 21 February [1861]

. . . Wagner is turning the men and women singers, the
orchestra and the chorus of the Opéra into goats. They cannot
disentangle the music of this *Tannhäuser*. They say that the
last general rehearsal was dreadful and didn't finish till one
o'clock in the morning. However they have got to get through.
Liszt is coming to prop up the charivari. I will not write the
article on *Tannhäuser*, I have asked d'Ortigue to do it. It is best
for every reason, and it will disappoint them more! Never did I
have so many windmills to tilt at as I have this year. I am

deluged with fools of every species, there are moments when I almost choke with anger.

To his son Louis

Paris, Monday morning 5 March [1861]

...Our musical world is in a great state of agitation at the scandal which *Tannhäuser* is going to cause. Everyone I meet is furious: the Minister left the rehearsal the other day in a rage. The Emperor is not pleased: and yet there are some genuine enthusiasts, even among the French. Wagner is clearly mad. He will die of a brainstorm, as Jullien did last year. Liszt has not come, he won't be at the first performance. I think he expects a fiasco. They have spent a hundred and sixty thousand francs putting on this three-act opera. Well, we shall see what Friday brings forth....

To Mme Massart

[Paris] 14 March 1861

...Ah! God in Heaven! What a performance! What bursts of laughter! The Parisians showed themselves yesterday in a new guise: they laughed at bad musical style, they laughed at crude and clumsy orchestration, at the naïveties of an oboe: in fact they understand that there is such a thing as style in music.

As for the "horrors", they were splendidly hissed.

To his son Louis

[Paris] 21 March 1861

...The second performance of *Tannhäuser* was worse than the first. They didn't laugh so much: they were furious and hissed unmercifully in spite of the presence of the Emperor and Empress, who were in their box. The Emperor is very amused. Coming out, on the staircase, people were inveighing against the wretched Wagner and calling him a scoundrel, an impertinent fool. If this goes on, one of these days the performance will stop in the middle and that will be the end of it. The Press is unanimous in damning it. As for me, I am cruelly revenged.

Two years later Berlioz heard a performance of *Tannhäuser* in Weimar and wrote to Morel: "There are very fine things in it, especially in the third act, which is profoundly sad and at the

same time grand : in that case why is it necessary—but no,
that would take too long..."

To his son Louis

Paris, 18 April 1861

Write, dear Louis, if you can without the cruel knife-thrusts
you gave me in your last letter. I am worse than usual to-day.
I have an article to do which I haven't the strength to begin.
I had an ovation at the Conservatoire after the performance of
the pieces from *Faust*.* I dined with the Emperor a week ago
and barely exchanged a few words with him. I was magnificently
bored.

To his son Louis

Paris, 2 June 1861

You are worried, and I can say nothing to reassure you.
Alexis is trying to find you a position in Paris, but is having no
success. I am as unable to do anything as he. It is for you alone
to make your life. They want me to put on *Alceste* at the Opéra
as I did *Orpheus* at the Théâtre-Lyrique, and offer me full
author's rights, but I have refused for various reasons. In that
world they believe that one can have things done for money
which are entirely contrary to the conscience of the artist : I have
just proved to them that this opinion was wrong. My obstinacy
has offended many people. They would do better not to amuse
themselves spending time and money on insulting a masterpiece
of Gluck and put on *The Trojans* straight away. But of course
they won't, since it's the obvious thing to do !

Liszt has conquered the Emperor : he played at Court last
week and has been given the Legion of Honour. Ah, if one
could only play the piano !...

To Humbert Ferrand

[Paris] Sunday 6 July 1861

...I declined the honour because of the transpositions and
alterations which had to be made to accommodate the role to
Mme Viardot's voice....

---

* Two excerpts from *Faust* were performed by the Conservatoire
Orchestra in April.

Yes, *The Trojans* have been accepted for the Opéra by the Director : but its production now depends on the Minister of State. They have first to produce a five-act opera by Gounod (which isn't finished yet) and by Gevaert (a little known Belgian composer), after which it will probably be the turn of *The Trojans*.... But I am determined to worry myself no more : I no longer run at Fortune's heels. I stay in bed and await her there.

All the same I couldn't resist a little uncourtly frankness when the Empress asked me, a few weeks ago at the Tuileries, when she would be able to hear *The Trojans*. "I don't know, Madame, I begin to think one must live a hundred years in order to get a hearing at the Opéra." The annoying part is that thanks to these delays my work is getting a kind of advance reputation which could impair its success....

I am getting on with a one-act opera for Baden, based on Shakespeare's *Much Ado about Nothing*. It is called *Beatrice and Benedict* : I promise there will not be much Ado in the form of noise in it. Bénazet, the "king" of Baden, wants it for next year....

To Humbert Ferrand

[Paris] 14 July 1861

...An American impresario has offered me an engagement in the *Dis*united States this year : but his proposals have come up against certain unconquerable antipathies of mine, and my passion for money is not sufficiently great to overcome them. I don't know whether your love for American utilitarian manners and customs is any more intense than my own. In any case it would be very unwise to go away from Paris for a year : at any moment they might want *The Trojans*....

The American Civil War had broken out by this time. Berlioz did supervise some rehearsals of *Alceste*, which opened on 21 October. In August Berlioz had gone to Baden, where he conducted the *Tuba mirum* and Offertory of his *Requiem, Harold in Italy*, and pieces by Verdi, Halévy and Donizetti. He returned to Paris in the autumn : there he received a letter from Louis with the news that he was married and had a child or children.

To his son Louis
Dear Louis,

Paris, Monday 28 October 1861

If I did not know what a bad influence sorrow can have on the best characters, I should feel inclined to answer you with home truths. You have wounded me to the heart most cruelly, and in cold blood, as appears from your careful choice of words. But I excuse you and embrace you : after all you are not a bad son. If someone who knew nothing about us were to read your letter, he might believe that I was "without real affection" for you, that people say you are "not my son", that I "could if I wanted to" find you a better position, and that I was wrong in not making you "come to Paris and ask for a post", and leave the one you have, and that I "humiliated" you by comparing you to some hero or other of Béranger's to whom you allude. Come now—frankly and without recrimination—you have gone too far and made me suffer in a way that you have never done before. Is it my fault that I am not rich, that I lack the means to let you live comfortably and idly in Paris with a wife and children? Is there a shadow of justice in reproaching me as you do? For nearly three months you keep silence, then comes this ironical letter! Ah, my poor dear Louis, it wasn't right.

Don't worry about your tailor's bill. It will be paid on demand. If you want to have it off your mind sooner, give me the man's address and I will settle it. It is true that I thought you were younger than you actually are. Is it a crime that I have no memory for dates? Do I know at what age my father, mother, sisters and brother died? No. Should one conclude from this that I didn't love them? Really! But I see that I sound as if I were justifying myself. Once again I tell you that unhappiness has made you go out of your mind, and that is why I can only love and pity you the more.

You ask me to try and get a post for you. What, and from whom? You know that there was never a more awkward person than myself at asking favours. Only tell me clearly what I can do and I will do it. . . .

Farewell, dear son, dear son, dear unhappy boy whose misery comes from yourself and not from me. I kiss you with all my heart and hope for news of you by the next post.

To George Hainl

4 rue de Calais [Paris] 9 January [1862]

My dear George,

I am very distressed not to be able to do what you ask of me, but everything prevents me. I am working without respite at a score which takes up all my time: besides it is contrary to everything I believe to put my hand to such derangements. The March from *Olympie* doesn't need vulgar military brass, it is quite richly enough scored. I pity you with all my heart for having to submit to such demands on the part of your public. Moreover, you won't have any harps for the hymn in the middle of the march, and without harps it will all seem colourless.

Farewell. Excuse me and don't be angry....

Berlioz finished *Beatrice and Benedict* on 25 February 1862. *Olympie* was an opera by Spontini (1819).

To Humbert Ferrand

[Paris] 8 February 1862

...The Minister has ordered Royer to put *The Trojans* in production after the opera by the Belgian, Gevaert, which will be given next September....

To Auguste Morel

Paris, Sunday evening 2 March 1862

Could you be good enough to give me some news of Louis? Has he left for the Indies? As I foresaw, he hasn't written me a single line. I can't tell you anything that you haven't already guessed, but I confess that this sorrow is among the most poignant I have ever experienced.

I write to you in the middle of one of those abominable reviews of the kind which it is impossible to do right. I am trying to support our unhappy Gounod, who has had a fiasco worse than any yet seen. There is nothing in his score, nothing at all. How can I support what has neither bone nor sinew? Still I have got to find something to praise. The poem is appalling—there isn't a shadow of interest or sense in it. And it's his third fiasco at the Opéra. Well, he'll have a fourth one. No one can write dozens of operas, not great operas. Paisiello wrote 170, but of what sort? And where are they now?...

Gounod's opera was *The Queen of Sheba*. On 13 June Marie died suddenly of a heart attack.

To his son Louis

[Paris, 17 June 1862]

You have received my letter and telegram. I'm writing to you again this morning to tell you that I am more or less all right, and there is no need for you to come... What I would like would be for you to come to Baden and join me on the 6th or 7th of August: I know that it would be a great pleasure for you too to come to the final rehearsals and the first performance of my opera. At least you would be my companion during the intervals in my hard labour: I could introduce you to my friends, in short, I would be with you. Can you leave your ship so near its sailing date?...

I am not sure how much money I can send you. The expenses of that sad ceremony, the transfer from St. Germain, are great. I am rather afraid too of bringing you to a gambling town, but if you will give me your word of honour not to bet a single florin I will trust you, and I will resign myself to the grief of parting when you leave....

My mother-in-law came back yesterday to find only her daughter's body. She is nearly frantic and is being looked after by a friend who came to our help. Think of the anguish! Write soon, my dear, dear Louis.

To Humbert Ferrand

Paris, 30 June 1862

In my bereavement I can write but little.

My wife is dead, struck down in half a minute by a heart attack. The dreadful loneliness, after this violent and sudden separation, cannot be described....

Marie was buried in the large cemetery at Montmartre: later her remains and those of Harriet were transferred to a perpetual resting-place which had been bought by Berlioz' friend Edouard Alexandre. Louis at once came to Paris and spent a week with his father.

To his son Louis

Paris, 12 July 1862

... I find it so comforting to talk to you. Yes, I agree, it was good at night to know that you were there close by. But I don't want you to feel sad. I would think of how your new position is going to improve your lot. You won't be making these endless trips which take you so far away from me. We shall see each other more often....

I had a letter from Baden this morning telling me that the chorus singers know their parts by heart and that they are found very effective. The manager is "sure of a great success"—as if he knew the rest of the score! Everything in this world is ruled by preconceived ideas. Yesterday we began the actual staging in the Opéra-Comique, with everyone present for a change....

To Princess Sayn-Wittgenstein

Paris, 22 July 1862

Your letter made me almost happy for a few hours, but such clearing of the skies is of short duration. Like you I have one of the three theological virtues—charity—but not, as you know, the other two. The insoluble riddle of the world, the existence of evil and pain, the mad fury of the human race, its stupid brutality, which it vents everywhere and at all times upon the most innocent people and often on itself, have reduced me to the state of dismal and desperate resignation of a scorpion surrounded by live coals. The utmost I can do is not to sting myself to death. And then, I suffer physically each day from seven in the morning till four in the afternoon in such a violent manner that my ideas are in complete confusion during these crises. It was this that prevented me from writing to you yesterday. I was quite incapable of it. Imagine, then, if I can think of composing, of committing myself to any sustained work.

You wonder how it is that you did not know of the existence of my two-act opera for Baden. It must be that I haven't written to you for a long time. The intervals of illness during its composition were so long that at the first rehearsals I was presented with music which I had completely forgotten. I have my work cut out in teaching the orchestra, for the thing is a caprice written with the point of a needle and it needs extremely delicate playing. Farewell, dear Princess, I will keep you informed....

To his son Louis

Baden, Sunday 10 August [1862]

...*Beatrice* was applauded from end to end, and I was recalled more times than I could count. My friends were delighted, but I was quite unmoved, for it was one of my days of excruciating pain and nothing seemed to matter. To-day I am better and can enjoy their congratulations. You will be pleased too, but why have you left me so long without a letter? Why do they keep transferring you from ship to ship? Don't write here again as I am going back to Paris soon. Now I am sent for and must go and thank my radiant singers.

To Humbert Ferrand

Paris, 21 August 1862

I am just back from Baden, where *Beatrice* had a real triumph. I always fly to you, whether my news is good or bad, I am so sure of your loving interest. I wish you had been there! it would have recalled the night of *The Childhood of Christ*. Enemies and conspirators stayed in Paris, but a large number of musicians and writers had travelled to Baden. Madame Charton-Demeur was perfect, both as singer and actress. But can you believe that my neuralgia was too bad that day for me to take an interest in anything? I took my place at the conductor's desk before that cosmopolitan audience, to conduct an opera of which I had written both words and music, in a state of deadly impassivity. As a result I conducted better than usual. I was much more nervous at the second performance.

Bénazet, who always does things royally, spent outrageously in all departments. He has inaugurated the new theatre splendidly and has created a furore. They want to give *Beatrice* at the Opéra-Comique, but there is no one to play the heroine as Mademe Charton-Demeur is going to America.

You would laugh if you could read the stupid eulogies which the critics are giving me. They have discovered that I have melody, that I can be gay and even comic. The story of the astonishment caused by *The Childhood of Christ* is beginning again. They perceived that I was not *noisy*, by *seeing* that the heavy instruments weren't in the orchestra. How much patience I would need if I were not so indifferent to it all!

Dear friend, I now suffer martyrdom daily from four in the morning till four in the afternoon. What is to become of me? I don't tell you this to make you patient under your own afflictions—my troubles are no compensation to you. I simply cry to you as one does to those who love and are loved. Farewell! farewell!

To Humbert Ferrand

Paris, 26 August 1862

...How I should love to come to you, as Madame Ferrand wishes! But I have a lot to do here owing to my wife's death, and Louis has resigned his commission and is stranded. Besides I am busy enlarging my *Beatrice*. I am trying to untie or cut all the bonds which hold me to Art, so that I may be able to say to Death, "At your service". I dare not complain when I think of what you have to bear. Are sufferings like ours the inevitable result of our organisation? Must we be punished for having worshipped the Beautiful throughout our lives? Probably. We have drunk too deeply of the enchanted cup: we have pursued our ideals too far....

Still, dear friend, you have a devoted wife to help you bear your cross.* You know nothing of the dread duet beating night and day into one's brain—the twin voices of world-weariness and isolation! God grant you never may! It is saddening music.

Farewell! my gathering tears would make me write words which would grieve you still more. Again, farewell!

To Vladimir Stassov

Paris, 10 September 1862

Dear Sir,

By good luck I have found one of my manuscripts in a fairly good condition, and I am happy to present it to the public library of St. Petersburg: it is in fact the *Te Deum* which you asked me about. If you will do me the honour of making a second visit to-morrow Thursday at noon I will give it to you.

When I wrote this work I had faith and hope: to-day I have no other virtue left than resignation. But I am nonetheless most grateful for the sympathy shown to me by true friends of art such as yourself.†

To Princess Sayn-Wittgenstein

Paris, 21 September 1862

...They supposed that I was in the grip of an intense emo-

---

* Ferrand also was very ill by this time.

† Stassov, the Russian music critic, was a propagandist for the Russian nationalist composers Borodin, Rimsky-Korsakov, Mussorgsky, etc.

tion when I came to conduct my orchestra on the first evening but I was in such pain at that moment that it was all of complete indifference to me, and as a result I conducted without making a mistake.

There was a host of fulsome Tartuffes there who obsessed me with their demonstrations, the *sincerity* of which I recognised perfectly. I had to put on the air of a simpleton and seem to believe them.

At present we are trying with the director of the Opéra-Comique to find the means of doing it in Paris, where these same fulsome gentlemen will send people to hiss me at the first performance. We can't find a singer. Mme Charton-Demeur was wonderful in it, and now she has gone off to Havana. Nobody wanted her in Paris. Liszt is right, it's only the second-rate who find the doors open to them. . . .

Yesterday I put down the last orchestral note with which I shall ever blot a sheet of paper. "No more of that. Othello's occupation gone". . . .

To Gustave Flaubert

Paris, 4 November 1862

My dear M. Flaubert,

I wanted to hurry over to your house to-day, but it was impossible. But I can't wait any longer to tell you that your book filled me with admiration, astonishment, even terror. I was frightened by it, I dreamt of it the last few nights. What style! what archaeological knowledge! What imagination! Your mysterious Salammbô, with her secret involuntary love, mixed with repulsion, for the enemy who has raped her, is an invention of the highest poetry, while remaining within the truest truth.

Let me shake your powerful hand and call myself your devoted admirer.

Hector Berlioz.

P.S. Now let anyone try to malign our language! . . .

To Richard Pohl

Paris, 28 November 1862

My dear Pohl,

You tell me strange things. It seems that a new opera, no matter who the composer, has less value for the German theatres than an album of drawing-room songs for a Paris publisher. I told you that I was depending on Dingelstedt as regards the sum which would be paid me to make the journey to Weimar. For 15 louis it's impossible. As for letting *Beatrice* be performed without my being at the general rehearsals and without conducting the first performances—that I can't consent to.

On the question of 500 francs for the full score there has been, of course, a mistake, through the fault of my copyist, who when I asked him what the copying would cost replied: at least 500 francs, thinking that I meant the score and orchestral parts. The whole copying, including the solo and chorus parts, cost Bénazet more than 800 francs. Now, to conclude, I will tell you quite frankly that we must give up the idea of putting on *Beatrice* in Weimar, since neither the play nor the music nor the composer's direction are of any value to the theatre! So I ask you to send me back the libretto and not to take the trouble of translating it. It is sad to recognise that in the land of intelligence, intelligence is so little esteemed. We are not slaves and we must not even give the appearance of being exploited.

Don't let's think about it any more.

Just occupy yourself with the translation of the book, of which the first edition will also bring in nothing: and in all doubtful passages don't fail to write to me to ask for an explanation.

Farewell, my dear friend, don't bother Dingelstedt any more with this business, and don't turn me into a nuisance.

Dingelstedt, the director of the Weimar theatre, wished to build up the dramatic side of the theatre as opposed to the operatic and so was suspicious of Liszt, who had left Weimar by this time, and also of Berlioz. However *Beatrice* was put on at Weimar on 8 April at the command of the Grand Duchess, and Berlioz went there to conduct the first performances. The book was *A Travers Chants*, published in Paris in July.

To J. W. Davison

Paris, 5 February 1863

...If within a week the Minister doesn't put *The Trojans* in rehearsal, I'll give in to Carvalho's urgings and start getting ready for production at the Théâtre-Lyrique, risking fate in December. For three years I have been kept dangling at the

Opéra, and I want to hear and see this great musical machine
before I die. I live like a man who may die any minute, who no
longer believes in anything, and yet who acts as if he believed in
everything. . . .

To Humbert Ferrand
                    Paris, midday, Sunday 22 February 1863
. . . Carvalho is busy at the moment engaging people for the
solo parts, orchestra and chorus. Rehearsals will begin in May
so that the work can be given in December.*. . .

To Humbert Ferrand
                              [Paris] 3 March 1863
. . . Your suppositions about my depression are fortunately
wrong : Louis has certainly worried me terribly, but I have forgiven him : he has found a ship and hopes to be a captain soon.
He is now in Mexico, and will be back in a month.

Once more it is a matter of love. A love that came smiling to
me, unsought by me, I even resisted it for some time, but the
loneliness in which I live and this inexorable need of tenderness
which is killing me overcame me : I let myself be loved, then I
myself loved even more, and a separation on both sides became
necessary, forced upon us : complete separation, without compensation, absolute as death. That is all. And I recover little by
little : but recovery is so sad. Let us talk no more about it.

I am glad my *Beatrice* pleases you. I am going to Weimar,
where it is now in rehearsal, to conduct a few performances in
April, then I shall come back to this wilderness—Paris.

I would be very anxious at this moment, if I could be anxious
at all, about the arrival of my Dido. Mme Charton-Demeur is
at sea, coming back from Havana, and I don't know if she will
accept the proposals made to her by the director of the Théâtre-
Lyrique : and without her the performance of *The Trojans* is
impossible. Oh well, who lives will see. But the Cassandra?
They say she has a good voice and some dramatic feeling. She's
still in Milan : it's a Mme Colson, whom I don't know. But
Mme Charton cannot play two parts, and that of Dido is even
bigger and more difficult.

Pray, dear friend, that my indifference will become complete,

* Berlioz had eventually agreed to let Carvalho put on *The Trojans*
at the Théâtre-Lyrique.

for otherwise I shall have a hard time while *The Trojans* is in rehearsal.

Good-bye: when I see your dear writing on my desk it calms me for the day. Never forget that.

This "unknown love" was called Amélie, and the episode happened about the time of the first production of *Beatrice and Benedict* in Baden. The only other reference to her is a passage in *Soixante Ans de Souvenirs* by Ernest Legouvé, to whom Berlioz confided the story. See also the letter of 30 August 1864 on p. 189.

To A. F. Marmontel

[Paris] 28 March 1863

Up to now I have had neither the time nor the strength to open the manuscript which you entrusted to me and I would make apologies if you didn't know well that I am telling the truth. But I promise to get at it and not to sting your friend with *sauce piquante*. Think of it! I have his work in my hand. I will have read it, what we call reading! For once I will write with knowledge of the case. If composers only knew with what casualness or in what somnolent states we licensed critics listen to their works, they would call us bastards and they would be right.

But if I dislike this score you must pity my embarrassment, as it involves a young composer dear to your kindly heart. Why the devil do you come to me, who am a *musician*, not any kind of musician, but one whose prejudices have vitiated his judgment? Do you think it is honest on the part of a militant to present the work of a colleague to the public? The critic may see nothing in the work, but it may be a good one. I have a vigorous hatred of certain kinds of music which nevertheless flourish, and I have already reversed more than one decision in which I proved a foolish judge. I hope for your sake that I shall like these three acts. But don't hang yourself, nor must the composer, if they bore me: it won't prove much. Weber said that Beethoven was mad.

Certainly the art of music changes. And that is necessary too....

The score was that of Bizet's *Pearl Fishers*: Berlioz reviewed it, favourably, on its first performance on 30 September: it was his last article. Marmontel was a pianist and composer who taught at the Conservatoire and was the author of *Les Grands Pianistes Célèbres*.

Berlioz left for Weimar on 30 March. The opera at Weimar and his concert at Löwenberg for Prince Hohenzollern-Hechingen were enormously successful.

To M. and Mme Massart

Löwenberg, 19 April 1863

...Here I am at Löwenberg, staying with the Prince of Hohenzollern, whom I hadn't seen since 1843. Alas, how much has happened in those twenty years! He himself has become feeble and gouty, but he has not lost his gaiety, and his love of music seems greater than ever. He literally adores me. His orchestra know all my symphonies and overtures inside out. And it's a delightful orchestra of fifty really musical musicians. The prince has had an exquisite concert hall built in his castle, with perfect acoustics, a green room behind and a music library, everything as it should be. He has given me an apartment right next door to it, and every day at four they come into my study to tell me that the orchestra is assembled. I open a double door and find fifty players seated and already in tune. They rise as I step to the rostrum. I lift my baton, give the first beat, and we're on our way. If you can believe it, at the first rehearsal they went through the finale of *Harold* without a mistake, the adagio from *Romeo and Juliet* without missing an accent. Seifriz, the Kappellmeister, told me after this, in French: "Sir, when we listen this piece we ever in tears".

Do you know, dear friends, what touches me most in these marks of affection? It is the discovery that I must be dead. So much has happened in twenty years which I have the impudence to call progress: I am played almost everywhere in Germany. My *Corsair* Overture is widely played though I myself have heard it only once. The others, *Lear* and *Benvenuto Cellini*, are often given and they are just the ones which are least known in Paris. The day before yesterday—laugh or smile if you like— I found myself unable to hold back a tear while conducting *King Lear*. I was thinking that perhaps Father Shakespeare would not curse me for having made his old British King and his sweet Cordelia speak in those strains. I had forgotten the work, which I wrote in Nice in 1831. As there is no harpist here one was sent

for from Weimar, 300 miles away. The Prince is kept in bed by
gout, so during meals he writes me pencilled notes which are
brought to me and which I must answer between fruit and des-
sert—there is no cheese here. He knows everything I have written
in prose and music. This morning he said, "Come and let me
embrace you : I have just read your analysis of the Pastoral
Symphony". But I am exhausted. This is because a theatre
orchestra is a slave stuck in a cave, while a concert orchestra
is a king on his throne : and then these great symphonic passions
upset me rather more deeply than the emotions of a semi-char-
acter piece like *Beatrice*....

Before returning to Paris Berlioz read to the Prince his poem of
The Trojans : the Prince died shortly afterwards and his
orchestra was disbanded.

To Humbert Ferrand

Paris, 9 May 1863
...On the 15th of June I shall go to Strasbourg to conduct
The Childhood of Christ at the Lower Rhine Festival on the
22nd. On the 1st August I shall again go to Baden, where we are
going to put on *Beatrice* again.

The Prince of Hohenzollern has given me his cross. The
Grand Duke of Weimar absolutely insisted on writing to his
cousin the Duchess of Hamilton a letter about me destined for
the eyes of the Emperor. The letter was read, I was asked to
come to the Ministry, and I said everything that I felt, without
veiling or mincing my words, and they were forced to agree
that I was right, and—that's as far as it will go. Poor Grand
Duke! He thinks it impossible that a sovereign should not be
interested in the arts....

To Humbert Ferrand

Paris, 4 June 1863
...Don't be at pains to send me long comments. Writing
must be for you as my feuilletons are for me. Miseris sucurrere
disco. It is enough if I have drawn your mind for a few moments
away from your sufferings.*

At last Carvalho and I are harnessed to this huge machine of
The Trojans. Three days ago I read the piece to the assembled

* Humbert Ferrand by this time was half paralysed.

personnel of the Théâtre-Lyrique and the chorus rehearsals are about to begin. The negotiations with Mme Charton-Demeur are complete : she is engaged to sing Dido. But I had to consent to letting the work be cut down to the last three acts only : they will be divided into five and preceded by a prologue which I have just written, the theatre being neither large enough nor rich enough to put on *The Fall of Troy*. . . .

The performance of *The Childhood of Christ* in Strasbourg was an immense success.

To Humbert Ferrand

Paris, 27 June 1863

. . . The hall, built ad hoc in the Place Kléber, held eight thousand five hundred people, and nevertheless one could hear everywhere. They wept, they applauded and spontaneously interrupted several of the pieces. You cannot imagine the effect of the final mystic chorus : it was the religious ecstasy which I had dreamed of and felt in composing it. An a cappella group of 200 men and 250 young women had rehearsed it for three months and they did not drop an eighth of a tone in pitch. At the last Amen, at that pianissimo which seems to lose itself in a mysterious distance, applause broke out such as I have never heard : sixteen thousand hands clapping. Then a rain of flowers and demonstrations of all kinds. I looked for you in that crowd.

Carvalho's enthusiasm for *The Trojans* is growing. The year began well : will it end the same way? Make a wish!

To Humbert Ferrand

[Paris] Tuesday 28 July 1863

. . . My son arrived yesterday from Mexico, and as he has got three weeks' leave I am taking him with me to Baden. The poor boy is never in Paris when they play anything of mine. All he has heard is one performance of the *Requiem* when he was twelve. So you can imagine how pleased he is to be going to two performances of *Beatrice*.

He is returning to Vera Cruz when he leaves Baden, but he will be back in November for the première of *The Trojans*.

I have made two enemies of two friends, Mme Viardot and Mme Stoltz, who were both pretenders to the throne of Carthage.

Fuit Troja. Singers won't recognise the irreparable ravages of time....

The rehearsals of *The Trojans* went in a way which irritated Berlioz exceedingly, and Carvalho made him make several more cuts. However eventually *The Trojans at Carthage* was produced on 4 November.

To Humbert Ferrand

[Paris] Thursday 5 November 1863

Magnificent success: profound emotion of the audience, tears, applause continual, and one hiss when my name was proclaimed at the end. The septet and the love duet knocked them over: the septet was encored. Mme Charton was superb: she was transformed: no one knew she had such dramatic talent. I am stunned by so many embraces. Only your hand was not there.

To Princess Sayn-Wittgenstein

4 rue de Calais, Paris, 19 November 1863

...Robinson's great canoe is launched...But I am ill and have been in bed for the last ten days. The strain of the rehearsals brought on a violent bronchitis which rest alone can soothe and cure. As a result I have not been able to go to the last four performances. I have just been told that yesterday's performance was splendid and that the whole third act aroused extraordinary excitement. Nothing equals the rage of my opponents. Yesterday two young people shouted furiously in the corridors of the theatre: "We cannot, we must not *allow* music like this!" Don't you think that the word *allow* is charming? On the other hand two ladies coming out after the fifth act, one saying to the other: "Yes indeed it's beautiful, it's very beautiful, but that's no reason for getting yourself in such a state, one must be able to *control* oneself. Your tears are attracting attention, it's not respectable"....

And you weren't there, and Liszt was not there.

Among the numerous letters I have received there is one which begins with this quotation from Shakespeare: "Well roared, lion!" Isn't that delightful?

But now let me lay myself at your feet, take both your hands in mine, and thank you with all my heart (and believe me, that is something!) for your sympathetic words, your constant friendship, your noble enthusiasm and your vibrant response to the distant echoes of *our* work. Again my thanks, dear intelligence, believe in the deep and grateful feelings of your devoted Berlioz.

To General Lvov

Paris, 13 December 1863

There remains the production of *The Fall of Troy*. I shall never write anything except for a theatre where I am obeyed blindly without reservation, where I am absolute master. And that will probably not happen. Opera houses are to music *sicut amori lupanar*....

To Princess Sayn-Wittgenstein

Paris, 23 December 1863

...Mme Charton is leaving us: she had already made a fairly considerable financial sacrifice in consenting to be paid only 6000 francs a month. She is going to return to her Verdi rôles at the Théâtre-Italien. Like all the other singers she has been most co-operative in rehearsal and neither she nor the others have made me change a single note. But the director, while protesting all the time that he only wanted to carry out my intentions, made me go through hell by demanding all sorts of cuts and changes. Nine numbers in all were removed. I have had enough....

Never mind, these 22 performances have sowed an enthusiasm in the musical world which I would very much have liked you to see. I have never witnessed such emotions. One can only compare them with the rage of my enemies....

To Humbert Ferrand

Paris, 4 May 1864

...If we could talk, I feel that, sitting near your armchair, I could make you forget your sufferings. Voices and expressions have a power that paper lacks. Have you at least some flowers and spring leaves outside your window? I have nothing but walls opposite mine. Across the street a dog has been barking for a full hour, there's a parrot squawking somewhere, and a parakeet imitating the sparrows: at the back some washerwomen are singing, and another parrot keeps calling out "Slo-ope arms!" What is there to do? The day is so long. My son has gone back to his ship, he leaves Saint Nazaire for Mexico in a few weeks' time. The other day he read some of your letters and congratulated me on having you for a friend. He's a fine fellow, whose feelings and mind have developed late, but richly.

Fortunately I have close neighbours who are cultivated musicians and full of kindness to me. I often spend the evening there. They allow me to stretch out on the sofa and listen to the conversation without having to take much part in it. There are never any bores there: or, if there are, it is understood that I can leave without a word.

...Theodore Ritter is playing the five concertos of Beethoven in a fortnightly series accompanied by a delightful orchestra. I go and hear those marvels. Our *Harold* has again been given with success in New York. What can be the matter with those Americans?...

To Princess Sayn-Wittgenstein

Paris, 3 August 1864

...If I were well I would embark on my son's ship and go with my son to Mexico, but when one can't even cross the Atlantic it's better to stay in our beautiful Paris which is getting more beautiful every day, and growing greener and more resplendent....

To M. and Mme Massart

[Paris] Monday 15 August 1864

Yes, really and truly! Marshal Vaillant has written a charming letter to tell me that the Emperor has appointed us officers of the Legion of Honour—yes, madame, both you and me. So arrange about changing your ribbon, etc. You would not go and dine with the Minister. Sixty of us were there, including His Excellency's dog, who drank coffee out of his master's cup. A great writer, M. Mérimée, said to me: "You should have been made an officer long ago, which shows that I have never been Minister".

You see I am a little better to-day and therefore more idiotic than usual: I hope this will find you the same. Paris is en fête and you aren't here! The Villerville beach must be very dismal, how can you stay on there? Massart goes shooting—he kills seagulls or perhaps an occasional sperm-whale—God knows how you kill time! You have deserted your piano and I would not

mind betting that when you come home you will hardly be able
to play that easiest of scales, B major! Shall I come and see you?
You can safely say "yes" for I shan't come. Forgive me! I'm
getting serious again, the pain is beginning and I must go to
bed. My best to you both.

To Auguste Morel

Paris, Sunday 21 August 1864

Thank you for your kind letter. The officer's cross and
Vaillant's letter pleased me, both for my friends' sakes and my
enemies'. How *can* you keep any illusions about music in
France? Everything is dead except the authority of fools....

I am almost alone here: Louis went back to Saint-Nazaire the
day before yesterday: all my friends and neighbours are in
Switzerland, Italy, England, Baden. I see only Heller sometimes:
we go and dine at Asnières, we are about as lively as owls: I
read, and re-read: in the evening I walk past the opera houses
so as to give myself the pleasure of not going in. The day before
yesterday I spent two hours in the Montmartre cemetery, I
found a very comfortable seat on a sumptuous tomb and went
to sleep there. From time to time I go to Passy, to Mme
Erard's,* where I find a colony of choice spirits who give me a
warm reception. I savour the pleasure of not doing reviews, of
not doing anything at all....

Paris gets more beautiful daily: it is a pleasure to watch her
blossoming out.

I hear there is to be a great festival at Carlsruhe: Liszt has
gone there from Rome and they are going to discourse ear-
splitting music. It is the conclave of young Germany presided
over by Hans von Bülow....

To Princess Sayn-Wittgenstein

Paris, 30 August 1864

... Should I tell you more confidences? No, that would be too
childish and would take too long. Know only that my favourite
walk, especially when it rains, when the sky floods with tears, is
the cemetery of Montmartre near my house. I often go there, I
have many connexions in that place. Recently I discovered a tomb
there which I did not know even existed. She had been dead for
six months and no one had been willing or able to tell me that

* Spontini's widow.

she was dead: she was twenty-six, she was beautiful, she wrote like an angel: I consented, we consented out of prudence not to see or write to each other again, to live completely separated. Wasn't that heroic? We saw each other in the distance one evening at the theatre, a sign with the head...that was all... she was already dying and I didn't know it...six weeks later she was dead...I didn't know that either. Not till six months afterwards...Enough, enough....

In September Berlioz returned to the Dauphiné, and there re-visited his childhood love Estelle, now Mme Fornier and a lady of nearly seventy. The story of their belated romance is told in the *Memoirs*.

To Princess Sayn-Wittgenstein

Paris, 24 September 1864

...The effect of this sublime Alpine Nature, and of the hills that lead up to it, the stillness of that immense orchard through which the Isère winds, the solitude of those rocky paths, over-whelmed me with a grief such as those who do not know my whole life can have no idea of. A sad and solemn episode in my visit to Lyons—forgive me, dear Princess, I am stupid: but I beg you, always remain your good and kind and understanding self...I go from one sorrow to another. God bless you for the prayer you said for the dead girl: her name was Amèlie.

To Princess Sayn-Wittgenstein

Paris, 19 October 1864

...The strange force of my feelings certainly astonishes her, but she understands them up to a point, and it has not occurred to her to think me mad...She has no active recollections: she thinks, like you, that my imagination is at work and I don't sup-pose she ever questions the conviction that it is false. But I think that perhaps unknown to herself she is coming to feel that the other one—myself as a child—is in control, and will remain master till the end, for he is real. In any case I shall do all I possibly can not to be importunate or indiscreet and not to alarm her: I shall be as reserved as possible, and perhaps some day she will secretly admit to herself that it would be a pity not to have been loved so well....

To Humbert Ferrand

Paris, 28 October 1864

On returning from my visit to the Dauphiné I found your sad letter. You must have had difficulty in writing, but your young friend M. Bernard tells me you are able to go out sometimes, leaning on a friendly arm. . . .

At first my neuralgia was better for a stay in the country with my nieces, but it came back, from eight in the morning till four in the afternoon, accompanied by a persistent sore throat. Still there are compensations. Louis is doing well, though our long partings are hard to bear, for we love each other dearly.

As for the musical world, the corruption in Paris is beyond belief, and I retire more and more into my shell . . . *Beatrice* is to be performed in Stuttgart and I may go to conduct it. I have also been asked to go to St. Petersburg in March, but I won't do so unless they offer me a fee tempting enough to make me brave that horrible climate. Then I will do it for Louis' sake, for of what use are a few thousand francs more to me? . . .

I can't imagine why some people have taken to flattering me so grossly. Their compliments are enough to scrape the paint off the walls, and I long to say to them: "Monsieur or Madame, you forget that I am no longer a critic. I don't write reviews any more".

The monotony of my life has been broken lately. Mme Erard, Mme Spontini and their niece begged me to read *Othello* to them. The door was firmly closed to all comers and I read the masterpiece through from beginning to end. I gave myself to it as if I had been all alone. There were only six people present and they all wept splendidly. Heavens! what a shattering revelation of the depths of the human heart! That angel Desdemona, that noble fate-haunted Othello, that devil incarnate Iago! And to think that someone of our own species wrote it! It needs long, close study to put oneself in tune with the author's point of view, to follow the magnificent sweep of his genius. And translators are such asses. I don't know how many of Mr Benjamin Laroche's mistakes I haven't corrected in my copy, and he is the best of them, the most faithful and the least ignorant.

Liszt has been here for a week and we dined together twice. As we kept off musical topics we had a pleasant time. He has gone back to Rome to play the Music of the Future to the Pope, who asks himself what it all means. . . .

To Humbert Ferrand

Paris, 10 November 1864

... Can you believe, dear Humbert, that I have a grudge against the past? I cannot understand why I didn't know Virgil. I seem to see him dreaming in his Sicilian villa: he must have been gentle, gracious, hospitable. And Shakespeare, the great dispassionate genius, impassive as a mirror, reflecting what it sees. Yet what ineffable compassion he must have had for all things! And Beethoven, contemptuous and rude, yet blessed with such profound sensitivity that I think I could have forgiven him all his contempt and his rudeness. And Gluck the stately! ...

Last week Blanche, the doctor of the Passy lunatic asylum, invited a party of artists and intellectuals to celebrate the anniversary of the performance of *The Trojans*. I was invited and was kept entirely in the dark. Gounod was there, Doli fabricator Epeus: in his sweet, weak voice, but with profound expression he sang "O nuit d'ivresse" with Mme Banderali and, by himself, Hylas's song. A young lady played the ballet music and they made me recite, without music, Dido's scene, "Va, ma soeur". It made a fine effect. They all knew my score pretty well by heart. I wished you could have been there.

To Mme Ernst

Paris, 14 December 1864

It really is kind of you to have written to me, dear Mme Ernst, and I ought to reply in a smooth, simpering style, neatly dressed, cravat well tied, all smiles and amiability. Well I can't.

I am ill, sad, disgusted, bored, boring, idiotic, wearisome, cross and altogether impossible. It's one of those days when I wish the earth were a loaded bomb so that I might divert myself by lighting the fuse. The picture you give me of your Nice pleasures doesn't attract me in the least. I should love to see you and your dear invalid, but I couldn't accept your offer of a room. I would rather stay in the cave under the Ponchettes. There one is free to growl alongside Caliban—I know he lives there, I saw him one day—and the sea doesn't often come and fill it up: whereas with friends, even the best, one is exposed to all sorts of unbearable attentions. They ask you how you survived the night but never how you survive your boredom: they stare at you to discover whether you are sad or happy: they

insist on talking to you when you are just muttering to yourself,
and then the husband says to the wife : "Do let him alone, you
can see he doesn't want to talk, don't bother him", etc. etc.
Then one takes one's hat and goes out, and on the way out
bangs the door too hard, and thinks : "Now there—what a brute
I feel. I shall be the cause of a domestic quarrel". Now in Caliban's grotto there is none of this. . . .

Well, never mind! Do you often stroll on the terrace and
along the shady walks? And then? Do you admire the sunsets?
And then? Do you breathe the sea air? And then? Do you
watch the tunny fishers? And then? Do you envy the young
English heiresses with their incomes of thousands of pounds
sterling a year? And then? Do you envy still more the idiots
without ideas or feelings who understand nothing and love
nothing? And then? . . . Why, can't I give you all that? We have
terraces and trees in Paris. There are sunsets, English heiresses,
idiots—they are even more plentiful than in Nice, for the popula-
tion is larger—and gudgeon to be caught with a line. One can
be almost as extensively bored as at Nice. It's the same everywhere.

Yesterday I had a delightful letter from some unknown man
about *The Trojans*. He tells me that the Parisians are used to
more *indulgent* music than mine. Isn't that an admirable phrase?

The Viennese sent me a telegram on Sunday to tell me that
they had just celebrated my birthday by performing part of
Faust and that the double chorus was an immense success. I
didn't even know I had a birthday! . . .

To Humbert Ferrand

Paris, 23 December 1864

. . . Only people like M. de Flotow, composer of *Martha*, receive nothing but panegyrics. His dull opera is sung all over the
world, in every language. I went to hear that delicious little
Patti sing *Martha* the other day : when I came out I felt I was
crawling with fleas, as one does after coming out of a dove cote.
I told the marvellous creature that I would forgive her for
making me listen to platitudes—that was the most I could do!
Fortunately it has that exquisite Irish air "The Last Rose of
Summer" in it, and she sings it with such poetic simplicity that
its perfume is almost enough to disinfect the rest of the score.

I will send Louis your congratulations: he will be very pleased....

As master-on-probation Louis had saved his ship in a severe storm and was congratulated on making port at Martinique. His promotion to captain was now assured.

To Humbert Ferrand

[Paris] 8 February 1865

...It is six in the evening and I have just got up, I took laudanum yesterday and am quite stupefied. What a life! I don't doubt that you are worse too. Nevertheless I am going out to-night to hear Beethoven's Septet: I am counting on it to warm my blood, and my favourite artists are playing it.

The day after to-morrow I am supposed to read *Hamlet* at Massarts. Shall I have the strength to go right through it? It lasts five hours. Of my audience of five only Madame Massart knows anything about the play. I feel almost afraid of bringing these artistic natures too abruptly face to face with this great manifestation of genius. It seems to me like giving sight suddenly to someone born blind. I believe they will understand it, as I know them well: but to have reached the age of 45 or 50 and not to know *Hamlet*—it's like having lived all one's years in a coal mine! Shakespeare says:

> Glory is like a circle in the water
> Which never ceaseth to enlarge itself
> Till, by wide spreading, it disperse to naught....

To Antoine Choudens

[Paris] Sunday 2 April [1865]

...A score is a book which many people wish to consult and read: unfortunately you have dissatisfied a number of your customers who wanted to have my work as I wrote it and not in a mutilated form. So follow your generous impulse, have all the scores of *The Trojans* corrected and don't do things by halves....

The publisher Choudens had bought the score of *The Trojans* from Berlioz, but he issued a piano score of it with many numbers cut out, and he never published the full score. This is only now (1965) announced for publication.

To Princess Sayn-Wittgenstein

[Paris] 23 April 1865

...You supposed it was one of those will o' the wisps that flicker across the marshes in the night and then go out? Oh no, it's my childhood, my youth, my first impressions, my sense of the infinite, which all come back to me. I love her as if she were young and beautiful. Sometimes I dare not write for fear of tiring her because she must then answer me. I know too well how embarrassed these replies must make her feel. She does not feel the same as I do: and, moreover, she is afraid (she admitted) of writing to me. So it's a month now since I sent her a couple of lines. But last week I couldn't resist it any more, and I bought her a lovely bunch of violets, and had them put in a box, and sent them—without any message. It made me feel wonderful, and I'm sure my flowers were appreciated....

To Humbert Ferrand

Paris, 26 April 1865

...How can I tell you what is cooking in the musical cauldron of Paris? I have got out of it and hardly ever get in again. I went to a general rehearsal of Meyerbeer's *Africaine*,* which lasted from half-past seven to half-past one: I don't think I am likely to go again. Joachim, the celebrated German violinist, has been here for ten days: he has been playing nearly every evening, at various different salons. So I heard Beethoven's piano trio in B flat, the violin sonata in A and the string quartet in E minor—the music of the starry spheres. You will quite understand that after such miracles of inspiration I am in no mood to listen to ordinary music, manufactured goods recommended by the Mayor or the Minister of Education.

If I possibly can I will see you this summer. I am going to Geneva, Vienne and Grenoble...I will do all I can. We're both still alive, we should take advantage of this extraordinary fact....

To Princess Sayn-Wittgenstein

Paris, 11 May 1865

Do you remember, Madame, the solemn exhortation you gave me one day in Weimar? I had just spoken of my desire to write a vast operatic composition based on the second and fourth books of the *Aeneid*. I added that nevertheless I would take good

* Meyerbeer had died, and *L'Africaine* was produced posthumously.

care not to undertake it, knowing too well the chagrin such a work must necessarily cause me, in France, in our age and the debased state of our literary and musical tastes.

You then forbade me to be afraid. In the name of my honour as an artist you called upon me to carry out this project, threatening to banish me from your esteem should I fail to do so.

I wrote *The Trojans*.

Without you, and without Virgil, this work would not exist.

You spoke, when sending me out to battle, like the Spartan women who said to their sons, as they handed them a shield: "Come back with it or on it".

I came back, weak and bleeding, with the shield!

The work, like myself, has suffered cruel wounds during the war. I have had the strength to bind and tend them. It is healed now, here it is whole and complete. It bears this votive inscription: *Divo Virgilio*. But could it not also bear your name?

So let it live under this double patronage!

This dedicatory letter accompanied a copy of the vocal score of *The Trojans*.

To Princess Sayn-Wittgenstein

[Paris] 30 June 1865

...I am still in the same state of health, which is only bearable at night when I have taken laudanum (which, however, I can only take occasionally). This persistent pain unnerves and brutalises me. I become more and more stupid, more and more indifferent to everything, or almost everything.

Yes, I saw the general rehearsal of *L'Africaine*, but I have not gone again. I have read the score.... I am fortunate in not having to write about it....

To his son Louis

Paris, 28 June 1865

I don't know why I am writing, as I have nothing to say. Your letter, which came this morning, worries me terribly. Now you say you dread being a captain: you have no confidence in yourself, yet you want to be appointed. You want a home instead of your solitary room: you want to marry, but not an ordinary woman. It's all easy to understand: only, it's no use if you shirk the tasks which alone can give you the freedom

you desire. You are thirty-two : at that age you should know the
realities of life, or you never will. You need money : it's not I
that can give it to you. I have just enough to make ends meet
and that's all... I will leave you what my father left me, perhaps a little more—but I can't tell you when I shall die. I don't
think it can be long. So don't speak to me of all the things you
want, because I can do nothing to satisfy your wishes. Remember, if you were married and had children you would be a
hundred times worse off than you are now. Learn what you can
from my example. Only a series of miracles—Paganini's gift,
my tour of Russia, etc.—saved me from the most ghastly privations. Miracles are rare, otherwise they wouldn't be miracles...

Your letter gives the impression that you are suddenly dis-
covering the full meaning of the world, society, pleasure, and
pain...

Louis had come back to St. Nazaire in the spring, where his
father met him. The marriage referred to in an earlier letter
(p. 172) was evidently a false alarm. Berlioz declined the usual
invitation to go to Baden, and was replaced by his protégé Reyer.

To his son Louis
                                      [Paris] 11 July 1865
Yes, dear Louis, let's talk whenever we can. Your letter this
morning is most welcome. Yesterday I had a dreadful day. I
went out and wandered up and down the Boulevards des Italiens
and Capucines for a couple of hours. At half-past eight I felt
hungry. I went into the Café Cardinal to have something to
eat, and heard my name called and saw a gay, smiling face : it
was Balfe, the Irish composer, who had arrived from London :
he asked me to dine with him. Afterwards we went to the
Grand Hôtel, where he is staying, and I smoked an excellent
cigar—which all the same made me ill this morning. We talked
and talked of Shakespeare, whom he says he has only really
understood during the last ten years or so.

I never read the papers, so please tell me where on earth you
saw those nice things you quote about me. The Baden programme is as I told you, Jourdain will sing Aeneas and Mme
Charton Dido. But there is some Wagner, Liszt and Schumann,
and Reyer doesn't know what is waiting for him at the
rehearsals....

Do you know that Liszt has become an abbé?

You shall have a bound copy of my *Memoirs* as soon as I get one, but I must have your solemn promise not to let it out of your hands and to return it when you have read it.

The Baden programme included two numbers from *The Flight into Egypt* and the duet from the fourth act of *The Trojans*. The *Memoirs* had been completed at the beginning of the year: they were printed, but were not to be published till after Berlioz' death. In August he went to Geneva to see Mme Fornier (Estelle).

To M. and Mme Damcke

Hôtel Metropole, Geneva, 22 August 1865

Dear friends,

I write just a few lines in case you should think you are forgotten. You know I don't easily forget, and if I did I could never bring myself to forget friends such as you.

Here I am in a state of agitation which I will not try to describe to you: there are moments of sublime calm, but many others full of anxiety and even pain. I was received with extreme eagerness and cordiality: they want me to be part of the family and scold me when I keep away. I stay there for four hours at a time, we go for long walks by the lakeside: yesterday we went in a carriage to a distant village called Yvonne, with her daughter-in-law and her youngest son who has just arrived: but I have never been able to be alone with her for an instant: I have only been able to talk about *other things*. This has given me an oppression of the heart which is killing me!

What can I do? I have no shade of reason, I am unjust, ridiculous. Everybody in the family has read and re-read the volume of *Memoirs*. She reproached me gently for having printed three of her letters: but her daughter-in-law said I was right and really I think that at heart she is not annoyed about it any more.

Already I dread the moment of departure. It is charming country and the lake is most beautiful, pure and deep: yet I know something deeper and purer and more beautiful still.

The Damckes were Berlioz' neighbours whom he often visited. Damcke was a Hanoverian violinist who had settled in Paris.

Before returning to Paris Berlioz visited his relations at Grenoble
and Vienne. Back in Paris he visited Mme Charton, whom the
director of the Théâtre-Lyrique was trying to persuade to take
part in a revival of *The Trojans*.

To Madame Fornier

Paris, 13 September 1865

...I have just been urging her not to accept. I shall oppose a
new assassination with all my power. The work is too big and
the theatre too small, they have not got the resources. I would
rather not be performed than performed in this way. Oh! God!
can't I be left in peace! I neither can nor wish to have anything
in common with the world of impresarios, directors, business
men, shopkeepers, grocers of a hundred sorts, disguised under
various names....

To his son Louis

Paris, 13 November 1865

Dear Boy,

Your letter has just come, and I want to answer it before I
go back to bed, because you will be busy on the 15th, and
today is the 13th. I hope you'll manage all right with all that
crowd of soldiers and civilian passengers. I very much approve
of your idea of having a home, a house to go to, and of buying
furniture for it : but aren't you afraid your ship might be
berthed in some other port than Saint-Nazaire? But of course
you must know. I wonder what you can have written to Mme
—— : I can guess what she replied. It's always money. One
should stay on land, at Grenoble or Claix, and be a justice of
the peace, a solid citizen, selling one's corn and sheep and wine :
then one is a man of substance, one plays *boules* on Sundays,
one has a brood of untidy children whom the grandparents consider badly brought up : one is so bored with this clamlike existence, one has a wife who is getting fat, and one ends by not
feeling anything, and one thinks : "If only I could begin again".
And then you feel a bitter resentment in the very marrow of
your bones : for you are getting old, you see your life slipping
by pointlessly : you have at last got plenty of money and you
don't know what to do with it : and then you die, and you are
back where you started.

How much I suffer! If I could I would fly off to Palermo or at least to Nice. It is horrible weather. I have to light a lamp at half-past three. To-night is our Monday dinner, and as I shall have to get up and go to it I want to snatch a little sleep first. I have had no letter from Geneva, but I didn't expect one. When one comes my heart lightens and my spirits rise.

My poor dear boy. What should I do without you? Do you know, that I always loved you, even when you were little? I, who find it so difficult to like little children? There was something about you which attracted me. It got less when you were at the awkward age and had no sense, but since then it has come back and now I love you, as you know, and my love grows every day.

To Humbert Ferrand

[Paris] 17 January 1866

I am alone this evening at my fireside, writing to you. I was greatly excited this morning—they're reviving *Armide* at the Théâtre-Lyrique, and the director begged me to supervise the rehearsals. It will hardly suit his commercial world. Mme Charton-Demeur, who is playing the overwhelming role of Armide, comes every day to rehearse with M. Saint-Saëns, a first-rate pianist and musician who knows his Gluck almost as well as I do. It is a curious thing to see the poor lady floundering about in the sublime and the light of her understanding gradually dawning. This morning in the Hatred scene Saint-Saëns and I could only clasp hands in silence: we were breathless! Never did a human being find such expression! And to think that this masterpiece is vilified, blasphemed, insulted, attacked on all sides, even by those who profess to admire it. Why aren't you here to enjoy it too?

Can you believe that since I have been plunged into music again my pains have gradually disappeared? I get up every day just like other people. But I am going to have a frightful time with the other singers and above all the conductor. It is coming on in April.

Madame Fornier writes that a friend she met in Geneva spoke warmly of *The Trojans*. That's good, but I would have done better if I'd written one of Offenbach's atrocities. What will those toads of Parisians say to *Armide*? ...

To Princess Sayn-Wittgenstein

Paris, 30 January 1866

... The Opéra administration and the Minister are now trying to prevent us proceeding with *Armide*. The Opéra neither can nor will put on *Armide*, but doesn't want any other theatre to put it on either. And always *l'Africaine*, and *Le Dieu et la Bayadère*, and *l'Africaine*, and then suddenly *l'Africaine*. And the advertising, relentless, maddening, nauseating, and idiotic! Where can one flee to escape it? I think one would even find it in an Eskimo's hut....

My salary as librarian of the Conservatoire has been raised from 1400 to 2800 francs. This more than makes up for the accursed articles, which I have given up. Ah! if only one could live for two hundred years one would end by becoming rich, wise, famous, perhaps even young, who knows?...

To Humbert Ferrand

[Paris] 8 March 1866

Dear Humbert,

I'm answering you this morning simply to tell you what happened yesterday at a big charity concert given, with trebled prices, in the Cirque Napoléon under Pasdeloup. They gave the septet from *The Trojans*, Mme Charton sang: there was a chorus of a hundred and fifty, and the usual fine orchestra. The whole programme was very badly received, except the *Lohengrin* march, and the overture to *The Prophet* was hissed so much that the police had to eject the malcontents. Then came the septet. Endless applause and an encore. The second time it went even better. The audience saw me on my three-franc bench—(I had not been sent a single ticket). This led to more calls, shouts, waving of hats and handkerchiefs. "Vive Berlioz!" they cried. "Get up, we want to see you." I meanwhile was trying to hide myself. On the way out a crowd surrounded me on the boulevard. This morning there were many callers and a charming letter from Legouvé's daughter. Liszt was there. I saw him from my perch. He hadn't heard any of *The Trojans*. He has just come from Rome. Why weren't you there too? There were at least three thousand people. At one time I would have been overjoyed. It made a tremendous effect, particularly the passage, impossible to reproduce on the piano, which evokes the sound of the sea, at the words:

And the sleeping sea
Whispers in dreams her deep sweet chords.

It moved me profoundly. My neighbours in the gallery, hearing
that I was the composer, shook my hands and thanked me. Why
weren't you there? It's sad, but beautiful. . . .

To Humbert Ferrand

[Paris] 9 March 1866

Just a word to add to what I wrote yesterday. A few amateurs
have written me a round robin of congratulation. The letter is
a slightly altered copy of the one I wrote to Spontini twenty-two
years ago after a performance of his *Fernand Cortez*. Isn't it a
nice idea to apply to me, twenty two years later, what I said to
him? I am greatly touched.

Liszt who had lately taken orders, had come to Paris to supervise a performance of his Graner Mass at St. Eustache. Berlioz
disliked the work: it represented the kind of religious music he
was very much against. Liszt attempted to justify himself in a
private meeting with Kreutzer, d'Ortigue, Damcke and Berlioz,
but Berlioz remained unconvinced. Princess Sayn-Wittgenstein
evidently took Berlioz to task about this.

To Princess Sayn-Wittgenstein

Paris, 13 July 1866

. . . You propound to me in respect of music a paradoxical
theory of ancestors and descendants which, if you will allow me
to say so, is a palpable absurdity and a libel against me. It is as
if you were calmly and philosophically accusing me of being a
liar and a thief. This has shocked me. I passionately admire a
number of works by "descendants" and I heartily detest many
famous "ancestors" who devoted themselves to the production
of the ugly and the false, ancient Ganymedes who under the
name of nectar dispensed lukewarm water all their life. Times,
periods, nationalities, ages are all one to me. Nothing would be
easier for me to prove it to you. But let us drop these arbitrary
systems designed to forward a particular cause—we might as
well talk theology.

You have the kindness to ask what I am doing, thinking and
reading. I do nothing except bear my incessant pains and my

unfathomable boredom. I ask myself night and day if I shall
die in great pain or with little pain : as for dying without pain,
I am not mad enough to hope for it.

To Mme Fornier

Paris, 25 July 1866

... I have been to Louvain for a musical jury which I was
more or less compelled to serve on. The object was to award a
prize for a religious composition. As a result I have read 73
masses in full score and chose, not the best, but the least bad. ...

To Madame Massart

[Paris] 3 September 1866

... I've been asked to supervise the rehearsals of *Alceste* at the
Opéra, but Perrin dawdles so, waiting for Society to come back
to Paris—as if there were any Society for *Alceste*—that I am
going to leave him stranded for a few days and run off to
Geneva. Ah, dear lady, how glorious it is ! how grand ! The
other day at the first ensemble rehearsal on the stage we wept
like stags at bay. "What a man Gluck was !" cried Perrin. "No,"
said I. "*We* are the men. Don't get confused." Taylor said
yesterday that Gluck had more heart than Homer : in truth he is
more thoroughly human. And we are going to offer this food of
the gods to rogues and peasant slaves ! ...

Berlioz made a short trip to the Dauphiné and Geneva in the
autumn, returning to Paris for the production of *Alceste* at the
Opéra in October.

To Humbert Ferrand

[Paris] 10 November 1866

I should be in Vienna, but I got a telegram the other day to
say that the concert had been unavoidably postponed until 16
December, so I won't be leaving until the 5th of next month.
I suppose *Faust* has not been rehearsed to their satisfaction, and
they don't want to offer it to me until it is nearly ready. It will
be a real joy to hear this work again, I haven't heard the whole
of it since Dresden, twelve years ago. ...

The *Alceste* rehearsals restored me a little. Never has it
seemed so grand, and surely never before has Gluck been so
worthily done. A whole new generation has arisen to worship ...

I have received a mass of letters thanking me for the care I lavished on Gluck's score. Ingres is not the only one of our Institute colleagues who comes constantly: most of the painters and sculptors have a real feeling for the antique, for that beauty which never ceases to be beautiful even in the moments of greatest woe...I am sending you the new pocket score: you will have no difficulty in reading it, and it will help to give you a few moments of pleasure.

To Ernest Reyer

Vienna, 17 December [1866]

Dear Reyer,

I only got up at four this afternoon, as yesterday overtired me.... It would be foolish of me to describe the recalls, encores, tears and flowers I received after the performance of *Faust* in the Redoutensaal: I had a chorus of three hundred, an orchestra of a hundred and fifty, and splendid soloists. This evening there is to be a great fête: two or three hundred artists and amateurs, among them the hundred and forty ladies (amateurs) who sang my choruses with their fresh, true voices. How well too they had been trained by Herbeck, who first had the idea of giving my work complete, and who would let himself be chopped to pieces for me. To-morrow I am invited by the Conservatoire to hear Hellmesberger conduct my *Harold*. This has been the most perfect musical joy of my life, so forgive me if I say too much! Well! this is one score saved at any rate. They can play it now in Vienna under Herbeck, who knows it by heart. The Paris Conservatoire can leave me in outer darkness and stick to its antiquated repertoire if it likes. You have drawn down this tirade on your own head by asking me to write!

Farewell: I have been invited to Breslau to conduct *Romeo and Juliet*, but I must get back to Paris before the end of the month.

To Humbert Ferrand

Paris, 11 January 1867

It is midnight, dear friend. I am writing in bed as usual: you will read my letter in bed, also as usual. Your last note made me sad: I read the suffering between the lines. I wanted to reply at once, but my tortures, medical stupidity, doses of laudanum—all useless and productive only of bad dreams—

prevented me. I see now how difficult it will be for us to meet. You can't move, and for three-quarters of the year the slightest moving about kills me. What are we to do?

My journey to Vienna nearly finished me—even the triumphant success, the delight of all that enthusiasm, the wonderful performance, couldn't save me. This awful climate of ours is lethal.

Dear Louis writes of his morning rides in the forests of Martinique and describes the lovely tropical vegetation—the really hot sun. That's what you and I both need....

Dear friend, the dull rumbling of passing carriages breaks the silence of the night. Paris is damp, cold and muddy—Parisian Paris! Now all is still: it sleeps the sleep of the the unjust....

Have you the full score of my *Requiem*? If I were threatened with the destruction of everything I have written save one work, I would beg life for that Mass. There's a new edition of it being printed in Milan: I could probably let you have it in six or seven weeks.... Farewell: I shall lie awake and think of you, for non suadent cadentia sidera somnos.

To Ferdinand Hiller

Paris, 8 February 1867

Dear Hiller,

You are the best of good friends! I will do as you tell me: take my courage in both hands and on the 23rd start for Cologne. I shall be at the Hotel Royal by the evening, but don't engage *rooms* for me, one tiny one is enough. If I can't possibly travel I will send on the orchestral score of the duet from *Beatrice* and you could conduct it. You speak just like my doctors: "It's a neuralgia"—like when Mme Sand pointed out to her gardener that one of the garden walls had fallen down. "Oh, it's not anything, madame, it's the frost that's done it." "Yes, but it will have to be rebuilt." "Oh, it's nothing, it's just the frost." "I don't dispute that, but it's lying on the ground." "Don't fret yourself, madame, it's the frost."...

On 26 February Berlioz conducted the extract from *Beatrice* and the whole of *Harold in Italy* in Cologne. Shortly afterwards *The Childhood of Christ* was given in Lausanne, and Mme Fornier was able to attend the performance.

To Mme Fornier

Paris, 6 April 1867

I have not yet seen anything of the Exhibition. I'm waiting for the arrival of my nieces: they will take me there willy nilly. Those girls are as eager as larks, and they're dragging their poor father to Paris, though he's not well and as little eager as I am.... A friend sent me a paper a few days ago containing a few friendly lines on the performance of my *Enfance du Christ* at Lausanne. It seems that the oratorio was tolerably well performed, but I prefer to believe it rather than to have heard it myself. I haven't heard this work since Strasbourg three years ago; there it was imposing, and Germany and France both took part. I would have liked you to have been in the audience then. Here I get performed a bit from time to time, and not too badly, in various concerts, but I don't go to them.

I have recently received news of my son, who is still sailing the waters of the Gulf of Mexico....

To Humbert Ferrand

[Paris] 11 June 1867

Thank you for your letter, dear friend, it did me good. Yes, I am still in Paris, so ill that at the moment I hardly have the strength to write to you. I am ill in all ways, anxiety torments me. Louis is still in the neighbourhood of Mexico and I have had no news of him for a long time: and I am afraid of all those Mexican brigands.

The Exhibition is turning Paris into an inferno. I have not been there yet, for I can hardly walk and at the moment it's very difficult to get a cab. At the Conservatoire I have been one of the jury awarding the musical prize of the Exhibition. We have heard a hundred and four cantatas, and now I have just had the very great pleasure of seeing the prize unanimously awarded to my young friend Camille Saint-Saëns, one of the leading musicians of our time....

I have been pressed to go to New York, where the Americans say I am popular. They played *Harold* five times last year with a truly Viennese success.

I am quite elated with our jury meeting. How happy Saint-Saëns will be! I hurried off to his house to tell him, but he was out with his mother. He is an astonishing pianist. At last our

musical world has done one sensible thing! It has given me fresh
strength. I could not have written you such a long letter if it
had not been for the delight I feel.

To Mme Fornier
                                    Paris, 29 June 1867
Dear Madame,
   Permit me to turn to you at the moment when I have suffered the most terrible sorrow of my life. My poor son has died
at Havana, aged thirty-three.
                                    Your devoted,
                                        H. Berlioz.

To Humbert Ferrand
                                    [Paris] 15 July 1867
   I send you a few words, since you ask for them: but it is
wrong of me to sadden you too. I am so much worse from the
return of my intestinal neuralgia that I am really hardly alive
and have barely sense enough to grasp poor Louis' business
affairs which the agents of the Transatlantic Company have
written to me about: fortunately one of his friends is helping
me. Thank you for your letter which did me good this morning. Forgive my stupidity. I am fit for nothing but sleep.
   Farewell, farewell!

To Mme Damcke, at Montreux
                                    Paris [24 September 1867]
Dear Mme Damcke,
   I would have written sooner if I had known your address, so
double thanks for your letter. My answer is short: I am as ill
as usual. After my fifth bath at Néris the local doctor, on hearing
me talk, felt my pulse and said "Get out of here as fast as you
can: the waters are the worst possible thing for you, you're on
the verge of laryngitis. This is really serious." So off I went the
same evening and was nearly choked by a fit of coughing in the
train. My nieces at Vienne nursed me devotedly, but when my
throat got better back came my neuralgia more fiendishly than
ever.
   I stayed in Vienne for a month: my elder niece was getting
married and insisted on my being a witness. The groom, who is
a major, is charming in every way, otherwise I would not have

witnessed. After the wedding dinner, they went off for a long honeymoon in the south of France, or again I wouldn't have witnessed. There were thirty three of us at the wedding, from every branch of the family, Grenoble, Tournon, Saint Geoirge, etc. We were all there except *one*, alas! It was the oldest whom I most enjoyed seeing again, my uncle, the colonel, aged 84. We both wept on meeting: he seemed almost ashamed of being alive: I am much more ashamed.

I spend most of my time in bed, but the Grand Duchess Helen has inveigled me into going to St. Petersburg. She wants to see me, and at last I have agreed to go. I shall leave on the 15th November and conduct six concerts at the Conservatoire, one of them of my own music....

To Messrs Steinway and Sons

Paris, 25 September 1867

I have heard the magnificent pianos which you manufacture. Allow me to compliment you on their excellence. Their tone is splendid and truly noble. Moreover you have found the secret of reducing to an imperceptible point the disagreeable harmony of the minor seventh, which hitherto was audible on the eighth and ninth vibration of the longer strings, thus producing a discordant effect. Like so many of your other improvements this marks a great step forward in piano making, and one for which every artist and amateur of sensitive ear will owe you a debt of gratitude.

To M. and Mme Massart

Paris, 4 October 1867

Yes, it is quite true. I am going to Russia. I have done a reckless thing. The Grand Duchess Helen was here the other day: she put an offer to me which after hesitating a little and consulting several of my friends I accepted. I am to conduct six Conservatoire concerts: five of the greatest works of the great masters and the sixth entirely of my own compositions. I am to have rooms in her palace and the use of one of her carriages, all my travelling expenses both ways and fifteen thousand francs. Why don't you come too? You could play your jovial Bach concerto in D minor and we would enjoy ourselves....

An American whose offers I had turned down six weeks ago, on learning that I was accepting offers from the Russians, has come back and three days ago offered me a hundred thousand francs to come to New York next year. What do you say to that? Meanwhile he's having a bronze bust of me made for a superb new concert hall which he's had built over there, and I go and sit for it every day. If I weren't so old, all this would give me pleasure....

The impresario was the German-American piano manufacturer Steinweg (Steinway) who had heard and seen Berlioz in Brunswick. The bust of Berlioz by his colleague Perraud is still in the Steinway Hall in New York.

During his visit to Dauphiné in the summer Berlioz had been three times to Mme Fornier's house at Saint-Symphorien d'Ozon : she had also just lost a son.

To Princess Sayn-Wittgenstein

Paris, 27 October 1867

...These three visits revived me each time, although Mme F...was very sad and desirous, she said, of seeing her tiresome life end....

To Choudens

St. Petersburg, 9 December 1867

...The day before yesterday, at the second concert, my *Symphonie Fantastique* had an immense success : all the movements were applauded. The March to the Scaffold was encored, and after the finale I was called back at least six times. The papers are splendid : the Grand Duchess and Prince Constantin are extremely warm, the artists overwhelm me....

To Mme Fornier

Palais Michel, St. Petersburg, 14 December 1867

...Every time I appear the applause is almost embarrassing. I have an admirable orchestra to conduct which is entirely devoted to me and with which I can do what I like. The Grand Duchess Helen asked me recently to come one evening and read *Hamlet* to her. She knows her Shakespeare in a way such as to inspire the reader's confidence. The poor woman possesses an income of 8 million roubles—32 million francs—in property : she does an immense amount of good for the poor and for artists.

However I often get bored in the beautiful rooms she has given me, and I can't always accept the invitations she sends me. I spend a lot of time in bed, especially after the rehearsals and concerts, which exhaust me. . . .

To Edouard Alexandre*

St. Petersburg, 15 December 1867

Dear Friends,

How kind of you to send me your news : I must seem very forgetful not to have done the same before this. I am loaded with favours from everyone—from the Grand Duchess down to the least member of the orchestra. They found out that the 11th was my birthday and sent me delightful presents. In the evening I was asked to a banquet of a hundred and fifty guests where, as you may imagine, I was well toasted. Both public and press are most eulogistic. At the second concert I was recalled six times after the *Symphonie Fantastique*, which was performed with tremendous spirit. What an orchestra! what ensemble! what precision! I wonder if Beethoven ever heard anything like it. In spite of my pain, as soon as I reach the conductor's desk and am surrounded by these sympathetic souls I revive, and I believe I am conducting now as I never did before. Yesterday we did the second act of *Orfeo*, the C minor symphony and my *Carnaval Romain*—all superbly done. The girl who sang *Orfeo* (in Russian) had an incomparable voice and sang well too. The Russians, who knew Gluck only from the mutilations committed by incompetent people, could hardly stop applauding. Oh, it is bliss for me to reveal to them the masterpieces of that great man. In two weeks we shall do the first act of *Alceste*. The duchess gave orders that I was to be obeyed in everything. I don't abuse her order, but I use it. She has asked me to come and read *Hamlet* to her one of these evenings, and the other day I happened to speak to her ladies-in-waiting in her presence of Saint-Victor's book, and now they are all rushing off to buy and admire *Men and Gods*. Here people love the beautiful : they live for literature and music : they have in their breasts some fire which makes them forget the snow and the hoar-frost. Why am I so old and tired?

Farewell all. I love you and press your hands.

* Well-known organ manufacturer, and (with Damcke) Berlioz' executor.

To Mme Massart
                    St. Petersburg, 22 December 1867
Dear Mme Massart,

I am ill as eighteen horses: I cough like six donkeys with the glanders: yet before I retire to bed I want to write to you. All goes wonderfully well here. The orchestra is superb and does exactly what I want. If you could hear them play Beethoven's symphonies, I think you would say things that don't occur to you at the Conservatoire...At the fifth concert I want to give the Choral Symphony, the first three movements at least: I am afraid to risk the choral movement as I am not sure enough of my chorus.

I have been invited to Moscow and the Grand Duchess is letting me go. The gentlemen of that semi-Asiatic city propound the most irresistible arguments whatever Wieniawski may say— he doesn't want me to jump at their offer. But I never could haggle and would be ashamed to do so now.

I have just been interrupted by a message from the Grand Duchess. She is giving a musical soirée to-night and wishes to hear the duet from *Beatrice*. Her pianist and two singers know it perfectly in French, so I have sent the score with a message to them not to be nervous as they will get through all right. I shall go back to bed. I could tell you a lot more if I weren't tired out, but it's nine o'clock and I'm not used to being up at such an unreasonable hour. I shall take three drops of laudanum so as to try to sleep.

You know that you are charming. But why the devil are you so charming? I can't make it out. Farewell, I am your
                                                    H. B.

To Mme Massart
                    St. Petersburg, 18 January 1868
Dear Mme Massart,

I found quite a pile of letters on my return from Moscow, among them one that gave me even greater pleasure than yours: you can guess who it came from. Nevertheless yours gives me joy too....St. Michael's Square is silent under its mantle of snow: the crows, pigeons and sparrows don't stir: sledges have ceased to run: there is a great funeral to-day, Prince Dolgorouki's, the Tsar and all the Court are going....

The programme for Saturday is settled. Oh! the joy when

I lay down my baton at the end of *Harold* and say: "In three days I start for Paris". I can't hold out against this climate, although I felt better in Moscow.

Don't speak of a concert in Paris. If I gave one simply for my friends and spent three thousand francs on it I should still be reviled by the Press. After seeing you I shall go to Saint-Symphorien and thence to Monaco, to lie down among the violets and sleep in the sun. I suffer so continually: the pain is so constant that I can't think what will happen to me. I don't want to die now, for I have something to live for....

To Mme Fornier

Palais Michel, St. Petersburg, 23 January 1868

...Oh! the day when I shall leave Vienne to lie at your feet in Saint-Symphorien! I will tell you then about my journey, which would be fatiguing for you now. I will only say that the Muscovites gave me an even warmer reception than the citizens of the capital. At the first concert which the organisers made me give in the immense Riding School there were ten thousand six hundred in the audience.

While in St. Petersburg Berlioz had renewed acquaintance with the critic Stassov, and also met the members of the new Russian nationalist school of composers, Balakirev, Cui, Rimsky-Korsakov and Mussorgsky, who became great admirers of his music.

To Vladimir Stassov

Paris, Sunday 1 March 1868

I haven't written to you since my return, I was too ill. And now I want to tell you that I am leaving for Monaco at seven this evening. I can't imagine why I don't die. But as I am alive I am going to see my dear Nice, the rocks of Villefranche and the sun of Monaco. Yesterday I dragged myself to the Academy, where I saw my sculptor and colleague. Perraud. He told me they are having three bigger than life-size copies of the bust cast for New York and Paris. I think it was you who suggested getting one for the St. Petersburg Conservatoire. If not, it must have been Kologrivov or Cui or Balakirev. More can easily be made.

Oh! to think that I shall soon be lying on the marble seats of Monaco, in the sun, by the sea! Don't be too strict with me. Write me long letters in exchange for my short ones: remember that I am ill, that your letters do me good : don't talk all this nonsense about me composing.

My kindest regards to your charming sister-in-law and daughter and to your brother. I can see you all so vividly as if you were here. Write soon. Your letter and the S U N will give me new life. Unfortunate that you are ! You live in the snow !

To Mme Fornier

Paris, 25 March 1868

I'm writing instead of coming to see you. I am at home in bed in Paris, after a week in Nice. It's very strange, I made the most absurd journey. My niece knows nothing about it, my brother-in-law knows nothing about it, at Grenoble they don't know either, but I can't leave you any longer in the dark about my accident. What happened was that I had been boring myself at Monaco for two days when one morning I tried to get down to the sea via some impractical rocks. I had not taken more than three steps when it became clear how rash I had been : I slipped and lost my balance and fell head first on my face. I lay a long time alone on the ground, unable to get up, and streaming with blood. Finally, after a quarter of an hour, I was able to drag myself back to the villa, where I was cleaned up and bandaged as far as possible.

I had kept my seat on the omnibus back to Nice the next day. I went back, but what do you think? When I arrived in Nice I decided, disfigured as I was, to go and see the terrace beside the water which I loved so much in the old days, and I went up there. I sat down on a bench, but as I couldn't see the sea very well from there, I got up to change my place, and I had hardly gone three steps when I fell flat on my face again, and I bled more than on the previous day. Two young men who were walking on the terrace rushed up horrified and set me on my feet and helped me to the Hotel des Etrangers, near the place where I had fallen. I stayed there a week in bed without moving, and when I had the strength I went back to Paris without worrying about what sort of sight I looked in the train. My mother-in-law and the servant cried out when they saw me. Since then I haven't left my bed, I have been in pain for a fort-night without getting better. My nose and eyes are in a pitiful state : the doctor, to console me, said it was lucky for me that I lost all that blood, otherwise I would have been finished,

especially the second time. Farewell, dear madame, I had to tell
you why I didn't come to see you. . . .

To Vladimir Stassov

Paris, April 1868

My dear Stassov,

You call me *Monsieur* Berlioz, both you and Cui! I forgive
you both. [Then follows the story of Berlioz' falls at Monaco
and Nice, as related in the previous letter.] Now I have had a
doctor and he has looked after me so well that after more than
a month of it I can just walk, holding on to the furniture. My
nose is nearly healed outside.

Could you find out why my score of *The Trojans* has not been
returned? I imagine the copying is finished and that it is no
longer needed.

I can write no more. If I wait till I am better it may be a
long time. Do write to me. It will be a real kindness.

To Auguste Morel

Paris, 26 May 1868

. . . I have been through a bad time and still find it hard to
write. My two falls, one at Monaco and the other at Nice, have
taken all my strength. The traces have almost gone now, but
my old malady has come back more painfully than ever. I would
have loved to see you and Lecourt when I was near Marseilles:
I would have come on my way back from Nice if I hadn't been
in such a bad state. But it wasn't possible—I should have been
broken up by your company more than by any other. Few of my
friends loved Louis as you did. And I can't forget. Forgive me,
both of you.

On 25 May Blanc Gounet, a boy who had been adopted as a
child by the Ferrands, strangled Mme Ferrand and disappeared
with her jewels. He was caught and guillotined in September:
shortly afterwards Ferrand himself died. Meanwhile Berlioz had
been entertained to an official banquet by the town of Grenoble.

To Vladimir Stassov

Paris, 21 August 1868

Dear Stassov,

You see I leave out the Monsieur.

I have just come back from Grenoble, where they had almost forced me to go and preside at a kind of musical festival and be present at the unveiling of a statue of Napoleon I. They ate, they drank, they painted the town red and I was ill all the time! They came to fetch me in a carriage, they drank toasts to me to which I didn't know what to reply. The Mayor of Grenoble overwhelmed me with compliments, he gave me a crown in silver gilt, but I had to sit there for a whole hour before the banquet began. Next day I left and arrived home at eleven at night, more dead than alive.

I feel good for nothing and I get such letters: they ask me to do impossible things. They want me to say something favourable about a German musician, which indeed I think deserves to be said, but only on condition that I say something unfavourable about a Russian one, whom they want the German to supplant, though the Russian too is very deserving. I will not do it. What the devil of a world is that?

I feel that I am going to die: I don't believe in anything any more! I should like to see you: you would act as a tonic, you and Cui might be able to cheer me up.

What can I do?

I bore myself in an exorbitant manner. No one is in Paris: all my friends have gone to the country, to *their* country for shooting: some of them invite me to visit them. I haven't got the strength for it.

How are you? And your brother? And your delightful ladies? Write, I beg: as briefly as you wish, but write! I still feel the effects of my fall on the rocks at Monaco: I also have vivid memories of Nice. If you are in St. Petersburg write me even six lines, I shall be so grateful. A thousand greetings to Balakirev. You are so kind: show it now. I must stop—writing is difficult.

I clasp your hand.

Berlioz went out almost for the last time in November to support the candidature for the Institute of Charles Blanc, who had helped him keep his Librarianship of the Conservatoire during the troubles of 1848. To Blanc he said: "My days are numbered: the doctor has even told me the number. But I will vote for you."

Berlioz died on 8 March 1869 at 12.30 in the afternoon.

SELECT BIBLIOGRAPHY

I. BERLIOZ' WRITINGS

Grand Traité d'instrumentation et d'orchestration, Paris, 1844
Les Soirées de l'orchestre, Paris, 1852, and modern editions up to 1927
Evenings in the Orchestra, trans. C. R. Fortescue and ed. David Cairns, London, Penguin Books, 1963
Les Grotesques de la Musique, Paris, 1859, reprinted 1927
A Travers Chants: études musicales, adorations, boutades et critiques, Paris, 1862
Mémoires de Hector Berlioz, Paris, 1870, 1878, and modern editions
Memoirs, trans. Rachel and Eleanor Holmes, ed. Ernest Newman, New York, 1932 and 1948
The Life of Hector Berlioz as Written by Himself in his Letters and Memoirs, ed. Katherine F. Boult, Everyman's Library, London, 1912 and 1923
Les musiciens et la musique, Paris, 1903. Contains extracts from Berlioz' articles in the *Journal des Débats*, 1835–63

II. BERLIOZ' LETTERS

Correspondance Inédite, 1819–68, ed. Daniel Bernard, Paris, 1879
Lettres Intimes, Paris, 1882
Life and Letters, trans. H. M. Dunstan, London, 1882. Translation of both volumes above
Letters 1819–1855, ed. Julien Tiersot, Paris, 1904–30
    Vol. 1, Les Années Romantiques, 1819–42
    Vol. 2, Le Musicien Errant, 1842–52
    Vol. 3, Au Milieu du Chemin, 1852–55
Briefe hervorragenden Zeitgenossen an Franz Liszt, ed. La Mara, Leipzig, 1895–1904
Briefe an die Fürstin Sayn-Wittgenstein, ed. La Mara, Leipzig, 1903
Lettres inédites de Hector Berlioz à Thomas Gounet, ed. L. Michoud, Grenoble, 1903
Une Page d'amour romantique. Lettres à Mme Estelle F. La Revue Bleue, Paris, 1903
Lettres de musiciens écrites en français du 15ème au 20ème siecle, ed. Julien Tiersot, Vol. 2, Turin, 1924–36
New Letters of Berlioz, 1830–68, ed. and trans. Jacques Barzun, New York, 1954. Contains a check list of Berlioz' letters which are still unpublished

Jacques Barzun's *Berlioz and the Romantic Century*, Vol. 2, also contains a list of Berlioz' letters which have appeared in books and periodicals

III. BOOKS ON BERLIOZ

Barzun, Jacques, *Berlioz and the Romantic Century*, Boston and New York, 1950, London, 1951

Boschot, Adolphe, *Histoire d'un romantique*, Paris, 1906 and 1946

Constantin, Léon, *Berlioz*, Paris, 1934

Davison, Henry, ed., *Music during the Victorian Era, from Mendelssohn to Wagner*, London, 1912

Ganz, A. W., *Berlioz in London*, London, 1950

Hopkinson, Cecil, *A Bibliography of the Works of Hector Berlioz*, Edinburgh, 1951

Jullien, Adolphe, *Hector Berlioz—sa vie et ses oeuvres*, Paris, 1888

Kapp, Julius, *Berlioz: eine Biographie*, Berlin and Leipzig, 1917

Massougnes, G. de, *Hector Berlioz et son oeuvre*, Paris, 1919

Pincherle, Marc, *Musiciens peints par eux-memes,* Paris, 1939

Pohl, Louise, *Hector Berlioz, Leben und Werke*, Leipzig, 1900

Pohl, Richard, *Hector Berlioz: Studien und Erinnerungen*, Leipzig, 1884

Prod'homme, J. G., *Hector Berlioz*, Paris, 1904 and 1927

Saint-Saëns, Camille, *Ecole buissonnière*, Paris, 1913

   Portraits et souvenirs, Paris, 1903

Tiersot, *Berlioz et la société de son temps*, Paris, 1904

Turner, W. J., *Berlioz: the Man and his Work*, London, 1934

Wotton, Tom S., *Hector Berlioz*, London, 1935

INDEX